TO MY FATHER

5/18/67   いと   6.36

THAILAND *and the* STRUGGLE *for* SOUTHEAST ASIA

By Donald E. Nuechterlein

CORNELL UNIVERSITY PRESS

Ithaca, New York

CORNELL UNIVERSITY PRESS

First published 1965

Library of Congress Catalog Card Number: 65–21996

PRINTED IN THE UNITED STATES OF AMERICA
BY W. F. HUMPHREY PRESS

Preface

THIS study of Thailand's role in the struggle for survival among the free nations of Southeast Asia is based on the author's residence in Bangkok from 1961 to 1963 and on his research at the University of California at Berkeley during the academic year 1963–1964. The year at Berkeley was made possible by a generous grant from the Rockefeller Foundation. Although many of the observations made and the conclusions reached are based on discussions the author had with distinguished Thai and American officials in Bangkok and Washington, the views expressed herein are solely his own.

No attempt has been made to use any one of the various methods of transliteration often employed by scholars in writing Thai place names and proper names. In general the spelling of such words is based on actual pronunciation in Thai, although in certain cases (such as "Thai" instead of the phonetic "T'ai" or "Tai") the conventional spelling is used to avoid confusion. If the names of Thai cities and some Thai leaders are spelled somewhat differently than is usual in newspapers and magazines, the author can only plead that his version probably is closer to the actual sound in Thai, and hope that it will be easier to read.

In this study of Thailand's foreign policy since World

War II, the author has given more than the usual amount
of attention to a discussion of Thai diplomatic history in
the belief that a clear understanding of Thailand's relations
with other countries, particularly during the past century,
will lead to a better appreciation of Thailand's current view
of the world and of its place in it. Similarly, considerable
attention has been given to internal political developments
since 1932, when the absolute monarchy was overthrown
and constitutional government was inaugurated for the first
time. The author believes that over the past thirty years
domestic politics in Thailand has been strongly influenced
by foreign policy considerations, and that a better knowledge of this relationship will result in greater understanding
of Thai politics. Finally, it is hoped that through this discussion of Thailand's relations with the United States since
World War II, Americans and Thais will better appreciate
the objectives and policies pursued by both governments.

A number of scholars with knowledge of Thailand have
read parts of this study in manuscript, and the author is
deeply indebted to them for their helpful suggestions. Among
them are: Professors Albert Pickerell and Robert A. Scalapino
of the University of California at Berkeley; Mr. Harry H.
Pierson of the Asia Foundation; and Colonel Aldon M. Hoff-
man of the United States Army. I also wish to thank Mr.
Bakdi Jittijudata, graduate student in political science at
Berkeley, for his assistance in spelling Thai names in English
as well as for his helpful comments on the manuscript. To
my wife Mildred goes credit for careful reading and criticism
of the original draft. Finally, the interest and encouragement
of my children—Jan, Jill, and Jeff—have been a real source
of inspiration.

Because events in Southeast Asia were moving so rapidly
at the time of writing, it was impossible to take account of

all the most recent developments affecting Thailand. Therefore, the major review of Thai foreign policy and of Thai-
American relations concludes with the year 1962, the crucial
year of readjustment within the SEATO alliance. A final
chapter entitled "Outlook" was added, however, before the
manuscript went to press; it reviews the major events in
Southeast Asia in 1963 and 1964 and their effect on Thailand's
policy. If this concluding chapter lacks the detail and perspective of the earlier chapters, the author begs the reader's
indulgence and trusts that the main part of the study will
help to place these recent events into a better framework
than might otherwise be possible.

DONALD E. NUECHTERLEIN

McLean, Virginia
May 1965

Contents

Introduction

IN September 1954 the United States made a historic commitment to come to the defense of the mainland of Southeast Asia by concluding a military alliance with Thailand and other interested nations: the Southeast Asia Treaty Organization, or SEATO. This decision to use American power to defend an area in which the United States had previously sought to avoid becoming involved was taken only after it became clear that the former great powers in Southeast Asia—the British and the French—were no longer able to carry the burden, and that the area probably would succumb to Communist power unless the United States was prepared to guarantee its security.

Strategically, the most important member of SEATO was the kingdom of Thailand, which is located in the heart of the Southeast Asia mainland and has a long border with the former Indochina states—stretching from northwestern Laos to the western border of Cambodia at the Gulf of Siam. In addition, Thailand was the only country in this area to retain its independence during the period of Western colonization, and it also seemed to have sufficient internal unity and sense of national purpose to convince American leaders that it could be a stable ally. To many observers Thailand appeared to be the key country in Southeast Asia, just as it had been in 1941 when Japan sought to conquer this area. They believed that if Thailand, with the help of the United States and other friendly powers, was maintained as a strong and prosperous anti-Communist bulwark in Southeast Asia, the growing threat from the Chinese and North Vietnamese Communists might be checked and contained within the area to which it was confined by the Geneva Agreements. On the other hand, if Thailand did not stand as such an anti-Communist bulwark, most observers considered that it would be extremely difficult, if not impossible, to prevent the Communists from taking control of the whole area, just as the Japanese did in 1942 after convincing Thailand that resistance was futile.

The difficulty of the SEATO alliance was that its commitments were seen in different ways by different members. For Thailand the alliance meant that, if necessary, American power would be used to prevent the former Indochina states of Laos, Cambodia, and South Vietnam from being absorbed into the Communist sphere either by overt aggression or through subversion. The British and French, however, were not at all sure that these three weak and unstable countries could be protected against Communist encroachments under any circumstances short of all-out war; and the British were more interested in having SEATO devote itself primarily to the defense of Thailand and Malaya-Singapore. From 1954 to 1960 these differences within the alliance did not have serious consequences, because the United States supported the Thai view that Laos and South Vietnam, which bordered on North Vietnam and were subject to Viet-Minh infiltration, must at all costs be preserved as non-Communist buffer states. Also, during most of this period Communist China and North Vietnam did not choose to put SEATO to the test in these areas.

Beginning in the summer of 1960, however, events in Laos caused a real crisis in SEATO and led also to a crisis in Thailand's relations with its principal ally—the United States. The issue revolved around the question whether a pro-Western and strongly anti-Communist Laos or a neutral Laos friendly to both the Communist and the Western powers was the better long-range solution to the stability of Thailand and hence the rest of Southeast Asia. Those SEATO members that argued for a neutral Laos—notably the French and the British—believed that China and North Vietnam could not tolerate an anti-Communist Laos on their borders, and that they would try to bring about the fall of such a government. Thailand, supported by the Philippines, argued strongly that a neutralist government in Laos would only pave the way for a Communist takeover, and that the best means to contain the Communists was to oppose them with overwhelming power if they tried to turn Laos or South Vietnam into Communist states, whether through overt aggression or through subversion and armed insurgency. To the Thais, Laos became the acid test of the SEATO alliance; for, if the United States, with its preponderant power and influence in SEATO, continued to support a pro-Western government in Laos and was determined to prevent the Communists from subverting that country, Thailand could feel secure in the fact that the Communist menace was not on its own doorstep. If, however, the United States decided to support a neutral Laos—particularly if the Communist Pathet Lao faction were permitted to be represented in the government—Thai leaders were afraid that Laos would soon succumb to the Communists, and then the Communist pressure on Thailand would be enormous. In the latter event, there was reason to believe that Thailand would lose faith in the efficacy of the SEATO alliance.

The critical point in the alliance for Thailand was reached in the spring of 1961 when the United States decided to negotiate with the Communist powers for a solution to the Laotian problem and thereafter agreed to a coalition government in which the Pathet Lao was represented. Although since then the United States has tried to reassure Thailand of its determination to defend it against Communist aggression and subversion and also to prevent the Pathet Lao from moving to the Mekong and thus taking over control of all of Laos, the Thai government has remained skeptical of long-term American intentions in Southeast Asia. Even though Thailand remained a good friend and ally of the United States, few observers doubted that future Thai policy would be governed by Bangkok's estimate of the extent of America's determination to prevent the Communists from taking over Laos and South Vietnam. The outcome of the confrontation in Vietnam in 1965 was, therefore, crucial to Thailand's future relations with the United States and to its position in SEATO.

Chapter 1

The Historical Setting

THE people who now inhabit the kingdom of Thailand are descendants of a racial group that includes the Shans of Burma, the Laos of the kingdom of Laos, and the Thai-speaking inhabitants of Yunnan Province in China. Although scholars disagree about the origins of the Thai race,[1] they generally agree that the Thai people lived in southern China for many years before beginning to migrate southward into the Indochina peninsula early in the Christian era. In the seventh century A.D. the Thais founded in Yunnan a powerful kingdom known as Nanchao; they challenged Chinese supremacy for several hundred years before making peace with China and accepting vassal status in the ninth century. Thereafter a steady flow of Thais moved southward. One group settled along the upper Salween River and became known as the Shans; another moved east into the upper Mekong Valley and called themselves Laos. A third segment

[1]D. G. E. Hall believes that the Thais as a racial group are cognate to the Chinese, and that their first appearance in historical records came in the sixth century B.C. (*A History of South-East Asia* [London, 1954], p. 144). Chula Chakrabongse, on the other hand, states that the Thais have been a distinct racial group for nearly five thousand years, and that they were well established before the Chinese came on the historical scene. (*Lords of Life* [New York, 1960], p. 16).

1

traveled directly south from Yunnan into the basin of the Chao Pya River[2]; they were the forefathers of the Thais. Much of the area along the Chao Pya and Mekong rivers was at this time under the control of the great Khmer Empire; the Thais settled there among the Cambodians and lived in peace with them for several centuries. In 1238 several of the most powerful Thai chieftains in the northwestern part of the Khmer Empire combined forces and defeated the Cambodian garrison at Sukhotai, the provincial capital. Subsequently they joined their small Thai communities into a new and independent state, the kingdom of Sukhotai.

Several facts help to explain the growth of the kingdom of Sukhotai: first, the Chinese encouraged it in order to reduce the power and influence of the Khmer Empire; second, the Burmese, who might otherwise have challenged the extension of Thai influence southward and westward, were defeated by the Mongols in 1287; third, Sukhotai produced an outstanding leader in King Ramkamheng (1283–1317), who by combining statesmanship with military skill built his kingdom into the most powerful state in the Indochina peninsula. In addition to conquering the length of the Chao Pya Valley south from Sukhotai and extending Thai influence into the Malay Peninsula, Ramkamheng defeated the Cambodian forces and removed Khmer influence from the eastern part of the area. He was also a great assimilator; during his reign he borrowed the best features of the Khmer and Mon civilizations to set the groundwork for a new Siamese civilization. One of his greatest contributions to Siamese culture was the written language.

King Ramkamheng has been described by Prince Chula Chakrabongse as "a brilliant diplomat."[3] By concluding a

[2]Sometimes erroneously called the "Menam" (Thai for "river").
[3]Chakrabongse, *op. cit.*, p. 24.

"blood brother friendship pact" in 1287 with several powerful independent Thai princes in the north, he was able to
extend the borders of Sukhotai far to the south and east
without having to worry about his northern flank. The influence of Ramkamheng was enhanced in the Mon states to the
south by the marriage of his daughter to a prince who later
became a Mon king. In addition, he was astute in his relations
with the emperor of China. Many diplomatic missions were
sent to China bearing suitable gifts for presentation at the
Chinese court, and trade began to flourish between the two
countries, first by the overland route and later by sea from
the Gulf of Siam. Ramkamheng is said to have visited Peking
twice during his reign and to have recruited Chinese artisans
who founded the famous Sukhotai ceramics industry. This
policy toward China was the linchpin of Ramkamheng's foreign policy; for, in return for accepting nominal Chinese
suzerainty, the kingdom of Sukhotai was at peace with its
northern neighbor, with whom it was able to enjoy the
benefits of a flourishing trade. This peaceful relationship
continued to the middle of the nineteenth century.

After Ramkamheng died in 1317, the fortunes of Sukhotai
began to wane. By the middle of the fourteenth century a
new and powerful Thai kingdom had grown up to the south,
at Ayutia, which was located in the middle of the Chao Pya
Valley, some fifty miles from the Gulf of Siam. Thereafter,
the king of Sukhotai recognized the authority of this new
power, and the kingdom of Ayutia, which eventually was
known internationally as Siam, developed into a great civilization by the end of the fifteenth century. Under strong
kings, Ayutia extended its influence from Sukhotai in the
north to the Bay of Bengal in southern Burma and far down
the Malay Peninsula. Although it is not clear whether Siamese
armies actually captured Malacca, the kingdom of Ayutia

claimed suzerainty over the whole Malay Peninsula at the end of the fifteenth century. Despite these successes, however, Ayutia was unable during this period to subdue the Thai state of Chiengmai in the north or to bring the Cambodians completely under its control. In 1432, Siamese armies finally conquered the Khmer capital of Angkor and enforced vassal status on their neighbors; but throughout the fifteenth century the Cambodians continued to fight against Ayutia.

The kings of Ayutia showed the same astuteness as had Ramkamheng in their relations with China. Hall believes that the rise of Ayutia to greatness on China's southern border was due as much to the diplomatic skill of the Siamese as to the weakness of the Mongol dynasty. When the Ming dynasty came to power in China, he writes, the king of Ayutia sent embassies to Nanking "and sedulously cultivated friendly relations." Hall concluded that "as diplomatists the T'ais have never been surpassed."[4]

Siamese relations with Burma, on the other hand, deteriorated during the sixteenth century into a series of disastrous wars over control of the Chao Pya Valley and of the northern Thai states. Burma had not presented a threat to Siam for several centuries because of internal conflicts among the various Burmese states. Early in the sixteenth century, however, they were united under powerful rulers who were determined to displace Ayutia as the major power in the Indochina peninsula. After a series of invasions of the Chao Pya Valley, the Burmese laid siege to Ayutia in 1569; and after a long battle they stormed the city and completely sacked it, carrying off thousands of prisoners, including the young Prince Nared, who was destined to play a major role in Siamese history. The fall of Ayutia marked the end of a

[4]Hall, *op. cit.*, pp. 151-2.

dynasty that had ruled Siam for 219 years; thereafter the country was torn by internal strife.

When Prince Nared was taken to Burma as a prisoner, he was placed in the royal military school, where he learned the art of war along with the Burmese princes. After several years the situation in Siam was so calm that the Burmese permitted him to return home and assume command of forces fighting the Cambodians. At the age of sixteen he distinguished himself so highly as a warrior that he was made king and crowned as King Naresuan. But his success in welding the Siamese people once again into a strong nation and his training of a large army alarmed the Burmese. In 1581 they launched another series of invasions of Siam, but in each case they were repulsed. Naresuan was unable to follow up his successful stand at Ayutia, however, because the Cambodians attacked his rear—a tactic that they employed whenever the Siamese were hard pressed by Burma. In a historic engagement in 1592, the Burmese made a last great effort to crush Siam; and in this battle King Naresuan killed the heir apparent to the Burmese throne in a combat involving elephants.[5] Thereafter Naresuan was free to re-establish Siam's power and influence in Southeast Asia. First, he settled with the Cambodians by routing their army and capturing the capital. To emphasize his contempt for Cambodia's treachery when Siam was fighting the Burmese, Naresuan executed its king in a humiliating public spectacle—an action that outraged the Cambodians then and that they have not forgotten. After securing his eastern border, Naresuan marched north and forced Chiengmai to accept Siamese control for the first time. He then invaded Burma and brought several provinces in the south under his control. He did not

[5]This famous battle, which is known to every Thai schoolchild, is described in detail in Chakrabongse, *op. cit.*, pp. 47–50.

succeed in destroying the Burmese capital at Pegu, but by the end of the century Burma was so torn by internal wars that it had ceased to be a threat. At the end of the sixteenth century Ayutia was once again the greatest power in the region. It then turned to the tasks of developing its culture and extending commerce with other nations.

Involvement with European Powers

The first contact between Siam and the West occurred in 1518, when the Portuguese sent an embassy from Malacca to Ayutia. Despite their apprehensions the Portuguese were accorded a friendly reception and concluded a treaty with the King, which gave them complete commercial freedom and trading facilities in Ayutia and several other ports. The Portuguese were also permitted to establish a Christian mission in Ayutia, and the King himself donated a large sum of money to build the first Christian church in Siam.

A century passed before the next European nation appeared in Siam; and when the Dutch came to Ayutia soon after 1600, they were granted the same hospitality and concessions as were the Portuguese. Shortly thereafter the English East India Company became interested in Siam; it, too, was given commercial concessions in Ayutia. However, after the Dutch concluded a commercial treaty with the King, their influence grew so rapidly that the East India Company found it unprofitable to continue its trade. As Dutch influence spread to various levels of Siamese life, relations between the nations became strained, and the Dutch felt obliged to use strong measures to obtain their demands. On one occasion they staged a naval demonstration in the Gulf of Siam as a means of bringing the Siamese into line. In contrast, the Chinese traders during the same period gained considerable favor because they worked unobtrusively and often married Siamese women. Local Japanese, however, caused great difficulties by becoming involved in court politics. As a result, in 1632 the Siamese massacred many of them and expelled the remainder from the kingdom.[6]

Dutch influence was so extensive when King Narai ascended the throne in 1657 that he decided to curb it. First, he induced the East India Company to reopen its factory in Ayutia; then he tried to conclude an agreement with the English to provide military assistance in case of hostilities with the Dutch. The English, however, were interested only in obtaining long-term trade concessions; and when the two sides failed to reach agreement, the Siamese decided to seek assistance from the French. In 1664 French missionairies were given permission to establish a church and a seminary and to extend their work to other parts of the kingdom. One of these missionaries returned from Europe bearing a letter from Louis XIV that hinted at the possibility of an alliance between France and Siam against the Dutch. King Narai received this news with great enthusiasm, and relations between him and the French community in Ayutia became increasingly cordial.

During this time there appeared on the scene one of the most colorful personalities in Siamese history, Constantine Paulkon, a Greek adventurer who had first come to Siam in the employ of the East India Company. In an effort to improve its relations with the Siamese court, the company obtained a position for Paulkon in the Ministry of Finance. So knowledgeable and energetic was he that he rose quickly and became chief of all foreign trade. Since, however, he

[6]These Japanese had fled Japan as religious refugees and were well treated by the Siamese. The good relations between the king of Ayutia and the Japanese imperial court apparently were not affected by this incident.

quarreled with his English associates, he was unable to bring about the agreement the King desired. Nonetheless Paulkon had the confidence of the King, who made him chief minister. As such he was deeply involved in King Narai's effort to conclude an alliance with France.

Louis XIV had been interested far less in aiding the Siamese against the Dutch than in turning Siam into a Christian kingdom. But when he learned that Paulkon had been converted to Catholicism and wielded great influence over King Narai, the French monarch consented to Paulkon's proposal that he send troops to Siam ostensibly to force out the Dutch but actually to Christianize Siam. In 1687 six French warships carrying 636 soldiers arrived and took up positions in Siam's trading port of Bangkok. Meanwhile French missionaries were working tirelessly, but in vain, to convert Narai to Catholicism. Slowly the King came to realize that France was not interested in helping him to oust the Dutch, and he began to look for ways to curb French influence. By this time also the Siamese nobles greatly resented Paulkon's influence on the King. Therefore, when the King fell ill in 1688, a palace conspiracy developed, and these Siamese "nationalists" staged a *coup d'état*. Paulkon asked the French to save him, but the Siamese were so stirred up that they prevented the French troops at Bangkok from coming to his aid. Paulkon was taken prisoner and publicly executed. The French were severely persecuted, and a number of missionaries, including the bishop, were put to death. France soon withdrew its troops and sought to restore good relations with Siam; but the Siamese were so outraged over the foreign intrigue that the government shut out Europeans, for all practical purposes, for the next one hundred and thirty years.

After the death of King Narai in 1688, Siam again became engrossed in internal conflicts, and its power declined under weak and incompetent kings. It also became involved with Vietnam for control over Laos and Cambodia. Its weakness became a real danger after 1750, when Burma once again emerged as a united and powerful nation and eventually turned against Siam. In 1767 Burmese forces completely ruined Ayutia, destroying precious art works and monuments and reducing its population from 100,000 to 10,000. Siam was then dismembered, and its various provinces were thereafter governed by the remaining royal princes and the nobility who set themselves up as independent rulers. The Burmese also imposed direct control over Chiengmai in the north and regained those territories in the south that they had lost during Naresuan's rule. It was the darkest hour in Siamese history.

The Siamese have shown a remarkable resiliency during their long history, and their recovery from the disaster of 1767 is the finest example of their resourcefulness. Wood has said that those who believe in the survival of the fittest "will admit that the Siamese, whatever their faults, must possess some special qualities which have marked them out to maintain this unique position."[7] One of the major factors in Siam's rapid recovery was the emergence of a great leader, just as the dark days of defeat two centuries earlier had produced Naresuan. The new leader was General Taksin, a remarkable military commander who had come from a humble background and risen rapidly in the King's service. During the Burmese seige of Ayutia, Taksin saw that matters were hopeless. He took five hundred soldiers, broke through the Burmese lines, and spent the next year training a new army near the Cambodian border. Then he marched on Ayutia and defeated the Burmese garrison stationed there. He quickly united the Siamese provinces under his rule and

[7] W. A. R. Wood, *A History of Siam* (London, 1933), p. 7.

had himself proclaimed king. After moving his capital to Tonburi, across the Chao Pya from the present capital of Bangkok, Taksin invaded Cambodia in 1771 and forced the King to accept Siamese suzerainty, which continued for nearly a hundred years.

Taksin's military successes worried the Burmese, who launched several invasions of Siam in an effort to crush this new threat to their supremacy. They were repulsed each time, and one of Taksin's best lieutenants, General Chakri, gained a great reputation for his defense of Chiengmai in the north. When the Burmese were defeated, Chakri continued his advance into the Laotian states of Wiengchan (Vientiane) and Luang Prabang and forced them to accept Siamese control. From 1778 until 1893, most of the territory of present-day Laos was under the jurisdiction of Siamese kings, and Chiengmai remains part of the kingdom of Thailand. These were remarkable achievements during a twelve-year period.

Unfortunately, as time went on, Taksin became tyrannical; and certain members of the nobility plotted his downfall. In 1781 he was deposed on grounds of mental incapacity and was executed. In his place the nobles chose General Chakri, the hero of the battle of Chiengmai, who ascended the throne in 1782.[8] Chakri moved the capital to Bangkok, where he built one of the most beautiful cities in the Orient as well as restored much of the old Siamese culture and traditions. In 1785 the Burmese made their supreme and last effort to crush the new Siam, but they were decisively defeated by Chakri's army. Although border fighting continued for some

[8]W. A. Graham writes that Taksin "was overtaken by the fate he had so often prepared for others and fell a victim to intrigue...he was dethroned by his courtiers, who gave out that he was mad, and offered the kingdom to one of their number [General Chakri]" *(Siam* [London, 1924], p. 209).

years, the British defeat of Burma in 1826 finally ended the Burmese threat.

When Chakri, who had taken the title of Rama I, died in 1809, Siam was the most powerful of all the states in Southeast Asia. Its position was being threatened, however, by the steady advance of British commercial interests in the Malay States and by the rise of a new and powerful Vietnam in the east, which threatened Siam's hegemony in Cambodia. In 1845, after many years of disputes and a number of armed conflicts over rights in Cambodia, Siam finally reached an agreement with Vietnam by which both countries guaranteed the protection of Cambodia. Some years earlier Siam had assumed control of territory along the eastern bank of the Mekong which had belonged to the former Khmer Empire and which constitutes southern Laos today. Vietnam did not contest Siam's right to this strip of land between Laos and Cambodia; Siam therefore controlled it until the French forced her to cede it in 1893. In the south, Britain sought repeatedly to reach an agreement with Rama II over rights in the Malay States; but it was not until the British defeated the Burmese in 1826 that Siam, under Rama III, signed a treaty. Under its terms Britain recognized Siam's rights in Kedah, Kelantan, and Trengganu, and Siam pledged neither to interfere with British trade in these states nor to challenge British control of Penang. Although the British had hoped for a more comprehensive agreement to open Siam up to British trade, the Siamese were not yet willing to go that far.

Trade negotiations with several Western nations took place during the next twenty years but in an atmosphere of suspicion on the part of the Siamese, a legacy of the period after 1688 when the French were driven out of the country and Siam had isolated itself from Western contacts and influences. Vella, in his study of Rama III's rule, states that the principal difficulties encountered by the Westerners in attempting to open relations with Siam stemmed from the fact that the Siamese felt no need for trade with the West—in fact, did not desire competition from Western merchants—and were reluctant to sign treaties with the West because of the possible political dangers involved.[9]

Although Rama III did conclude a limited trade agreement with Great Britain in 1826 and another with the United States in 1833, these did not result in substantial trade because the Siamese managed to circumvent the undesirable sections in order to keep to a minimum the impact of the trade on its economy and culture. During the eighteen-forties the British and Americans tried again to open up Siam to large Western trade and to conclude comprehensive treaties, but Rama III steadfastly refused. When Rama IV, King Mongkut, ascended the throne in 1851, relations with the West were at a critical juncture. Britain had gained control of the Malay States up to the area under Siamese influence. There was now a serious possibility that the British might use force to accomplish their objectives in Siam.

Accommodation with the West (1851–1893)

Mongkut had spent twenty-seven years in the priesthood prior to his accession[10] and had made many contacts with Western missionaries, particularly Americans, from whom he learned to speak and write English. He also had time to read Western books, and he took a keen interest in scientific and technological developments. With the vast changes being wrought in Southeast Asia by the new power of the West,

[9]Walter Vella, *Siam under Rama III* (Locust Valley, N.Y., 1957), p. 115.

[10]He had a greater claim to succeed his father on the throne than did his half brother in 1824; but the latter seized power, and Mongkut chose to enter the priesthood rather than contest him.

Mongkut became intensely interested in inte
tions. When he came to power in 1851, he
that Siam would have to accommodate itself to t.
be subdued by it. Hall probably paid him the su⊢
compliment when he wrote: "It is perhaps not too muci.
to say that Siam owed to Mongkut more than anyone else
the fact that she preserved her independence when by the
end of the nineteenth century all the other states of Southeast Asia had come under European control."[11]

The event that seems to have been decisive in the thinking
of Mongkut and a few other liberal Siamese leaders was the
defeat of China by Great Britain in 1842. If China, to whose
power and prestige Siam deferred for many centuries, could
not hold out against Western pressures, Mongkut and his
advisers reasoned that Siam also could not expect to resist
these pressures and survive as a nation. Therefore, almost
immediately upon his accession, Mongkut set out to cultivate
the friendship of the greatest power, and therefore the greatest threat to Siam's security, at that time—the British.

The Treaty of Friendship and Commerce of 1855 with
Great Britain was a turning point in Siamese history, not
only in her relations with Western countries but also in her
internal life. The treaty gave important financial concessions
to the British, which had a direct effect on Siam's economic
life and caused a revolution in the traditional means of
conducting business and trade within Siam. The treaty also
necessitated profound changes in the internal administration
of the country and in the implementation of justice. The
major concessions limited Siam to an ad valorem duty of 3
per cent on goods imported by British merchants; permitted
opium to be imported duty free, subject to some restrictions;
limited export duties to an agreed schedule; gave British

[11]Hall, *op. cit.*, p. 578.

subjects the right to rent or own land near the capital; granted British subjects extraterritorial rights—that is, the right to trial under British rather than Siamese law for violation of criminal and civil codes; and recognized the right of the British consul in Bangkok to handle cases involving British subjects. These latter two provisions became the most serious threat to Siamese independence during succeeding decades and were the source of much subsequent resentment of Western influence in Siam.

The reception accorded the British envoy, Sir John Bowring, by King Mongkut has been described in detail by many writers. It seems clear that the Siamese monarch outdid himself to impress upon Queen Victoria's representative that Siam was an enlightened and progressive kingdom which welcomed contacts with the West; furthermore, Siam, unlike its Asian neighbors, was prepared to do business with the British and to make whatever internal adjustments were required to maintain cordial and fruitful relations. To a large extent Mongkut succeeded in this effort, and relations with the British remained cordial. Mongkut paid a heavy price for this friendship, in the subsequent disruption of Siamese life, but he had set out on this course determined not to make the same mistakes as had the Burmese and Chinese; and because he was so powerful a ruler, he was able to overcome the opposition of the conservative Siamese nobility.

The year after the conclusion of the British treaty, Siam negotiated similar treaties with the United States and France. The American envoy, Mr. Townsend Harris, had been commissioned to go to Japan to negotiate a treaty with the emperor for trade and commerce. He was sent first to Siam, however, when word of Bowring's success reached Washington. Harris was accorded a similar reception to that given

Bowring; but according to his own account, he had first to persuade Siamese officials of the size and importance of the United States. Once negotiations on the treaty began, it was clear that the Siamese desired something more than a commercial arrangement; Harris stated in his diary that they wanted a commitment from the United States to act as arbiter on Siam's behalf in case it became involved in trouble with Great Britain. Harris refused to be drawn into such an arrangement and threatened to leave Siam without an agreement. Finally Mongkut signed the treaty without reservations. Harris reported that most of his difficulties were the result of Siamese fear and distrust of the British, whom they characterized as "rapacious tyrants who were seizing the whole of Asia." On the other hand, Harris quoted the Prime Minister as saying, "We love the Americans, for they have never done us or anyone else in the East an injury."[12]

If Harris' account of Siam's attitude is a fair appraisal, it would support the view that Mongkut's policy toward Great Britain was based on fear rather than on respect and admiration, as some writers have argued. Although he recognized clearly that Siam must accommodate itself to British power, Mongkut was not willing to trust the British. Thus he sought guarantees from other powers to help ensure Siam's independence during this critical period. It was a policy based on a sober assessment of Siam's weakness in the face of pressure from a powerful nation.

When the French negotiated with Siam in 1856 for a treaty of trade and commerce, their envoy was also approached with a plea for protection from the British. He refused to be drawn into any commitment on this matter, and the treaty he finally concluded was similar to those obtained by the

[12]*The Complete Journal of Townsend Harris* (Garden City, N.J., 1930), pp. 111, 150, 151.

British and the Americans, except that it gave considerable freedom to French missionaries to carry on their work in Siam. However, the French representative came away from the negotiations with the impression that the Siamese would have welcomed French assistance to counterbalance British influence.

After these three treaties were concluded, Siam made similar arrangements with many other European countries. Britain, however, became the most important commercial country in Siam, and within a few years British merchants had invested large sums of money and had established many firms there.

If fear of British encroachment dominated Siamese foreign policy in the eighteen-fifties, the intervention of the French in Cambodia and Laos beginning in the eighteen-sixties became Siam's principal worry in the latter part of the century. By 1861 France had established itself firmly in South Vietnam and then laid claim to suzerainty over Cambodia because the latter had paid tribute to Vietnam as well as to Siam. The French pressed their claim strongly, with both the Cambodians and the Siamese. Finally, in 1867 King Mongkut agreed to a treaty whereby Siam gave up its rights in Cambodia in return for French recognition of Siam's control of the two formerly Cambodian provinces of Siemrat and Pratabong (Siemreap and Battambang). Before Mongkut died in 1868, it was clear to him and his advisers that France was becoming the real danger to Siam's independence, and that Siam would need the fullest support of the British to resist the French advance.

Mongkut was succeeded by his son, Chulalongkorn, who reigned for forty-two years, until 1910. A minor when his father died, he used the period prior to his formal accession in 1873 to read widely and to travel to Java and to India

in search of knowledge of Western technology and administration as they were exercised in Asian countries. When
he assumed control of the government, he greatly speeded
up the modernization that his father had begun. Hall states
that the young king "realized forcibly that if his country
were to preserve her independence she must, willy-nilly, put
her house in order according to the prevailing European
notions, or at least keep up the appearance of doing so."[13]
The changes instituted during his long reign were truly
remarkable. One of the most far-reaching was his insistence
that the children of royalty be educated by Western standards
at the palace school. He also sent many of his sons to Europe
for their education, and when they returned, they assisted
in accelerating the modernization of Siam. In addition,
Chulalongkorn hired many foreign technicians and advisers
to assist in this silent revolution until such time as Siam had
enough trained people to do the job itself. Some of these
foreign advisers were given wide responsibilities and were
honored accordingly by the King with noble titles.

Failure of the Policy of Accommodation

The greatest threat to Siam during this period lay in
foreign affairs. The British completed the annexation of
Burma in 1886 and were steadily extending their influence
in the Malay States. Despite their fear of the British, the
Siamese were able to negotiate most differences in an ami-
cable manner. The French, however, used any pretext to
extend their control over all territories that had at any time
been part of Cambodia or of Laos. After France completed
the subjugation of Vietnam in the eighteen-eighties, Siam
began to worry about its own hold on the Laotian states and
sent a strong army to Luang Prabang to put down a local up-

[13]Hall, *op. cit.,* p. 584.

rising. Incidents followed involving a Laotian chieftain, which France used as an excuse for annexing a number of Laotian cantons. In 1890 France set forth new and extensive claims in Laos, based on the fact that Laotian kings had once paid tribute to the King of Annam. Siam rejected these claims and reinforced its garrisons in Laos. At the same time the British became concerned because the area in dispute reached to the northern border of Burma and because they wished to avoid border difficulties with the French in Southeast Asia.

When in 1893 France laid claim to all Siamese territory east of the Mekong River, Britain did not reject this claim but only raised with the French the question of Siamese rights in the area. Without active British support, Siam's position was hopeless. France then exploited various incidents in Laos and demanded that Siam evacuate all territory east of the Mekong. The Siamese offered to submit the dispute to arbitration, but French forces from Vietnam moved across the border and began to occupy Siamese territory. Siam appealed frantically to Great Britain for help, but London counseled moderation and asked Siam not to provoke the French into a war. France knew, however, that the Siamese were helpless to stop its advance and in a show of force sent several warships to the mouth of the Chao Pya River early in July 1893. There is some dispute whether the French naval commander received instructions to remain outside the mouth of the river; but the ships did proceed up the river, and the Siamese fortress at Paknam fired on them. The French returned the fire, and casualties were suffered on both sides. After this exchange the French were in the command-ing position.[14] The French government issued an ultimatum

[14]Hall concludes that "the Siamese committed the serious blunder of firing the first shots in the encounter" and thereby "played into the hands of the French." *Ibid.*, p. 607.

to Siam which demanded three things: evacuation of all territory east of the Mekong—from the river basin in northern Laos down to the Cambodian border; payment of an indemnity of three million francs; and punishment of the officers responsible for the firing on French ships at Paknam. Siam was willing to accept the latter two points but asked for negotiations on the border question, because much of the territory demanded by France had been under Siamese control for many years: Even France had recognized Siam's rights in Luang Prabang several years earlier. In desperation Siam pleaded with Great Britain to intercede and ask France to moderate its demands.

Britain did indeed become alarmed as the Siamese situation appeared to be drifting toward war; it sent several warships to the Gulf of Siam to demonstrate its interest in the dispute. It also asked France for an explanation of its intentions; but after obtaining a promise that Siamese independence would be respected, Britain urged Siam to accept the French demands. The Siamese government had delayed its decision in the hope that Britain could influence the French, so the latter proceeded to blockade the Chao Pya River. Siam finally capitulated in August 1893, but now France decided to increase its price and demanded that Siam also evacuate all armed forces from the provinces of Siemrat and Pratabong, which had once been part of Cambodia. It also demanded that Siam withdraw its forces twenty-five kilometers from the west bank of the Mekong River; pending the withdrawal, French forces occupied the southeastern Siamese province of Chantabun. In October 1893 a treaty was finally agreed to which embodied all these concessions; but the Siamese were bitterly disappointed over the lack of support from Great Britain in their hour of need.

Soon afterward Britain and France negotiated to determine

their spheres of influence in Southeast Asia, but efforts to create a buffer zone in northern Laos came to naught. For a time it appeared that these two nations might be drawn into a war over rival claims in the area, and that Siam might be caught in the middle. However, in 1896 Britain and France reached an agreement that gave France all territory east of the Mekong, in upper Burma, and in Laos; and both nations then agreed to guarantee the independence of Siam in the Chao Pya Valley.[15]

The danger period for Siam did not finally end until 1904, because France continued to press demands and to interpret the 1893 treaty in an extreme manner, particularly regarding the status of Asian subjects of the French empire, or protégés. When France and Great Britain concluded the Entente Cordiale in 1904, they also settled the Siamese question. In that year Siam concluded a limited treaty with France by which it agreed to give up sovereignty over all the Laotian states in return for French concessions on the protégé question and evacuation of Chantabun. A final settlement was reached in 1907, when Siam gave up all claims to the provinces of Siemrat and Pratabong, and France relinquished jurisdiction over its Asian subjects resident in Siam. Britain and Siam settled their differences in 1909, when Siam surrendered sovereignty over the four Malay states of Kelantan, Trengganu, Kedah, and Perlis, and Britain gave up jurisdiction over its Asian subjects in Siam.

During this period two visits by King Chulalongkorn to the major European capitals, in 1897 and again in 1907, enhanced Siam's international prestige. He was warmly received by European royalty and by the French President. The Siamese government hoped that through such contacts King Chulalongkorn could induce the various great powers to

[15]*Ibid.*, p. 610.

accept Siam as a soverign state and to accord it equal rights in the international community. This was a continuation of King Mongkut's policy of personal diplomacy with the Western powers of the day; but at the turn of the century the necessity for Siam to obtain international recognition of its sovereignty was even greater than it had been fifty years earlier.

In recent years considerable controversy has arisen among both Thai and foreign scholars over the diplomatic history of Siam in the eighteen-eighties and nineties. Because this period continues to arouse strong emotions among the Thais, it is well to clarify the record in order better to appreciate Thai thinking about current problems of Southeast Asia. King Mongkut's policy of accommodation to the West clearly was based on an erroneous assumption—namely, that Siam could preserve its independence in the face of Western imperialism by playing Britain and France against each other. Another assumption was that a policy of appeasement would be to Siam's advantage. In line with this view Mongkut gave the British what they wanted in 1855; at the same time he and his advisers sought to establish close relations with France in order to counteract the growing economic and political influence of Britain. It was the same policy that King Narai had tried in the seventeenth century, in order to curb Dutch influence, except that King Mongkut went much farther in accepting a policy of change and modernization. However, the French had ambitions of their own in Southeast Asia, not excluding Siam; and when these became apparent in the eighteen-eighties, the Siamese seriously tried to establish the closest possible relations with the British in order to counter the growing French threat from Indochina. A policy of appeasement did not work with the French: it seemed only to whet their appetite for more concessions. Neither did a policy of alignment with Britain work out to Siam's satisfaction, because the British were not willing to defend Siamese interests at the risk of bringing on a war with France. It is also possible that the British may even have considered absorbing Siam into the British Empire if an agreement could have been worked out with the French.

Some observers believe that King Chulalongkorn made a serious mistake in 1893 in ordering the shelling of the French ships at Paknam. If, so the argument goes, these ships had been allowed to sail up the river, Siam would have emerged from this crisis in better condition because the French would have had no pretext for their ultimatum. Negotiations would then have taken place in which the British could have brought their influence to bear on Siam's behalf. This writer believes this view to be too simple, for it is based on two assumptions that are not necessarily valid: first, that the French would have been more moderate in their demands for control of all of Laos and Cambodia, including Siemrat and Pratabong; and second, that the British would have been willing to bring, and effectively could have brought, real pressure to bear on France. It seems clear that Britain did not consider Siamese possessions in Laos and Cambodia worth the risk of war with France, and it is indeed questionable whether Britain would have been willing to go to war with France to protect Siamese independence. The shelling of the French ships at least had the effect of forcing the British and other European powers to recognize that France might be bent on annexing the whole Chao Pya Valley. By precipitating a clash with the French, the Siamese probably lost no more territory than they would have by continuing to appease the French; and it probably jolted the British into realizing that France might take over all of Siam and threaten the

large British economic investment there, unless some agreement were reached quickly to guarantee the integrity of
Siam as a buffer between the two colonial empires. Surely
the British were not pleased by the prospect of having an
ambitious and proud France facing them across the Burmese
border and of losing their large commercial stake in Siam.
In sum, it may be said that Siamese independence was
preserved by a combination of factors, not least of which
was sheer luck. Appeasement had not worked on France,
and close cooperation and skillful diplomacy had failed to
sway Great Britain. In the final analysis, Britain and France
came to an agreement because of their mutual desire to avoid
a confrontation in Southeast Asia, not because of any great
attachment for Siam. Those who had been responsible for
Siam's foreign policy at the turn of the century were well
aware of this; and after the crisis of its independence was
over, they began to reassess Siam's international position and
to look around for new friends.

Search for International Recognition

The Siamese have often been described as highly pragmatic people, strongly influenced by events rather than by
theories or speculation. This national trait was clearly opera-
tive in the field of foreign policy during the nineteenth
century. Until 1842 the most important power in the world
for the Siamese was China; and each Siamese monarch was
careful to pay formal respect to the Chinese emperor by
sending him tributary gifts.[16] After China's military defeat
by the British, however, Siam's policy was one of accommodation to Great Britain, which it considered to be the most powerful of the European nations. Siam, however, was sufficiently

[16]This practice continued until after Siam concluded the treaties of
1855–1856 with the western powers.

impressed with French power to seek to establish good relations with France and even to appease her by giving up
Siamese claims in Cambodia during the eighteen-sixties. The
period after 1893 saw Siam searching for additional friends
among the great powers as a means of avoiding dependence
on Britain. It gave increasing attention to the United States
as a possible ally after the latter defeated the Spanish in the
Philippines and acquired territories in Southeast Asia. Shortly
thereafter, in 1903, Professor Edward H. Strobel of the Harvard Law School was recruited as the first foreign policy
adviser to the Minister of Foreign Affairs—a position that
was maintained until 1940.[17]

Perhaps the most significant event in the long run in respect to Siamese foreign policy was the defeat of Russia by
Japan in 1904 and the subsequent peace treaty which conferred on Japan the status of a great power. Prior to this,
Siam had cultivated friendly relations with Russia in the
hope of persuading it to counsel France against pressing new
claims in Southeast Asia. King Chulalongkorn and several
royal princes had sent their sons to Saint Petersburg as military cadets, and there were friendly exchanges between the
Czar and the Siamese king. Russian prestige and influence
declined rapidly after the Japanese victory, however, while
that of Japan rose rapidly. In many ways Siam's and Japan's
experiences with the West had been similar. Both were old
monarchies that until the mid-nineteenth century were in-
ward-looking and highly suspicious of Western nations. Both
were opened to Western trade and influence by outside
forces, and both sought immediately to modernize their
countries in order to avoid losing their independence. By

[17] A British adviser was attached to the Ministry of Finance, a French-
man was retained in the Ministry of Justice, and other nationals were
hired as consultants and advisers in various other ministries.

the end of the century Siam and Japan were the only independent countries remaining in the Far East. Siam was therefore tremendously impressed that Japan, in the short span
of fifty years, had so modernized itself that it could defeat a
major European power in war. Japanese prestige was also
increased by a treaty of commerce concluded in 1898, in
which Japan agreed to give up all extraterritorial rights in
Siam. Japanese influence therefore increased substantially
during the early part of the twentieth century.

In the period preceding World War I, the primary objective of Siam's foreign policy was to gain international recognition of the nation's independence and boundaries and to
regain full sovereignty over its internal administration, particularly over foreign nationals living within its borders. The
war provided Siam with an opportunity to achieve both
objectives. When war broke out, Siam declared its neutrality;
but Britain and France were anxious to have it join the Allies,
because of the large quantities of food it could contribute,
and because both Allied powers could then withdraw troops
from Southeast Asia for use on the western front. Although
King Wachirawut (Rama VI), who had ascended the throne
in 1910, was sympathetic to Britain as a result of his long
years of schooling in that country, the army officers tended
to be sympathetic to Germany because many of them, including several royal princes, had received their military training
there. Furthermore, the Siamese elite was opposed to both
the British and the French because of their treatment of Siam
during the eighteen-nineties. The Germans, on the other
hand, had never infringed on Siamese sovereignty, had been
good traders, and had assisted Siam with its internal development, notably its railroads.

By 1917, however, it was clear that the Allies would win—
particularly after the United States declared war on Germany

and Austria. In July, Siam declared war on Germany on the pretext of its unrestricted submarine warfare. Eventually Siam sent to France about 1,200 men, most of whom were in a motor transport corps, while the others were pilots and airplane mechanics. These men arrived in France only a few months before the Armistice. They returned home as heroes, however, and the Siamese took considerable pride in their participation in the war.

Siam gained after the war the right both to be represented as an equal at the Paris Peace Conference and to participate as a charter member of the League of Nations. Its international status had improved enormously from what it had been a decade earlier, and the stage was now set for negotiations with the European powers to terminate the extra-territorial and "special privileges" provisions of those treaties concluded in the eighteen-fifties and sixties that had caused Siam a considerable loss of sovereignty.

Negotiations concerning Siam's sovereignty commenced at the Paris Peace Conference when the Siamese approached the American delegation and asked for a revision of the treaty of 1856. President Wilson agreed with the Siamese position, and in 1920 a new treaty was signed that gave Siam full jurisdiction over all American subjects living there. This was agreed to as Siam's right, and the United States asked no compensation or concessions in return. The latter also agreed to revise the economic clauses of the 1856 treaty and to give Siam the right to levy any duty on the import of American goods, provided that other nations also agreed to waive their treaty rights in this matter. By its generosity the United States greatly increased its prestige among the Siamese and contributed to improved relations between the two countries.[18]

[18]For a description of the negotiations with the United States and

Negotiations with the ten European nations that had similar treaties with Siam proved more difficult. A major reason was that none of the treaties had a time limit, and no method had been provided for terminating or modifying them except by consent of both parties. In effect Siam had no recourse but to appeal to the sense of justice of each treaty nation. The King decided to entrust these negotiations to the current American adviser in the Ministry of Foreign Affairs, a young Harvard law instructor named Francis B. Sayre. The fact that Sayre was the son-in-law of Woodrow Wilson may have been a factor in choosing him for the job of persuading European governments to renegotiate these unfair treaties. Sayre spent a year visiting European capitals and in 1925, despite great frustrations and many delays, succeeded in negotiating agreements on behalf of Siam which closely followed the American treaty.[19] Certain minor restrictions on Siamese sovereignty were retained in some of these documents, but the new treaties provided for abrogation by either party after ten years. By 1939 Siam had renegotiated these treaties, thus finally regaining, after eighty-four years, its full sovereignty.

---

other treaty powers, see Francis B. Sayre, *The Passing of Extraterritoriality in Siam* (Institute of Pacific Relations, 1928).

[19]The role played by Francis Sayre in getting these treaties revised has a prominent place in Thai history books and contributes to the friendly feeling the Thais have for the United States today.

Chapter 2

The Political Climate

WHEN King Mongkut concluded in 1851 that Siam either had to modernize or perish as an independent nation, he set in motion forces that neither he nor his successors could clearly foresee or easily control. During the next eighty years Siam experienced tremendous economic and social changes and the complete revision of its administrative machinery. In the political sphere, however, there was almost no change: Siam remained an absolute monarchy—one of the few remaining in the world in 1932. The most significant aspect of the political revolution in that year was the absence of violence with which it was accomplished; to some observers, an equally important feature was that political change had been so long in coming. Both factors indicated that the Siamese were not a politically oriented people, and that they had a deep respect for the institution of the monarchy.[1]

Among the causes of the revolution that occurred on June 24, 1932, the most frequently mentioned are: (1) the weakness of King Prachatipok (Rama VII), who came to the throne in 1925 without previously expecting to succeed his brother

[1] A plot to depose Rama VI and set up a constitutional monarchy under another prince was discovered and crushed in 1912. The plot included both military and civilian officials and was remarkably similar to the 1932 *coup d'état* in its aims and plan of execution.

and therefore had not prepared himself for the demanding tasks of ruling an absolute monarchy; (2) the economic retrenchment necessitated in part by the extravagance of King Wachirawut (Rama VI) and later by the world-wide economic depression. King Prachatipok made strenuous efforts to keep the national budget in balance, but in so doing he was forced to reduce the size of the civil service and the army and to delay promotions for those who remained; (3) the resentment felt by many officers over King Wachirawut's private military corps, the Wild Tigers, which he had created and on which he lavished attention and funds—money that the regular army felt should have been used to strengthen the nation's defenses. Although King Prachatipok tried to restore the prestige of the armed forces, he was not able to overcome the general discontent among many army officers.[2]

Probably the most important cause of the revolution of 1932 was the determination of a small group of foreign-trained young intellectuals to modernize Siam's political structure and to institute a program of radical economic reform. These men, who had studied in Europe during the nineteen-twenties, were impressed with the ideas of liberal government and political freedom that permeated Europe after World War I. In a real sense the key men in the June conspiracy were political idealists who believed the time had come for Siam to rid itself of outmoded ideas of kingship. Whether these young liberals were republicans at heart is not entirely clear, for they were willing to retain the mon-

[2]Another factor that created a psychological climate favorable to the revolution was a superstition that the Chakri dynasty would last only one hundred and fifty years. Chula Chakrabongse relates that in April 1932, on the occasion of the anniversary of the coronation of Rama I in 1782, "rumors were rampant," and people "were talking of an impending revolution or at least of assassinations of high personages." (Lords of Life [New York, 1960], p. 309.)

archy so long as the King agreed to accept a much reduced role; but it is certain that the group of some fifty Siamese students who had returned from France by 1932 was determined to remake Siam politically and was fully prepared to abolish the monarchy if it proved to be a stumbling block to their program.[3] The leader of this group was a brilliant young lawyer who had studied law in Paris—Pridi Panomyong, also known by his title name Luang Pradit Manutam.[4] When he returned to Siam in 1928, after having obtained a Doctor of Laws degree, he was appointed professor of law at Chulalongkorn University and soon became secretary of the bar association. At the time of the revolution in 1932, Pridi was only about thirty years old; yet he was regarded as the brains of the revolution.

There is reason to believe that if King Prachatipok had been permitted to follow his own political instincts, he would have granted a constitution before the conspirators could take matters into their own hands. Sir Josiah Crosby recalls that King Prachatipok told him personally that his uncles and brothers, "who could not bring themselves to believe that there was anything untoward in the air," dissuaded him from granting a constitution.[5] The ultimatum the King

[3]Walter Vella states that the most politically minded students were those who studied in France, primarily in law. "These students were doubly vulnerable to liberal political influences" he writes. "They were surrounded by a republican atmosphere and they were studying a subject closely allied to politics." (*The Impact of the West on Government in Thailand* [Berkeley, 1955], p. 363.)

[4]Titles such as Luang, Pra, and Pya were conferred by the King on commoners who achieved a certain rank in the civil service or the armed forces. After 1932 this practice was abandoned, but many people continued to use the titles they already had. Since Pridi Panomyong is the name by which he is better known, it is used in this study.

[5]Crosby, *Siam: The Crossroads* (London, 1945), p. 78. Vella has observed, "It is ironical that if Prachathipok had been more of an

received at his summer residence on June 24, 1932, left no doubt that unless he capitulated to the demands of the People's Party (as the revolutionary group called itself) and accepted a constitution, he would be deposed, and another prince would be installed as monarch.[6]

It seemed clear on the day of the revolution that the People's Party was split into two factions: a leftist group that was made up primarily of young civil servants and led by Pridi Panomyong; and a conservative group composed mainly of older army and navy officers and led by Colonel (Pya) Pahon Ponpayuhasena, one of the three colonels who signed the ultimatum to the King. He was joined by another influential army officer, Colonel (Pya) Song Suradet, commandant of the Army Staff College—a highly important position through the influence it gave him over younger army officers. Colonel Song, who was even more conservative than Pahon, did not trust Pridi and his group of intellectuals. A younger army officer, Major (Luang) Pibun Songkhram, also joined the People's Party and later became its most powerful leader; in 1932 he played a minor role in the revolution, working primarily behind the scenes. The mil-

autocrat—more strong-willed than his advisers—the monarchy might have been able to introduce a democratic regime to Thailand." (Op. cit., p. 360.)

[6]For the texts of this ultimatum and of the King's reply, see Kenneth P. Landon, Siam in Transition (Chicago, 1939), pp. 9, 10. Some writers have concluded that the events of June 24 and 25 did not constitute a revolution in the true sense, because the King accepted the demands of the revolutionists and pardoned all of them. It cannot be denied, however, that the King was under great duress, and that there surely would have been some bloodshed had he not capitulated. For all practical purposes the overthrow of the absolute monarchy in 1932 was a revolution, but the term coup d'état has been used extensively in order to preserve the fiction that the King acted of his own free will in granting a constitution.

itary leaders of the revolution were essentially conservative officers who respected the institution of the monarchy and believed that Siam needed a strong king as a unifying force to avoid the dangers of political instability. At heart they probably were not interested in representative government of the Western type; their main reason for joining the revolutionary group was their dissatisfaction with the arrogance of the royal princes who occupied most of the top positions in the government. Once they achieved positions of power and prestige, these officers were prepared to resist any further progress of the revolution. Pridi and his radicals could not have staged their revolution without army support; and after the *coup d'état* he had to accept, for the time being at least, the conservative views of the army in formulating government policies and in drafting a permanent constitution.

The provisional constitution that King Prachatipok accepted a few days after the revolution was largely the work of Pridi; it remained in effect for six months, while a constitutional drafting committee worked on a permanent basic law. Under its terms the country was governed by a king, an assembly with a special executive committee which later became the cabinet, and law courts; but the king was reduced to acting only as a figurehead. The provisional assembly consisted of seventy members, appointed by the People's Party. At its first meeting it elected Pya Manopakorn, the respected chief judge of the Court of Appeals, as chairman of the executive committee (Prime Minister). Pya Mano, as he was usually called, was not involved in the revolution but was sympathetic with its limited aims.

It may seem strange that the intellectual leaders of this revolution permitted the policy of the provisional government to be determined largely by conservative civil servants, most of whom had taken no part in the overthrow of the government. The reason is that the older and conservative army leaders opposed a sharp change of policy and of administration, especially in view of the king's willingness to cooperate with the People's Party. Another important, and perhaps crucial, reason for the moderation with which the new government approached its tasks was the fear that foreign powers might not recognize it if it appeared too radical. King Prachatipok warned in his reply to the ultimatum of June 24 that "if I decline to continue in my office as king, the foreign powers will not recognize the new government. This might entail considerable difficulty for the government."[7] The People's Party wanted the new government to be accepted by foreign powers, and it wished to avoid at all costs giving any of them cause to intervene in Siamese affairs.[8]

Constitutional Government (1933–1938)

The permanent constitution of December 10, 1932, represented a compromise between the views of the young liberal element in the People's Party and the moderate views of the King and of the conservative army elements in the party. As a result it was a conservative document which gave the monarch a more prominent role in governing the country than did the provisional constitution. This basic law embodied the six principles of the People's Party, which were enunciated in the original manifesto distributed in Bangkok on June 24, and were accepted by all subsequent Thai governments: (1) freedom and equality of all people in politics, in business, and before the law; (2) internal peace and

[7]Landon, *op. cit.*, p. 10.

[8]Crosby writes that when he took up his duties as British Minister in Bangkok in 1934, many in the new government still feared that Britain and France might intervene to restore the absolute monarchy. He says it was one of his first tasks to dispel this fear from the Thai leaders' minds. (*Op. cit.*, p. 92.)

order; (3) economic well-being for everyone through adoption of a national economic policy; (4) equal privileges for all classes; (5) freedom and liberty for everyone where they did not conflict with the first four principles; (6) the most complete educational opportunities possible for all people.

A unique feature of this constitution was the provision that half the members of the assembly would be appointed by the king and would serve until half the eligible voters had completed four years of schooling, or for a maximum of ten years. The reason given was that since the country was not prepared for full democracy, a period of tutelage was required in order to ensure a peaceful transition. This may have been a sound decision in view of the inexperience of the nation in representative government; but it meant that the ruling political group, the People's Party, could maintain itself in power for at least ten years and perhaps longer. The other members of the assembly were subject to general elections every four years—or sooner if the King dissolved an assembly—and had to fulfill certain educational requirements as well as be residents of their districts. The powers given to the executive indicate how far the provisional cabinet of Pya Mano had accommodated the wishes of the King. The King was empowered to dissolve the assembly—even without the cabinet's approval—with the stipulation that general elections must be held within three months. He was also given the right of pardon and of vetoing legislation, although the assembly could override his veto. He was empowered to promulgate emergency decrees provided they were countersigned by one responsible minister. The cabinet was appointed jointly by the King and the assembly, rather than exclusively by the assembly. The December 10 constitution thus was the first step toward representative government in Siam; it also contained the seeds of a political philosophy that would later serve to cloak political elements that opposed democratic government and sought to control the nation.

Although the constitution was promulgated with great pomp and ceremony by the King and the government, the underlying differences of political philosophy between the cabinet and the assembly[9] soon broke into the open and resulted in a serious split between Pya Mano and Pridi Panomyong. The immediate issue was a national economic plan that Pridi had drafted in accordance with the third principle of the June 24 manifesto. His radical plan for revolutionizing the nation's economic system represented the supreme effort of the young civilian intellectuals in the People's Party to wrest control of the revolution from the older conservative faction and to institute those social and economic reforms that they had hoped to effect in the June 24 revolution. Pridi was strongly influenced by Marxist ideas in formulating his plan, and the way he proposed to carry it out verged on totalitarianism. One writer has stated that Pridi's aim was to establish a "pyramidal economic dictatorship 'for the good of the people,' " and that he condoned "an authoritarian system as a means to an end because he hated and was impatient of his people's backwardness."[10] The key element in Pridi's plan was that the government should take over and operate the economic system, own all the industries and all the land, and decide how it should be divided and worked. The difference between this and a Communist economic plan lay in its implementation. Instead of confiscating all land and industries, the government would be empowered to compensate the owners with government bonds, and all

[9]The seventy members of the assembly whom the People's Party had appointed the previous June continued to serve until elections could be held.

[10]John Coast, *Some Aspects of Siamese Politics* (New York, 1953), p. 6.

its actions would be accomplished in accordance with the law. Pridi left no doubt that state socialism was his goal; he conceded that this would result in a loss of freedom for the people, but he justified these harsh measures by promising "overwhelming happiness" for the people, who would benefit richly from state management of the means of production.

Pridi's economic plan, although never implemented, is significant for two reasons: (1) it split the People's Party wide open within nine months of the June revolution, causing such a severe strain between cabinet and assembly that he was obliged to retire temporarily from politics; and (2) it showed clearly that contrary to the views of some writers, Pridi was at heart neither a democrat nor even a liberal. Although it may be argued whether he was a Moscow Communist, there can be little doubt that he was strongly influenced by Marxism. Few people have doubted Pridi's patriotism, which he demonstrated so well during World War II; but it would be false to assert that he was a great liberal idealist who sought freedom and democracy for his people.

The upshot of Pridi's bid for power in the spring of 1933 was a sharp conflict between the cabinet, controlled by Pya Mano, and the assembly, in which there was considerable support for Pridi's economic plan. The cabinet became alarmed at the possibility that the assembly might take matters into its hands and declare "no confidence" in the government. Therefore, Pya Mano called Pridi a Communist and started a rumor that Pridi's followers were planning a *coup d'état*. The situation was further complicated by publication and wide distribution of the King's objections to Pridi's economic plan, which seriously compromised the King in the eyes of the moderates and made him a target in subsequent attacks on the Mano government. Pya Mano persuaded the King to issue a royal decree on April 1, 1933, proroguing the assembly and giving Mano dictatorial powers. To accomplish his ends, Mano had to solicit the support of the army, which he did by raising the specter of Communism. Moderate army officers such as Colonel Pahon were won over, and their signatures on the royal decree were decisive in implementing Mano's plan to crush Pridi.

Pridi and four supporters resigned from the cabinet, and he was persuaded to take a long trip to Europe. To ensure that Pridi's followers and radical ideas did not disturb the peace, Mano imposed strict press censorship and closed down several newspapers for criticizing him. A law was promulgated making it a crime, punishable by ten years in prison, to be a Communist. By the end of April 1933, the older conservative faction was clearly victorious in its power struggle with the young radicals.

As often happens in situations of this kind, Mano's tactics soon caused anxiety among the military leaders, who began to fear that he would not be content until he had restored the absolute monarchy. On June 20, 1933, the military group arrested Mano and other conservative leaders, imposed martial law on the country, and informed the King that it was "necessary for the army and navy to seize the control of the government with the intention merely to convene the assembly." They insisted that they were "as always filled with respect and have faith in His Majesty."[11] Colonel Pahon signed this message to the King, along with two brilliant younger officers, Lieutenant Colonel Pibun Songkhram and Navy Commander Supa Chalasai, who played key roles in the overthrow of the Mano government. Pibun, especially, had become keenly aware that control of the military was the key to Siamese politics.

Although Pahon reconvened the assembly and prepared

[11]Landon, *op. cit.*, pp. 31, 32.

for the first general elections, the new government did not abolish the restrictive measures of the Mano regime, such as press censorship, the anti-Communist law, and the ban on public discussion of Pridi's radical economic plan. The government also opposed the formation of political parties, fearing that divisions along political lines in the assembly might lead to political chaos.[12] Clearly, Colonel Pahon and his military group were no more prepared than Pya Mano had been to accept the kind of economic radicalism that Pridi advocated.

Once the military faction was in firm control of the situation, Prime Minister Pahon was persuaded to permit Pridi to return home. He was not allowed to hold high office until a special commission had investigated the charges of Communism against him. After a well-publicized investigation in the spring of 1934, Pridi was officially cleared; it was not decided, however, whether his economic plan was communistic, and therefore many Thais still suspect that Pridi was working toward a communistic system of government, with or without ties to the Soviet Union.

The return of Pridi to Bangkok was a signal to a royalist group to make one last bid for power. These reactionaries rallied around the former Minister of Defense, Prince Boworadet, who quietly gathered together the army officers who favored restoration of the absolute monarchy. Although it is doubtful that the King had any part in the rebellion, many Siamese believed that he must have known of the plan and had not tried to prevent it. On October 12, 1933, Prince Boworadet led his troops from Korat toward Bangkok, proclaiming that his aim was to oust the military oligarchy,

[12]A request by military officers to form a political party was rejected by the Mano government early in 1933, and thereafter the People's Party was divested of its status and became largely a political association.

which had violated the spirit of the revolution and deceived the people with promises of democracy. The Pahon government was equal to the situation, and within a week the rebellion was crushed. (A key figure in the successful defense of Bangkok was Colonel Pibun Songkhram, who was thereafter an exceptionally popular leader both in the army and among the population.) Prince Boworadet fled to Indochina, where he lived in exile, but other members of the rebellion were captured and tried. In typical Siamese fashion the prisoners were well treated, and none were sentenced to death, although the leaders were sent to prison.

In November 1933, a month after the rebellion had been crushed, the first general elections in Siam were held to fill seventy-eight seats in the assembly (the assembly had been expanded in 1932). The vote was light, and the elections produced little enthusiasm among the public; but they were significant in that they showed the government's willingness to carry out the provisions of the 1932 constitution—despite the unsettling effects of the Mano dictatorship and the royalist rebellion. Most of the elected deputies were respected civilians, many of them lawyers and retired officials. The appointed half of the new assembly was composed largely of military officers. Pahon continued as Prime Minister.

At the beginning of 1934 it appeared that the political situation in Siam had finally been stabilized. One last act in the political drama that had commenced with the 1932 revolution was, however, yet to be played. In January 1934, when King Prachatipok and Queen Rampai left for England, it became clear that public sentiment had cooled toward the royal family. The King chose to delay his return to Siam, and in March 1935 he signed a letter of abdication. It is to his lasting credit that he sought, against the counsel of his advisers, to work out a compromise solution to the constitutional problem. Even when he realized that he had outlived his usefulness to the country, he showed great wisdom in suggesting, in the letter of abdication, that his successor should be young enough not to interfere in political affairs until the government had time to implement its new policies. This advice was accepted, and the government selected his ten-year-old nephew, Prince Ananta Mahidon, to be king. A council of regency was established to act for him until he could assume full royal powers.

The five-year period from early 1934 to the end of 1938, when Pahon stepped down as Prime Minister, was one of consolidation and domestic reform in Siam. The feuding between the Pridi forces and the army group—dominated increasingly by Pibun Songkhram—was minimized by Pahon, who acted as moderator between these two dynamic young men. He selected Pibun for Minister of Defense in 1934 and thereby cemented the military's support of his government; while by appointing Pridi Minister of Interior in 1935, Pahon ensured the support of the young liberals whose skills the government desperately needed. Pridi was so successful in this job and made so great an impression on foreign officials during a trip abroad in 1936, that Pahon appointed him Foreign Minister in 1937 and placed him in charge of re-negotiating Siam's treaties of friendship with foreign powers —which finally erased all traces of extraterritoriality in Siam.

Because the period from 1933 to 1938 is frequently referred to as the "hopeful years" of constitutionalism in Thailand— compared with the period from 1939 to 1944, which witnessed a military dictatorship—it is well to assess the progress made toward democratic government during these five years. The major reason for the success of the Pahon government was that the army and the navy were willing to support it against the radicals and the monarchists. It was clear to most political observers at the end of 1933 that the person or clique that controlled the armed forces would control Siamese politics for the foreseeable future. Thompson has cited examples of the elected members of the assembly challenging the government on legislation and on scandals involving ministers, and even forcing the cabinet to resign and reconstitute itself along lines acceptable to the assembly;[13] but the evidence indicates that if there was a democratic trend during the nineteen-thirties, it was carefully controlled by the government and was never permitted to get beyond a rather well-defined line. The fact was, as Vella states, that the power of the cabinet was supreme and "the Assembly understood the bounds of its activities."[14] In the field of personal liberties and freedom, the government showed that it was not prepared to permit democratic ideas to seep down very far: there was no freedom of the press, the government exercised strict censorship, and in one year (1933–1934) there were seventeen occasions on which the government closed newspapers. When the question was raised in 1936 whether newspapers could print news from sources other than those approved by the Bureau of Censorship, the government refused permission. Similarly, the government steadfastly refused to permit political parties to organize because, it said, the time was not yet ripe for party politics.

The truth seems to be that the so-called democratic experiment in Siamese politics following the overthrow of the absolute monarchy was primarily a change of elites rather than a basic change in government policy. Wilson, in his study of Thai politics, has suggested that those who engineered the revolution of 1932 sought to find ideological and

[13]Virginia Thompson, *Thailand: The New Siam* (New York, 1941), pp. 89–95.
[14]Vella, *op. cit.*, p. 378.

legal justification of their actions in European ideas of democracy, constitutionalism, and revolution—with which many of them were familiar through their studies abroad. "They found the current notion of constitution a device which in part served them admirably. A constitution limits a king. But a constitution also has a representative assembly whether representation is in demand or not. Thus they had an assembly."[15] Although this may appear to be a cynical view of the development of constitutionalism in Thailand, it is closer to the truth than the view of those who saw these years as a promising beginning for representative government in Southeast Asia. The drift toward military dictatorship which began in 1939, after Pibun Songkhram became Prime Minister, should not be surprising: it was a logical outcome of political developments throughout the decade combined with the war clouds that began to gather in the late thirties. The fact that Pridi Panomyong, who was thought to be the champion of democratic government, accepted a cabinet post in the Pibun government and cooperated closely with him until the Japanese occupation in 1941 is clear indication that Pridi was not alienated by Pibun's nationalism and authoritarianism, as might be expected of a strong opposition leader.

One might conclude that the revolutionaries of 1932, despite differences of opinion on how the new government should be run, were agreed on one fundamental point, namely, that Siam was not ready for true representative government and hence needed a strong regime—even an authoritarian one—to guide it in domestic as well as in foreign affairs. When it became certain that the world was drifting into war and that Siam might well become involved, the leaders concluded that a strong military, rather than civilian, government would be best for the nation in such a time of crisis.

[15]David A. Wilson, *Politics in Thailand* (Ithaca, N.Y., 1962), pp. 119–26.

Rise and Fall of the Military Faction (1939–1944)

In December 1938 the Pahon government received an adverse vote in the assembly; and the Prime Minister, who had served for nearly six years, decided to step down in favor of his protégé, Pibun Songkhram, who had by this time consolidated his control of the army. Pibun had several major attributes that qualified him for this powerful position. First, he was an excellent military officer, who had risen from a humble family background and won a scholarship to study military science in France. Second, he was a master politician who had won the respect and confidence of his fellow officers by cleverly using his position as Minister of Defense to make promotions and give out decorations and other honors to key personnel in the army and navy. Third, Pibun shrewdly took advantage of a nationalist awakening among the educated class following the revolution of 1932, and built it into an ideology patterned to a large extent on the German and Japanese models of state worship. Endowed with a pleasing personality, good looks, and a sharp mind, Pibun seemed to personify what the Thai people look for in a national leader; but it is difficult to say whether he would have risen so high as Prime Minister without the active support of Colonel Pahon.

Much has been written about the various forms that this new nationalism and chauvinism took during Pibun's tenure as Prime Minister, from 1939 to the summer of 1944. Basically Pibun's philosophy was antidemocratic: he believed that authoritarian government based on military strength was the most efficient way to achieve progress in an underdeveloped nation such as Siam. Like Pridi and other younger officials who had studied in the West, Pibun was determined that Siam must break out of its backwardness and achieve a larger role in Asian affairs. Pibun and his supporters looked to Germany and Japan, which had so successfully built up their strength and challenged Britain and France, as models for Siam's future. To achieve similar success, Siam's economy had to be made self-sufficient, the Chinese minority had to be divested of its commercial monopoly, the people had to be taught patriotism and inculcated with faith in the military as the protector of the nation, and the leader—Pibun—should be revered as the national genius who would bring back the glories of old Siam. As Crosby has so aptly stated: "It is a characteristic of the Siamese that they like to be in the fashion, and Luang Pibul [Pibun] proved no exception to this rule. If dictatorships were to be the order of the day, then it suited his book perfectly to develop into a dictator himself!"[16]

Pibun's assumption of complete power shattered the small beginnings that had been made toward constitutional government in Siam; in an age when totalitarianism seemed to be the wave of the future, there was little room in Pibun's scheme of things for the principles of democratic government. From the time he took over the reins of government from Pahon, Pibun's attitude toward the assembly was one of tolerance and then of indifference. During 1939 the assembly passed every measure the government submitted; and few of the elected members sought to organize any opposition to Pibun—as they had to Pahon. Pibun rewarded the compliant assemblymen with a salary increase at the end of 1939, and in this and other ways he obtained their full cooperation without resorting to coercion.[17]

[16]Crosby, op. cit., p. 89.

[17]Even before Pibun became Prime Minister, a majority of both the cabinet and the appointed half of the assembly were military men. This trend became even more pronounced after his accession and helped to ensure his control of the legislature.

Pibun's selection of a cabinet is perhaps the best indication of his skill in placating dissident elements and gaining cooperation through persuasion rather than through force. To his potential rival, Pridi, went the post of Minister of Finance and considerable freedom to institute rather sweeping reforms in the nation's financial system. Another well-known participant in the 1932 revolution, Khuang Apaiwong, became Minister of Communications; another, Admiral Tamrong Nawasawat, was appointed Minister of Justice. Pibun retained for himself the key posts of Defense Minister and Minister of Interior, which gave him control over the national police. Finally, Pibun took the portfolio of Minister of Foreign Affairs, although he chose as deputy minister one of Pridi's able supporters, Direk Chaiyanam, who became Foreign Minister in 1941. By 1940 Pibun was in complete control of the government, he had virtually no opposition within the country, and he was thus in an excellent position to turn his attention to foreign affairs and to play the game of international politics which he hoped would bring him and his country unprecedented influence in Southeast Asia.

When in December 1941 Japanese forces occupied Thailand, Pibun decided to cooperate with them.[18] Pridi and his followers were ousted from the cabinet to make room for pro-Japanese ministers. Direk Chaiyanam, who as Foreign Minister had steadfastly opposed any policy other than simply permitting Japanese troops to cross Thailand, was sent off to Japan as ambassador and was replaced by the ultranationalist and opportunistic (Luang) Wichit Watakarn.[19] Pridi was

[18]The official name of the country was changed to Thailand in 1939. For a fuller account of Pibun's wartime policy, see Chapter 3.

[19]Luang Wichit is usually credited with having been the archapostle of the Pan-Thai movement to expand Thailand's borders into neighboring states and also the author of many of the nationalist excesses that Pibun carried out before and during the war.

appointed to the politically innocuous office of Regent, while the young King continued his studies in Europe. Nevertheless this position afforded Pridi an excellent opportunity to work secretly with the Allies and thus, when later it appeared that Japan would not win the war, to become a suitable alternative to Pibun. Pibun retained Khuang Apaiwong in the cabinet, however, even though he was not pro-Japanese.

After Pibun[20] decided in December 1941 to link Thailand's destiny to that of Japan, there was little more he could do in foreign affairs except to wait for the outcome of the war. During 1942, when the Japanese armies swept over all of Southeast Asia, and when Pibun's power and prestige were at their peak, his ardent nationalist disciples intensified their efforts to emulate the fascist states by instituting strange customs and regulations which ran counter to Thai culture and traditions and were greatly resented by the people.[21]

When it became clear in 1943 and early 1944 that Japan would eventually be defeated, Pibun's political fortunes began to wane. In fairness to Pibun, it should be stated that he was no great friend of the Japanese during the war years, and that they did not hold him in high esteem. Apparently they were as aware as the Allies of his opportunism, and as time went on, they found him increasingly difficult to work with.

In July 1944 most of the Thai leaders realized that Pibun had to be replaced if Thailand was not to be bombed into submission by the Allies and occupied as a defeated enemy for many years after the war. Pridi had for some time been working actively behind the scenes to build up his own

[20]He was now Field Marshal Pibun Songkhram.

[21]See Coast, op. cit., pp. 25–6, for a description of some of the customs instituted during the war. Whether Pibun actually knew the extent of these regulations is not clear; an irate public nonetheless forced him to take the blame for them.

support; but the Allies had made it clear that they would not aid his underground forces until Pibun was ousted. Also, the Japanese, who distrusted Pibun and knew about the contacts with the Allies, were threatening to take full control of Thailand. Pibun was persuaded that it was imperative for the good of the nation that he step aside and permit new leaders to negotiate with both the Japanese and the Allies for Thailand's survival. In July 1944 he reluctantly resigned, after losing on a key vote in the assembly—and only three days after Premier Tojo resigned in Tokyo. Pibun retired from politics, a discredited and disappointed man. In four years he had gone from the pinnacle of power to seeming political oblivion.

Government under Civilian Leadership (1944–1947)

From August 1944, when Khuang Apaiwong became Prime Minister, until November 1947, when the military staged a *coup d'état,* the dominating personality in Thai politics was Pridi Panomyong. Pridi engineered the adverse assembly vote that resulted in Pibun's resignation; he then persuaded Khuang Apaiwong to head a new government and try to reach an accommodation with the Japanese occupation authorities during the remaining months of the war—to prevent them from assuming direct control of the country at a time when it was obvious that an underground was being organized. In August 1945 Pridi issued the royal proclamation disavowing Thailand's declaration of war on the United States and Britain in 1942.[22] When in August 1945 Khuang decided that he should resign and make room for another man who could deal effectively with the Allies, Pridi sent for the Thai minister in Washington, Seni Pramot, and prevailed upon him to accept the job at the end of September

[22]See Chapter 3.

1945. During the month that it took Seni to travel home, Pridi installed Tawee Bunyaket, an able lieutenant, as interim Prime Minister. After the general elections of January 1946 resulted in a clear victory for his supporters, Pridi remained in uncontested control of the national assembly and of the government until November 1947—even though he personally served as Prime Minister for only a few months. The rise and fall of Pridi was even swifter than that of Pibun and must be explained in some detail.

When the Pacific war ended in August 1945, Pridi and his Free Thai colleagues emerged as the dominant political force; and he was hailed throughout the country as a national hero. The last four months of 1945 saw a burst of popular enthusiasm and political activity that had not been known since the 1932 revolution. Stimulated by the prospect of general elections and the government's granting of full freedom of speech and of the press, the public became absorbed in political affairs. Political parties were permitted for the first time, and there were no curbs on electioneering. Pibun and several collaborators were under arrest as war criminals, and Pridi took steps to ensure that the military would not interfere in his plans to build a mass following to support his political program. To many observers this seemed to be a period of considerable promise for constitutional government in Thailand.

In the elections of January 6, 1946, to fill the seats of the elected half of the national assembly, candidates supporting Pridi won a large majority and subsequently elected Khuang Prime Minister after Pridi decided to remain in the background. Khuang, who resented being dominated by Pridi, resigned, however, in March and founded the Democratic Party, a conservative and pro-monarchist group. This minority party became a vocal segment in the assembly, and for the first time in Thailand's constitutional history there was an organized parliamentary opposition. In April 1946, at the urging of his supporters, Pridi became Prime Minister in name as well as in fact; but by stepping down from the lofty position of Regent to involve himself with a parliament that he could control but not silence, Pridi exposed himself to direct attack and was forced to take responsibility for mismanagement and corruption in the government. Also, some of Pridi's liberal followers were dismayed when, just before he accepted the premiership, a special court set up to try war criminals dismissed the case against Pibun and several of his chief lieutenants on the grounds that the law did not apply retroactively. Pibun and the others were allowed to go free. Although technically this was a case for the courts and not for the government, it was widely believed that the court action could not have occurred at the height of Pridi's power without his personal consent.[23]

Shortly after Pridi assumed power, the government presented to the assembly a new draft constitution to replace the constitution of 1932. To those who had expected Pridi to promote liberalism and true representative government, the 1946 constitution proved a disappointment. The essential difference between the 1932 and 1946 constitutions was that the latter provided for a bicameral assembly, in which members of the upper house (senate) were elected by the lower

[23]Some observers have speculated that Pibun's release was the result of an oath taken by members of the People's Party in 1932 never to harm the person of any other member of the revolutionary group. Another theory is that Pridi was so confident early in 1946 that Pibun was out of the political picture for an indefinite period that he believed it was safe to release him. Another possibility is that Pridi and Pibun were working in closer harmony during the war period than most people realized, and that Pridi simply did not believe Pibun's actions in 1941 and 1942 made him a war criminal insofar as Thailand was concerned.

house. Because Pridi's supporters had a solid majority in the elected lower house, there was little doubt that the senate would also be packed with them. As Wilson has pointed out, Pridi's source of strength lay with the assembly where his oratorical skills could be used to fullest advantage; it was therefore in his interest to shift more power into the hands of the elected members of the assembly to ensure his continued control of the political situation.[24]

The new constitution was approved after some debate in the assembly, and it came into force in May 1946. The elected members then chose the members of the senate, most of whom, as predicted, were loyal supporters of Pridi. Although Vella observed that the new constitution "proved that liberal Thai leaders were willing to compromise their democratic principles in order to retain power,"[25] it might be more accurate to say that this constitution proved that Pridi was no liberal, and that his real objective was to retain power at any cost. The fact that Pridi based his power on a packed legislature rather than on the armed forces gave his government a more respectable aura; but it would be wrong to say that Pridi was prepared in 1946 to place the fate of his government or of Thailand in the hands of a popularly elected assembly.

The mysterious death of the twenty-year-old King Ananta Mahidon on the morning of June 9, 1946, severely upset the political scene in Thailand and started Pridi on the road to ruin. The exact circumstances of the King's death have never been revealed. Although it was never proved that Pridi had any direct part in the tragedy, the fact that not only did he make no public statement to clear himself but instead inspired stories that it had been an accidental death, cast doubt

[24]Wilson, *op. cit.*, p. 263.
[25]Vella, *op. cit.*, p. 389.

on him in the public eye. Pridi's imposition of press censorship in order to silence the wild speculation that was rampant
in Bangkok only added fuel to the flames and tended to
implicate him further. It seemed to many observers that he
was running away from his responsibilities at a time when he
should have launched a complete investigation of the King's
death and reported fully to the assembly and to the public
on the facts. Pridi's strange behavior gave rise to a slashing
attack by Khuang and his Democratic Party in the assembly,
which made Pridi's position nearly untenable.[26] Finally, in
August 1946 Pridi resigned as Prime Minister and removed
himself from public life.

The new Prime Minister was retired Admiral (Luang)
Tamrong Nawasawat, a member of the 1932 revolutionary
group, who after leaving military service had become a successful lawyer and politician. He was exceptionally popular
with members of the assembly—principally because he shut
his eyes to some of the most flagrant cases of corruption and
profiteering among assemblymen ever known in Thailand.
Although a Pridi supporter, Tamrong was an independent
political figure in the assembly and sought to build a following by permitting members to make personal fortunes at the
public's expense. In Tamrong's defense it may be said that
the economic problems in this postwar period would have
been staggering for even a tough-minded administrator; but
Tamrong was not one to quarrel with fellow politicians or
high government officials when they used their positions to
enrich themselves. There were few arrests and trials during
his tour in office, despite widespread smuggling of rice and
misappropriation of public funds. As a result, government

[26]For an authoritative account of events surrounding this case, see
Alexander MacDonald, *Bangkok Editor* (New York, 1949), pp. 42–53,
81–93.

under civilian rule became generally discredited; and the way was open for the military faction to return to power.

It was surprising that the Tamrong cabinet lasted as long as it did—from August 1946 until November 1947. But while the assembly remained loyal to Pridi and Tamrong, there was no constitutional way that the government could be upset— despite the best efforts of the opposition Democratic Party to unseat it. By 1947 the public optimism and enthusiasm that had been so prevalent in 1945 and early 1946 were gone, and representative government was in disrepute. In this situation it was not remarkable that rumors began to circulate that Pibun was thinking of returning to politics. Few residents of Bangkok, however, would have predicted that the army's bid for power would have been so bold, so secret, and so threatening. MacDonald writes that the *coup d'état* which took place on the night of November 8, 1947, was so well planned that "even Pridi Phanomyong could not have known just who the enemy was." No blood was shed and no lives were lost; but "those who saw the tanks rattling along the street or the machine-gun nests springing up, or saw the bare blades of the bayonets knew how ugly and serious it could have been."[27]

Return of the Military Faction

The military *coup d'état* of November 8 made no pretense of being in accordance with constitutional principles. The available evidence suggests that it was organized originally by a few high-ranking army officers who were disgruntled by the minor role the civilian government had imposed on the army, and who saw in the King's death and the scandals of the Tamrong government an opportunity to stage a coup that the public would accept. Since the conspirators were

[27] *Ibid.*, p. 154.

relatively unknown, they needed a national popular leader. Field Marshal Pibun Songkhram was the logical person because of his continued high prestige among military men. When approached by the plotters, Pibun apparently agreed to join the conspiracy; but he did not accept a position in the new government: he preferred for the time being to work from behind the scenes in his proposed job of supreme commander of the armed forces. Following the coup and after Pridi and Tamrong as well as other leaders of the civilian faction had fled the country, the Coup Group, as it was called, publicly announced that Pibun was in charge during the emergency which it claimed was precipitated by the previous government's failure to stop inflation and curb corruption. A new interim constitution was put into effect, and the regency council was forced to approve of measures taken. The Coup Group promised to hold elections within three months and to draw up a new constitution. Meanwhile, the announcement warned the nation to remain calm and not to oppose the efforts of the military to apprehend key members of the previous government. It was significant that the navy did not participate in this coup; but neither did it oppose it.[28]

The military group ousted the Pridi group from the government with remarkable efficiency.[29] The real problem, however, was to ensure public and foreign support for the new regime. Again, Pibun showed himself to be a master politician. Sensational stories were circulated by the Coup Group,

[28]Wilson, *op. cit.*, p. 177, states that out of thirty-six leading figures in the 1947 coup, thirty-three were army officers, two were air force officers, and one was a member of the national police.

[29]MacDonald, *op. cit.*, p. 175, recalls that in an interview shortly after the coup, Field Marshal Pibun told a group of reporters that since "public opinion wanted the change" and "as it could not be done by constitutional means...the army decided unanimously to get rid of it."

claiming that it had prevented both a Communist and a republican takeover of the country. Pridi was accused of having plotted the assassination of the late King and of planning similar action against the new King, the younger brother of the dead monarch, as part of a plan to set up a Thai republic. Pibun also persuaded his wartime cabinet minister, Khuang Apaiwong, to become Prime Minister. Khuang's Democratic Party was just as anxious as the military faction to get rid of Tamrong's corrupt regime, and it clearly had no respect for Pridi because of his implication in the death of the King; but Khuang was not in sympathy with the Coup Group's methods and was therefore unwilling to become a front man for Pibun and his cohorts. Because of the strongly adverse foreign reaction to the *coup d'état,* Pibun decided it was expedient temporarily to install in power a respected civilian. Therefore he pledged Khuang that he and the Coup Group would not interfere in his administration; the latter then accepted the government leadership.

It would be wrong to conclude the the *coup d'état* of November 8, 1947, was not welcomed by many people in Thailand. The army, of course, was enthusiastic because, after nearly four years of being humiliated and ignored, it was now back in power—or nearly so. But the lower classes and the royalists also had much sympathy for the coup. Mac-Donald, who admitted his deep opposition to Pibun and to the military's return to power, recalls that "there would be many who saw the coup as a good thing, especially the lower classes," because for them "there had been nothing good about the Tamrong rule. A change of almost any kind would be for the better." Similarly, he found that the royalists "rejoiced to some extent," because "Pridi was the archenemy of the throne," and it gave them considerable satisfaction to see the group that had created the 1932 revolution now "at one another's throats."[30]

The general elections of January 29, 1948, part of the Coup Group's effort to legitimitize the coup, drew little popular participation. One reason was that many Pridi men who occupied seats in the previous assembly were in jail, in hiding, or in exile. But the real significance of these elections, which appear to have been relatively honest, was that Khuang's Democratic Party obtained a small majority of seats in the lower house of the assembly, while the military party, *Tamatipat,* made a very poor showing. With the support of some independents in the assembly, Khuang was now in a position to rule on the basis of a parliamentary majority, elected in free elections. Khuang's gamble two months earlier in accepting the Prime Minister's portfolio had paid off handsomely; so he agreed to serve in this capacity again, but with an entirely different and more legitimate basis of support. Khuang's new cabinet was strong but not linked with the military; and when he presented the list along with his reform program to the new assembly in February 1948, he won an overwhelming vote of confidence.

If Khuang thought that he could now rule the country on the basis of a parliamentary majority, however, he was badly mistaken: the Coup Group was not prepared to let him steal its *coup d'état.* On April 6, 1948, four army officers who had participated in the November 8 conspiracy appeared at Khuang's official residence and advised him to resign at once. After conferring with his cabinet and recognizing that no military support would be available to him to defend his government, Khuang stepped down. The Coup Group then urged that the Regent ask Pibun Songkhram to form a government because, they said, he was the only person who could

[30]*Ibid.,* p. 164.

maintain order in the country. Thus Pibun, who had been discredited and in police custody only two years earlier, was back at the helm of the government. He gave as his reason for accepting the top government job that a clash between the military group and Khuang's civilian government was inevitable, and that he was probably the only person who could control both sides and prevent bloodshed. He said that the younger army officers were in favor of decisive action, and that he, Pibun, could not stand in their way and survive.[31]

It is not clear why the Coup Group waited nearly five months before unseating Khuang, especially after the Democratic Party won in the general elections. It appears that a primary consideration influencing the senior officers who plotted the coup was the negative reaction of foreign powers. First reports from Washington and London showed that these nations disapproved strongly of the coup and especially of the re-emergence of Pibun, who was still in bad repute for his wartime actions. Even the nomination of Khuang as Prime Minister failed to satisfy the British and American governments. Only after the January 1948 elections gave the new government a popular mandate and after the assembly had given Khuang a vote of confidence, did these powers finally extend recognition. Once this was achieved, the military group concluded that the time was ripe for a second coup. At first the United States reacted coolly to Pibun's assumption of power, even suspending consideration of Thailand's request for financial assistance; but in May 1948, after Pibun received a vote of confidence in the assembly,[32] the State Department announced United States recognition of his government.

[31]Coast, *op. cit.*, p. 47.

[32]When Pibun presented his government to the assembly for a vote of confidence, he received only 70 affirmative votes out of a possible 200; of the remainder, 26 were opposed, 67 abstained, and 37 were absent.

What was the strong hand Pibun held that enabled him to return to power and to gain international acceptance so soon after the war? Some writers have argued that the United States made a crucial mistake in granting recognition to Pibun and his military group because the coup signaled an end of the experiment in popular government in Thailand and thereafter permitted the military to manipulate politics with no regard for the constitutional process.[33] The author believes that the political events of 1947 and 1948 within Thailand cannot be adequately explained or appreciated without a consideration of the international situation at that time. Although the threat of international Communism to Thailand's security in the postwar period is discussed in detail in Chapter 4, it is well to recall here that in 1947 and 1948 Thailand was an island surrounded by revolutions and guerrilla wars. To the east the Viet-Minh Communists had launched a full-scale war against the French; in Burma and in Malaya the Communists were making great efforts to take over the governments by terrorist tactics; in Indonesia a critical situation had developed between the nationalist forces and the Dutch colonialists. Most ominously to the Thais, the Chinese Communists were slowly extending their control over the mainland. China had historically been Siam's most powerful neighbor, and the specter of a strong and united China always haunted the Thai. In Europe the cold war was in full swing, and the Russians were threatening the Marshall Plan nations. Finally, in February 1948, about the same time that Khuang won his vote of confidence in the assembly, the Communists seized power in Czechoslovakia and produced

[33]The most recent exponent of this view is Frank C. Darling, who argues that American postwar policy is largely responsible for curbing democratic development and encouraging the military to rule the country. See his article "American Policy in Thailand," *Western Political Quarterly,* March 1962, pp. 93–110.

fear in Western capitals that the Soviet Union would use force in Europe to gain its objectives. A few months later the Berlin blockade was imposed, and the United States began to rearm. If the year had been 1946, it is doubtful whether Pibun could have obtained recognition for his government; but in the world situation of 1948 it is not surprising that he who considered himself the most effective anti-Communist in Thailand, should speculate that he might be acceptable to the United States and other Western governments if he convinced them that Thailand was a bastion of anti-Communism in Southeast Asia and that he was the most strongly anti-Communist leader available there. The British, who had been even more resentful of Pibun for his collaboration with Japan during the war, also needed a sympathetic and effective government in Thailand to assist in their struggle to crush the Communist terrorists who threatened to overrun the Malay Peninsula. For these reasons the United States and Britain concluded that Pibun and the military group were by far the least threatening of the many evils that might engulf Thailand in 1948, and therefore granted recognition to his regime.

Decline of Constitutionalism

The return to power of Pibun Songkhram and the military faction marked a turning point in Thai politics. Political power remained in the hands of influential army and police officers until the army under Marshal Sarit Tanarat emerged as the uncontested victor in the power struggle in September 1957. Pibun's position during this period was far different, however, from what it had been in 1938, when he came to power for the first time. While he was then in full control of the army and police and held almost dictatorial power, in 1948 he was a moderator among several factions that controlled these sources of power; and to maintain his position, he was obliged to use political methods such as compromise rather than direct force. The period from 1948 to 1951 was one of marked political instability, resulting from various attempts by rival groups to oust the 1947 Coup Group from power. The most serious challenge occurred in February 1949, when Pridi, backed by the royal marines and some navy elements, attempted to overthrow the government by force and reinstate the civilian faction. The rebellion was well planned and had the support of some key civilian officials of the Pibun government. The plan was poorly executed, however; and after three days of sporadic fighting and several hundred casualties—many of them civilians—the insurrection was crushed by loyal army forces. Pridi fled into exile in China, where he remains at the present writing. Unlike the coups that had been attempted previously, this one in early 1949 not only precipitated serious fighting and considerable bloodshed but also resulted in extensive reprisals against the plotters. For several months thereafter the police carried out investigations; some former cabinet ministers and assemblymen associated with Pridi were shot while in police custody, and many others were held in prison. The extensiveness of the plot and the great secrecy with which it was undertaken stunned the army; and it was only by good luck that loyal army commanders seized control of the tank battalions near Bangkok before the Pridi forces could turn them against the government.[34] As a result of this near overthrow, the Coup Group took steps to entrench itself more firmly, dealt harshly with all opponents to the regime, and demanded ever higher military budgets to maintain order and root out suspected

[34]The army commander who organized the resistance to the rebellion was General Sarit Tanarat, who thereafter rose rapidly in the army and in 1958 became Prime Minister.

subversive elements. Pridi's appeal to the liberals and his political organization were irreparably damaged by this abortive coup, and he has remained out of the country ever since. Idealists who had looked to him as the embodiment of hope for democratic government in Thailand unhappily concluded that he was "a political adventurer" who would use force if necessary to achieve power.[35] After February 1949 it was clear to most observers that civilian control of government would be impossible for an indefinite period, and that politics would be dominated by various factions in the army and police.

One of the initial programs instituted by the Pibun government in 1948 had been the repression of the Chinese minority within Thailand. Pibun entrusted this program to his efficient and ambitious protégé, General Pao Siyanon, who was Deputy Director General of the national police. As the threat of Communist China grew from 1950 to 1954 and the Pibun government adopted an increasingly anti-Communist foreign policy, General Pao's responsibilities for combating subversive influences within Thailand grew proportionately. By 1954 he had built the police into a paramilitary force, rivaling the army as a source of political power; and it was apparent that he planned to use this force as a springboard to becoming Prime Minister when Pibun decided to step down. Pao had the added advantage of being the son-in-law of General Pin Chunhawan, who as Commander in Chief of the Army had been a leading figure in the 1947 *coup d'état* against the Tamrong government. In addition to these assets, General Pao possessed a certain ruthlessness and audacity that commanded his subordinates' respect and seemed to mark him as a future leader.

A second serious threat to the regime occurred in June 1951, when the navy made a desperate effort to challenge the

[35]MacDonald, *op. cit.*, p. 222.

army's political power and to regain some influence in national affairs. In a bizarre scene aboard a ship in the Chao Pya River, where Prime Minister Pibun was participating in a ceremony to mark the transfer to Thailand of a United States dredger under the military assistance program, a group of navy men kidnaped Pibun and held him hostage on board a warship for several days, while navy officers sought to negotiate with the army and police regarding the formation of a new government. This effort failed, and heavy fighting broke out. Nearly a thousand civilians were killed or injured in the streets of Bangkok, and unofficial estimates placed the military casualty toll at several hundred. It was the worst episode of violence Bangkok had ever seen; and it served as a sobering reminder to those who assumed that Thais are generous toward opponents that when large political issues are at stake, they are not unlike other peoples in their willingness to spill blood. In this case the opposing sides were so evenly matched that the outcome was in doubt for two days. On the third day the air force, which had previously remained aloof from political struggles because it lacked the means of power, took an active part on the side of the army. New planes, which had been supplied by the United States as part of the military aid program, were used to bomb and strafe navy ships and installations. Even the ship on which Pibun was held prisoner was bombed and sunk—so desperate was this struggle for power. Marshal Pibun escaped by jumping overboard and swimming to shore.

This episode served to dramatize the weakness of the Prime Minister's position as moderator of the various factions in the armed forces. From then on Pibun's personal influence declined, while real political power passed to his two powerful lieutenants, General Pao and General Sarit. Pao was appointed Director General of Police, and Sarit soon became

Commander in Chief of the Army. Between them, these men were in a position to run the country as they pleased; but they found it expedient to have Pibun continue as Prime Minister while they built up their own political organizations. The navy revolt also resulted in the virtual disbanding of the Thai marine corps and in a wide purge of navy officers. From then on the navy ceased to play any significant role in Thai politics.

The consolidation of power by the army and police resulted in the decline and near extinction of constitutional government in Thailand. A new constitution, drafted by a team of experts appointed by the Khuang government, had been promulgated in March 1949. Since this constitution was a bold effort by the Khuang government to curb the military's power by constitutional means, it is surprising that the document remained in force for two and a half years before being challenged by the Coup Group. One reason was that Khuang and his Democratic Party majority in the assembly were extremely careful to avoid a confrontation with the military faction. The political situation came to a head, however, on November 29, 1951, only five months after the army and the police, with air force support, had crushed the navy revolt. General Sarit and General Pao cooperated once again, apparently unknown to Pibun, to eliminate the last important source of opposition to their control of the country—the assembly. This was known as the "radio coup" because it was reported on the radio without further elaboration: a group of military and police officers issued an announcement saying that they had decided to abrogate the 1949 constitution, close the assembly, and reinstitute the 1932 constitution with its government-appointed upper half of the assembly. They reaffirmed their support of the constitutional monarchy but said that the 1949 constitution was too advanced for

Thailand. The immediate reason given for this abrupt action was the danger of internal Communism and the serious world situation. In foreign policy, the announcement said, Thailand would continue to accept military and economic aid from the United States and would adhere to the principles of the United Nations Charter. There was little public reaction, and the coup was entirely successful. Pibun remained Prime Minister, but with reduced influence.

Early in 1952 the government appointed the upper half of the new unicameral assembly; not surprisingly, most of these appointees were military men who had been loyal to General Pao and General Sarit during their efforts to put down revolts. The government held general elections in February 1952 to elect the lower half of the assembly, but Khuang and many of his followers refused to stand for election because they strongly disapproved of the Coup Group's cavalier treatment of the assembly and of the 1949 constitution. The elections of 1952 resulted, therefore, in a sweep for the government party, *Tamatipat,* and the military group had no cause thereafter to worry about opposition from the assembly. In fact, from 1952 to 1955 there was no real opposition to the government from any quarter. So long as the police and the army, under Pao and Sarit, continued to cooperate, a period of stability in Thai politics seemed assured.

The attitude of the King toward the November *coup d'état* was of some importance to the leaders. King Poumipon had been living in Switzerland in order to finish his education. When he returned to Thailand for a short visit in 1950, there was such widespread public enthusiasm for him that the military must have been impressed, and also fearful of his potential influence if he should decide to resist its growing power. Most observers believed that it was no mere coincidence that the November coup occurred only two days before the King returned to Thailand permanently to assume his full responsibilities as monarch. According to this view, the army and the police, which had consolidated their power in the summer of 1951, were apprehensive about the role the young King intended to play upon his return. The King expressed his displeasure by refusing to acknowledge the new political situation for four days after his return; during this time negotiations went on between the government and the palace. The King held one important card: the threat of non-recognition by foreign powers if he failed to approve the coup. A solution was reached, however, and the King approved of the new constitution. The regime was thereafter granted recognition by other countries. Although the King at this time was nearly powerless, his delay in granting approval of the government was seen by many as a sign that he would not in the future stand completely aloof from politics.

The years 1952–1955 witnessed growing corruption and political intrigue in Thailand, coupled with strongly repressive measures on the part of the police against anyone suspected of leftist sympathies. With public opinion muted, with bribery of a compliant national assembly by the government on a large scale, and with a world situation that made it convenient for the regime to use the threat of Communism to silence all opposition, politics in Thailand steadily deteriorated. As the police obtained great power and were led by the ruthless and irrepressible General Pao, it was not surprising that they became involved in some of the largest scandals ever known in Thailand—notably opium smuggling, which was highly organized and brought into the pockets of key officials untold millions in Thai currency.[36] At the same time

[36]The widespread corruption and arbitrary practices of the Thai police during this period are described in D. Insor, *Thailand: A Political, Social, and Economic Analysis* (London, 1963), pp. 69–74.

some members of the ruling military group around General Sarit seized the opportunity to go into commercial enterprises and reap large rewards. From 1948 until 1953 there was general prosperity in Thailand, because rice was in great demand as an export commodity; and the public was not seriously aroused. By 1953, however, the price of rice had dropped on the world market; and the country was thrown into an economic depression. As the huge profits of government officials became more obvious, criticism became open and widespread and was directed principally against General Pao and the police.

At the risk of appearing to condone the excesses of the Thai government during this period, the writer believes that it is important to emphasize that Thailand was at the same period faced with the most serious threat to its national security since World War II, and that the government was forced to resort to arbitrary methods to resist the real efforts launched by the Communists to undermine the government. On all sides of the country—in Indochina, Malaya, and Burma—Communist-led insurrections were in progress; and early in 1953 the Chinese Communists announced the establishment of an autonomous Thai state in southern China, in an obvious effort to encourage subversion and defections in Thailand. After the Pibun government joined the Western powers in recognizing the Bao Dai government in Vietnam, and in sending troops to Korea, it became a prime target of Communist propaganda and infiltration. The Pibun government was so hard pressed to deal with the growing threat to the nation's internal security that the police were given wide authority to ferret out suspected Communists, especially following passage of a strong anti-Communist law by the assembly in 1952. Inevitably many non-Communist leftists were arrested and held for indefinite periods. Sympathizers of the

Pridi policy were considered subversives, because they es-
poused neutralism and anti-Western sentiments at a time
when government policy was strongly pro-Western. The line
between loyalty and disloyalty was a fine one, and the Pibun
government during these critical years was not prepared to
be charitable in dealing with opposition groups.

Such was the political climate in Thailand in the early
nineteen-fifties, when the government made the critical decision to join the Western powers in a defensive alliance against
the spread of Communism in Southeast Asia. In one sense,
the question whether Thailand would join the West in opposing the Communist powers in this area or take a neutralist
position had been largely determined in 1948 when the
military faction took control of the government and installed
Marshal Pibun as Prime Minister. The Korean War and the
efforts of Communist China to undermine the Thai government in the early fifties reinforced the Pibun government's
view that China presented the greatest threat to Thailand's
security and that keeping the protection of the United States
was the best way to prevent Thailand from being absorbed
into the Chinese sphere of influence. In order to bring about
an alliance with the United States, however, it was essential
that Pibun maintain a tight control over opposition groups
which favored neutralism or a pro-Chinese policy. For this
purpose General Pao and General Sarit held the necessary
power. That is why the Pibun policy of aligning Thailand
with the United States and Britain in the SEATO alliance in
1954 did not produce serious opposition within the country.[37]

[37]See Chapter 4 for a discussion of Thai foreign policy during this
period.

Chapter 3

Thailand in World War II

BY 1939 Siam[1] had regained its full sovereignty after nearly a century of encroachments by European powers, and had begun to experiment with Western ideas of constitutional government in order to bring itself politically up to date. Before it had a real opportunity to develop modern political institutions, however, world war loomed as a threat to national independence; and by 1940 foreign affairs was the major preoccupation of the government. When Britain and France, Thailand's most powerful neighbors, became involved in the European war, Japan moved to exploit their weakened position in Southeast Asia and thus became a new factor in Thailand's security. The problem for the government was to preserve the nation's neutrality; and failing this, the next task was to reach an accommodation with whatever power presented the greatest danger, and also try to avoid the experience of 1892 and 1893, when Siam sought unsuccessfully to play one great power against another.

During the nineteen-thirties the main objectives of Thai foreign policy were: protection of national independence, extension of trade relations, and promotion of Thai interests in Southeast Asia, particularly in Laos and Cambodia. So

[1]The name of the country was officially changed to Thailand in that year.

long as France remained in firm control of Indochina, there was little prospect that Thailand would be able to press its claims; however, a new power was emerging in Asia—namely, Japan; and as it extended its influence into China and challenged British and French supremacy in Asia, Thailand slowly shifted its policy. At first, friendship with Japan seemed to be an excellent means of countering British and French influence; as Japan became more powerful, and particularly after it launched a full-scale invasion of China in 1937, some Thai leaders saw in a policy of cooperation with Japan an opportunity to regain lost territories in Indochina and to advance Thai interests in Burma and in Malaya as well. Although Thailand's trade with Japan had grown steadily during the nineteen-twenties and early thirties, not until 1933 did it take the first step toward accommodation with Japan. At the League of Nations, Thailand abstained from a vote of censure against Japan for invading Manchuria; shortly thereafter it exchanged trade commissions with Japan. Rumors began to circulate that Japan had offered to assist Thailand in constructing a canal across the Isthmus of Kra in the Malay Peninsula. Since such a canal would have bypassed Singapore as the shortest route from the Indian Ocean to the Far East, the prospect alarmed Great Britain. Although the Kra canal never materialized, there were growing contacts between Thailand and Japan during the thirties: many Thai students went to Japan for their education, and many Japanese businessmen, journalists, and tourists visited Bangkok.[2]

When the military faction headed by Pibun Songkhram

[2]The growth of Japanese influence in Siam during this period is described in Josiah Crosby, *Siam: The Crossroads* (London, 1945), pp. 62-9. See also Virginia Thompson, *Thailand: The New Siam* (New York, 1941), pp. 123-37.

came to power in December 1938, there was a definite shift in domestic as well as in foreign affairs. The armed forces were greatly expanded, the local Chinese were placed under heavy restrictions, constitutional government lost much of its validity, foreign business firms were increasingly harassed, and some were forced out of business; and the government instituted a program of chauvinistic nationalism that strongly resembled policies in Germany and Japan. Certain government leaders began to talk openly of closer ties with Japan and of Thailand's need to be militarily strong in order to resist Britain and France. One of the first things Prime Minister Pibun did was to change the name of the country to Thailand—an action that carried with it the nationalistic implication that Siam was the political and cultural home for the thousands of Thai-speaking peoples living outside its borders—in Laos, Cambodia, Burma, and in the Yunnan province of China.

When war broke out in Europe, and Britain and France became absorbed in it, the Pibun government recognized that Thailand might be able to benefit from this situation insofar as its aspirations in Southeast Asia were concerned. Initially, Thailand declared its neutrality; then it sought to negotiate nonaggression pacts with the three most powerful nations in Asia—namely, Great Britain, France, and Japan. Treaties were concluded with all three early in June 1940; but within a few weeks the situation in Europe had changed profoundly with France's defeat by the Germans and its withdrawal from the war. In addition, Britain was preparing to defend itself against an invasion from the Continent, and no one could predict the outcome of the European war. For the Thai government, therefore, the summer of 1940 appeared an opportune time to adopt a revisionist policy in Southeast Asia in the hope of regaining its "lost territories" in Laos and

Cambodia and of generally enhancing its position in respect to France and possibly to Britain.

Although the nonaggression treaty with France had already been signed, the Thai government refused to ratify it until France agreed to negotiate concerning two enclaves of Laotian territory on the west bank of the Mekong—one in the north near Luang Prabang and the other near the Cambodian border—both of which Thailand claimed. This was a modest request, in view of the large areas in Indochina that Siam had been forced to cede to France in 1904 and 1907; regaining these enclaves would have established the Mekong as the boundary between Laos and Thailand along the entire length of their long border.[3] Vichy France was not, however, sympathetic to Thailand's request, so the latter then sought support from a number of great powers, including Great Britain, the United States, Germany, Italy, and Japan. Meanwhile, in the summer of 1940 Japan began to move into Indochina as a means of carrying its war to southern China. Thailand saw in this an opportunity to reach some agreement with the Japanese by which the latter would respect Thailand's claims in Laos and Cambodia if Japan occupied the whole area.

By the autumn of 1940 the United States and Britain were becoming apprehensive over Thailand's policy in Indochina, and they warned the Thai government against using force to obtain its demands from France. On the other hand, in order to curry favor with Thailand, the Japanese encouraged it, because they believed that country would be of key importance in their plans to invade Malaya and Burma.[4] After France refused to negotiate and Japan had indicated sympathy for

[3]The basis of Thailand's claims in this dispute is clearly stated in Vichitr Vadakarn, *Thailand's Case* (Bangkok, 1941).

[4]These diplomatic moves are described in some detail by James V. Martin, Jr., "Thai-American Relations in World War II," *Journal of Asian Studies*, August 1963, pp. 452–5.

Thailand's position, the Pibun government decided on a show of strength and mobilized its armed forces. In addition, it increased its demands to include all territories surrendered to France in 1904 and 1907—namely, the disputed provinces in Cambodia; and it demanded a commitment from France that, in the event the latter relinquished its sovereignty over Indochina, it would turn over control of Laos and Cambodia to Thailand. The Pibun government was clearly betting that the Japanese would eventually oust France from Indochina, and so wanted to stake out its claim to the two areas it had previously controlled. By October 1940 nationalist feeling in Bangkok was running high, and the government subtly encouraged a popular demand for armed action. In late October the situation between Thailand and France was so critical that the United States decided to cancel delivery of ten bombers that Thailand had bought from an American firm. The Thai population was outraged, and an anti-American propaganda campaign was launched with government support. To make matters worse, the Japanese then agreed to send Thailand an equal number of planes, complete with Japanese mechanics to service them.[5]

Fighting between Thai and French forces broke out along the eastern border in November 1940, and Thailand occupied the two enclaves in Laos it had claimed on the western side of the Mekong. After some weeks of skirmishing and a small French air attack on Bangkok, Japan arranged for a ceasefire. Negotiations took place in Tokyo during the spring of 1941, and Japan exerted pressure on both sides. In May a treaty was finally signed in which France agreed to return to Thailand territories taken in 1904 and 1907, including the Cambodian provinces of Siemrat and Pratabong. Thailand did not, however, obtain a guarantee of the future disposition of

[5]*Ibid.,* p. 455.

Laos and Cambodia. The real gainer from these negotiations was Japan: in return for a promise that neither France nor Thailand would conclude an alliance with a third power against Japan, the Japanese agreed to guarantee the new border in Indochina. Japan also greatly enhanced its prestige by effecting a treaty between a European colonial power and an independent Asian nation.

Fear of Japanese designs in Southeast Asia alarmed the British and American governments. In the summer of 1941 they were forced to take a new look at Southeast Asia, and at Thailand in particular. Japanese occupation of Cambodia at that time was also a danger signal. Whereas in 1940 the United States viewed Thailand as an upsetter of the status quo in Asia, by the summer of 1941 American policy was based on the assumptions that Japan had military designs on Southeast Asia, and that Thailand should be strengthened militarily and encouraged to resist Japanese pressure. The Thai government also was having second thoughts about a policy of close cooperation with Japan. In August Prime Minister Pibun told the American ambassador that Thailand would oppose any military aggression against his country. He also formally asked for American assistance. The national assembly passed a bill calling on all citizens to resist invasion, and the government loudly proclaimed Thailand's determination to protect its neutrality by all possible means. By autumn Pibun was frantically calling for planes and arms from the United States and Britain, and he sought also to coordinate Thai defense plans with those of Britain in Burma and Malaya. But military assistance was not forthcoming; British forces were very short of arms in Malaya and Singapore, and the United States decided it would be wiser to make its defense effort in the Philippines than on the Asian continent. Thus, when the Japanese ambassador presented the Thai government with an ultimatum on December 7 to permit Japanese troops to transit the country, it had little choice but to agree—which it did after a few hours of deliberation. Sir Josiah Crosby, British minister in Bangkok at that time, believed that "in the final resort it was our military weakness in the Far East which...led to the alliance between Japan and Siam. Had we been able to hold our own against our adversary, I have no doubt that Siam would have continued to maintain her neutrality."[6]

Alliance with Japan

Once Thailand became convinced that the Allies were in no position to help her, it moved very swiftly to cooperate with the Japanese. Japan's ultimatum of December 7 stated that it did not regard Thailand as an enemy nation but wished to cooperate with it. The Japanese offered the Thai government three alternatives: it could allow the Japanese to use its territory for moving troops and supplies into Burma and Malaya, in return for which Japan promised not to interfere in Thailand's internal administration; or Thailand and Japan would form a defensive military alliance, under which Thailand would assist the Japanese war effort, in return for a guarantee of assistance in case Thailand were attacked by a third party; or Thailand would join Japan in the war against the Allies, in return for which Japan would agree to the return to Thailand of all territories in the Malay Peninsula ceded to Britain in 1909.[7] The latter offer was indeed a large incentive to the nationalistic Pibun government, and the

[6]Crosby, *op. cit.*, p. 127.

[7]A detailed account of the Japanese ultimatum and the Thai government's reaction is contained in Nicol Smith and Blake Clark, *Into Siam: Underground Kingdom* (New York, 1946), pp. 261–6. Their account is based on an interview with the Thai foreign minister, who participated in the cabinet discussions.

temptation to go the whole way was too great to resist. But since it was necessary to prepare public opinion for so complete a shift of policy, Pibun accepted the Japanese offer in stages. On December 8 the cabinet agreed to the first alternative—Japanese use of Thai territory; on December 10 martial law was proclaimed throughout the country, and the Prime Minister in a radio address to the nation said that Thailand must adjust itself to the new world situation and also hinted at the possibility of a military alliance with Japan. Two days later Pibun again addressed the nation and explained the reasons for a military alliance between the two countries. He blamed Britain for having deprived Thailand of its territory, and concluded that true friendship could not exist between the two countries. On the other hand, Pibun thought that Thailand would benefit from an alliance with Japan because the latter would help it to regain all the lost territories in the south.[8] On December 21, 1941, a treaty of alliance was formally concluded between Japan and Thailand and immediately went into effect.

The final step that Thailand took to align itself firmly with Japan came on January 25, 1942, when it declared war on Great Britain and the United States. The reason given for this action was that the participation of British and American fliers in bombing attacks against civilian as well as military targets in Thailand constituted an act of aggression. Britain was also accused of economic manipulation of the national economy to the detriment of Thailand; and the United States was accused of refusing to deliver airplanes, previously paid for by Thailand, and of having failed to come to Siam's assistance in 1893 when it was threatened by France. Sir Joseph Crosby observed that the communiqué issued by the

[8]Japan's assistance earlier that year on behalf of Thailand's claims against France served as a strong incentive to Pibun in this case.

Thai government "can only be held to have set up a record for childish insincerity which must be well-nigh unique in the history of international relationships, and future generations of Siamese will assuredly blush to recall it."[9] From that time on until 1944, Thailand cooperated fully with Japan, and during the war the two countries exchanged many missions of good will. Thailand retained nominal control of its internal administration; but Japan made ever greater demands on its economy, inflicting considerable economic hardship on the country before the war's end. Thailand did obtain from the Japanese alliance the four Malay states ceded to Britain in 1909—Kedah, Perlis, Kelantan, and Trengganu— as well as control over the two Shan states of Burma—Kengtung and Mongpan.[10] A formal treaty covering the transfer of these territories to Thailand was signed by the Japanese and Thai governments in Bangkok on August 20, 1943.

In appraising Thailand's policy toward Japan in 1940 and 1941, the question of the government's motivation inevitably arises. Some observers have contended that as a long-time admirer of the Japanese, Prime Minister Pibun was naturally disposed toward a fascist point of view in foreign policy. They believe that as soon as Pibun became Prime Minister in 1938, he set about paving the way for an alliance with Japan which would lead, he thought, to Thailand's becoming the dominant power in Southeast Asia; and that therefore the neutrality policy of 1939 and 1940 was only a smokescreen for the real objective of bringing about a close working relationship between Thailand and Japan. A second theory is that Pibun was guided purely by opportunism: that he realized early in the summer of 1940 that Japan would eventually displace

[9]Crosby, op. cit., p. 137.

[10]Thai forces participated in the Japanese invasion of the Shan states, which are inhabited primarily by people of Thai racial stock.

Britain and France as the predominant power in Asia, and that this shift in the balance of power would provide a chance for Thailand to enhance its own position as well as to regain territories seized by the British half a century earlier. A third theory, which is a variant of the second, is that Pibun was not sure until the autumn of 1941 whether Japan would take the final plunge against the United States and Britain and mount a full-scale invasion of Southeast Asia, and that Pibun had no affection for the Japanese but in fact feared them as much as in an earlier period Siam had feared British and French power. It is said also that British and American warnings to Japan in the summer and autumn of 1941 and the possibility of obtaining Allied support gave Pibun some hope of being able to maintain a neutral policy. Crosby, who had no reason to be charitable to the Pibun regime, described Pibun as "a born opportunist." "Since," Crosby continued, "it is power-politics which count for most with him and his like, it will be understood that he was not going to quarrel with us unless and until he was quite sure we were 'down and out.' " Crosby believed that Pibun would "come down from his fence on the side of the victor" when he was convinced which side that would be.[11] It is also worthy of note that Thailand was not the only occupied country to declare war on the United States: the Philippines also took this step after the Japanese had conquered them.

This writer is of the opinion that prior to December 1941 Prime Minister Pibun's policy was neither pro-Japanese nor anti- British and French. He was first and foremost pro-Thai, and his policy was not inconsistent with traditional Thai foreign policy. If Japan had won the war, Pibun would probably have been a national hero, just as King Naresuan and King Taksin were hailed in earlier periods of Thai history

[11]Crosby, *op. cit.*, pp. 123–4.

for regaining lost territories and thus restoring the nation's power and prestige.[12] Although it is probably true that Pibun was authoritarian by nature, and leaned toward a Japanese type of government rather than toward British parliamentarianism, there is little solid evidence to support the view that he admired the Japanese or that he looked upon them as liberators of Asian peoples, despite the Japanese propaganda about "Asia for the Asians." Pibun's folly lay not in his efforts to accommodate to Japanese power in 1941 but rather in that he pursued this policy too far. If he had simply bowed to pressure and permitted the Japanese to use Thai territory, and even if he had cooperated with them to some extent he could have claimed justly that he wanted only to preserve the independence of his country, and that such cooperation was a small price to pay. But Pibun went farther and willingly joined Thailand in an alliance with the invader—to the extent of declaring war on two previously friendly nations.[13] Historians might well ask whether such an "all or nothing" course was in the best interests of Thailand, regardless of which side won the war. Also, in this case Pibun's policy ran counter to the traditional Thai foreign policy of keeping open various alternatives in case international conditions should change. His decision can best be explained on the basis that he was awed by the startling victories of Japan at Pearl Harbor, followed by the sinking a few days later of

[12]This assumes, of course, that after the war the Japanese would have withdrawn their forces from Thailand and permitted it to keep its newly acquired territories.

[13]Nicol Smith quotes Foreign Minister Direk Chaiyanam as saying Prime Minister Pibun called the cabinet together on December 11 and informed it that he thought "it was best to cooperate [with the Japanese] to the extent of a military alliance"; otherwise " 'the Japanese will not be convinced of our sincerity.' " He then told the cabinet he had already consulted with the Japanese about an alliance. (Smith and Clark, *op. cit.*, p. 265.)

two British warships in the Gulf of Siam—the *Prince of Wales* and the *Repulse.* Pibun was then convinced that Britain was finished as a power in Asia, and that Thailand could benefit considerably from an open alliance with Japan.

Even if Pibun's policy in 1941 and 1942 is justifiable in terms of Thailand's interest in becoming a power in Southeast Asia, he can still be criticized for acting too precipitately and shutting the door to future possibilities for maneuver. If Pibun was certain that Japan would eventually win the war, there was no real advantage to be gained by joining an alliance and declaring war on the Allies immediately. Would it not have been prudent for Pibun to wait for a year or more before deciding to go all the way with Japan? Thailand did not get control of the four Malay provinces and the two Shan states, which had been promised by the Japanese, until the summer of 1943. If Pibun had waited until then to conclude an alliance with Japan, he would have been able to see more clearly who was going to win in the Pacific. Although under these circumstances Japan might not have permitted the Thais to maintain their internal administration indefinitely, Pibun would have emerged from the war as a great patriot if the Allies won, and Thailand would have had few problems in normalizing its relations with them. Or, if Japan had been winning the war in 1943, Pibun could have then joined in the war effort and reaped the benefits at the end of hostilities. However, Pibun decided not to wait.

After Thailand succumbed to the Japanese ultimatum of December 7, the Thai minister in Washington, Seni Pramot, took it upon himself to inform the State Department that he believed his country to be under Japanese coercion. He asked for assistance to form a "Free Thai" movement from among Thai students and officials then in the United States, in order to work for the liberation of his country. Martin states that "the anti-Japanese, pro-western policy of the Thai Minister in Washington was to affect profoundly the policy of the United States toward Thailand throughout the war and during the negotiations at its end."[14] It also produced a divergence of views between the United States and Great Britain regarding a postwar settlement with Thailand. When Seni Pramot was instructed by his government to deliver the declaration of war to Secretary of State Hull in January 1942, he told Hull that as he did not consider this to be the will of the Thai people, he preferred not to deliver it. Whereupon the United States chose not to consider itself at war with Thailand despite the declaration of war issued in Bangkok. Thereafter Seni was given financial help when frozen Thai assets were released by the State Department; and he built up a Free Thai group of about fifty persons, which worked closely with the United States Office of Strategic Services (O.S.S.) to infiltrate agents into Thailand. Despite its refusal to recognize a state of war with Thailand, the United States Government decided to treat as enemies any Thai forces opposing United Nations troops; and it considered Thailand, for economic warfare purposes, as enemy-occupied territory. One factor influencing the decision of the United States regarding Thailand was a recommendation from the Chinese Nationalist government, which held that nonrecognition of a state of war would indicate to the Thai military that the United States believed Japan was coercing Thailand—thus making it easier for China to carry out military operations against the Japanese in Thailand.[15]

While the Free Thai movement was being organized in the United States, efforts were also being made within Thailand to organize an underground movement to assist the Allies. The leader of this movement was Pridi Panomyong,

[14]Martin, *op. cit.*, p. 466.   [15]*Ibid.*, p. 461.

one of the organizers of the 1932 revolution. Pridi resigned his cabinet post when the Pibun government decided to capitulate to Japan in December 1941, and was then appointed Regent in the absence of the young King, who was in Switzerland completing his education. Early in 1943, several of Pridi's men escaped from Thailand into China, made contact with O.S.S. agents, and subsequently were sent to the United States. Thereafter contact was established between the Free Thai and the underground, and during 1944 agents were filtering in and out of Thailand on an ever-increasing scale.[16] The contribution of the Free Thai and the Thai underground to the Allied war effort was significant: it enabled British and American forces to penetrate Thailand, to obtain information on Japanese capabilities and troop movements, and to rescue several hundred American and British fliers who had been forced down over Thai territory. More important, the Free Thai movement, with O.S.S. support, supplied well-trained guerrilla warfare officers to the underground; they in turn recruited a Thai force of some 50,000 men who were prepared to attack the Japanese whenever the Allied headquarters gave the command. This force did not play its intended role in the liberation of Thailand, however, because of a basic divergence of policy between the British and the American governments, a split that carried over into the postwar period and affected Thailand's efforts to rehabilitate itself within the international community.

Adjustment to Allied Victory

In 1944 a real crisis occurred in Thailand's foreign policy, as it became increasingly clear that Japan would eventually be defeated by the Allied forces and that Thailand might

[16]An authoritative account of the exploits of Thai agents in Thailand is given in Smith and Clark, op. cit., Chapters 11–15.

then be treated as an enemy nation rather than as an enemy-occupied nation. Prime Minister Pibun had gambled heavily on a Japanese victory, and the problem was how to extricate Thailand from this situation with the minimum of damage. The real obstacle was Great Britain, which, unlike the United States, had suffered considerably from the Thai government's declaration of war and was in no mood to be charitable. In Thailand British commercial interests were extensive, and there were many British residents. Furthermore, the British felt with considerable justification that Thailand's cooperation with the Japanese had contributed measurably to the latter's success in conquering Malaya and Singapore and in pushing through Burma to the eastern gates of India. The British also resented the blatant opportunism of the Pibun government in taking over control of four Malay and two Burmese states in 1943. Finally, in 1942 the Thais had chosen to break the nonaggression treaty they had signed with Britain in 1940. The British viewed the Thais during World War II much as the Siamese had traditionally viewed the Cambodians: as opportunists taking advantage of weakness to seize territory and enhance their own position. For all these reasons the British were not prepared to overlook the Thai declaration of war; and the Thai government became increasingly concerned that they might refuse to recognize the independence of Thailand at the conclusion of the war.

It is a matter of some disagreement among observers of this period whether Pibun Songkhram and Pridi Panomyong were working in concert during World War II or were following opposite courses of action. Most writers have concluded that there was a basic divergence of views between the two men, that Pridi was both ideologically opposed to the Axis forces as well as convinced that the Japanese would be defeated by the British and the Americans. Therefore, it is stated, he either resigned from the cabinet, or was forced out, in December 1941 because Pibun decided to join the Japanese in the war against the Allies. He was then given the nonpolitical job of Regent, from which position he eventually set about to organize the underground and to pave the way for the downfall of the Pibun government in 1944. A second view is that Pridi and Pibun were agreed on the basic objectives of Thai policy in 1941, even if they differed on political philosophy. According to this version, the Pibun government accepted the Japanese offer of participation in the war in order to place Thailand in a good bargaining position when the Japanese took over British and French colonial possessions in Southeast Asia; but in order to allow for the possibility that the Japanese might not win the war, Pridi was appointed Regent and eventually made contact with the Allies when it appeared that things were going poorly for the Japanese. Pridi was well suited for this job because, in addition to being a popular political leader, he had been Foreign Minister during 1937 and 1938 and had visited many Western capitals to negotiate new friendship treaties. When the Japanese war effort began to slow down in 1943, and it became doubtful whether they could win, Pridi was able to use his position as Regent to organize his followers and to seek aid from the Allies. His position offered him immunity from the Japanese authorities, and Pibun was careful not to interfere with him. How much Pibun knew of Pridi's actual operations is uncertain; what seems clear is that Pibun apparently had no objection to Pridi's activities, because he certainly could have taken steps against the underground if he had wanted to do so.[17]

Although Pridi was successful in making contact with the

[17]Pridi apparently made no real effort to organize this force and to seek help from the Allies until early 1943, when American successes in the Pacific were beginning to turn the tide of the war.

Allies and in obtaining considerable support for building up his underground, he was not successful in his major objective, namely, the creation of a Thai government in exile which would receive recognition by the United Nations as the lawful Thai government. The United States was willing to see Thailand emerge an independent nation after the war, and was prepared to supply the underground with equipment and training; but it was unwilling to recognize a Thai exile government, partly because of the strong opposition of the British. The United States was even willing to assist Pridi to escape from Thailand, if he wished to do so, without political commitments. The British, however, were not willing to give unconditional support for Thai independence after the war. British policy held that the Thais must work themselves back to their prewar status, and that independence could be secured only at a price. Pridi's plan never materialized, therefore, and the British and Americans continued to disagree about the peace terms that should be offered Thailand at the end of the war.[18]

In July 1944, a few days after the Tojo government fell in Japan, Prime Minister Pibun was persuaded to resign. By this time Pridi was the most powerful opposition leader in Thailand, and he realized he would not get full cooperation from the Allies until Pibun was ousted. Pibun's political head was the first price Thailand had to pay to get back into the good graces of the Allies, and Pridi skillfully engineered his downfall. Pridi then persuaded his friend and collaborator in the 1932 revolution, Khuang Apaiwong, to become Prime Minister and see Thailand through the difficult period until the end of the war. His task was both to keep the Japanese from taking over and administering the country directly, and

[18]For an account of wartime correspondence between the British and the American governments relating to Thailand, see Martin, *op. cit.*, pp. 463–7.

at the same time to permit the build-up of the underground. It was a dangerous role for any political leader to play, and it is to Khuang's credit that he was able to satisfy the Japanese. It may seem surprising that the Japanese authorities permitted Pibun to be ousted; but the reason probably lies in the likelihood that Pibun had become unpopular with the Japanese as well as with the Thai people for his nationalistic excesses and his chauvinism. Khuang, on the other hand, was known for his candor and honesty, and the Japanese probably preferred him at a time when they themselves realized that they could not win the war.[19]

During the last months of the war Pridi tried repeatedly and unsuccessfully to obtain permission from the Allies to launch an uprising against the Japanese so that Thailand could gain the prestige of fighting Japan. Thailand came under the jurisdiction of the British Allied Commander for Southeast Asia, Lord Mountbatten, whose headquarters in Ceylon was making preparations for an invasion of Malaya and Indochina in 1945. The O.S.S. persuaded Pridi not to act without coordinating his efforts with those of Mountbatten; and the war ended in August 1945 before the Thai underground was able to get into action. In their account of this period Smith and Clark state that the British did not want Pridi's force to fight because it would have given Thailand a reason to demand treatment as an occupied country during the peace negotiations.[20]

[19]The Japanese commander in Thailand apparently was an able officer, whose objective during the final year of the war was to build friendship between Thailand and Japan for the postwar period. As a result Japanese troops were well behaved, and at the end of the war they handed over their weapons to the Thai underground without resistance or incidents.

[20]Nicol Smith, the O.S.S. agent smuggled into Thailand during the last month of the war, relates how eager Pridi was to stage an uprising before the Japanese took serious steps to curb his underground organization. (*Op. cit.*, pp. 231-3.)

The Thai government was unprepared for the war's sudden end and thereafter made frantic efforts to redeem the nation in the eyes of the Allies for the misdeeds of Pibun in 1941 and 1942. On August 16, one day after the Japanese surrendered to General MacArthur, Pridi Panomyong issued a proclamation as Regent of Thailand. This document, approved unanimously the same day by the national assembly, declared that

the will of the Thai people does not approve of the declaration of war and of acts adverse to the United Nations, [and that the Regent, acting for the King,] proclaims on behalf of the Thai people that the declaration of war on the United States of America and Great Britain is null and void and not binding on the Thai people as far as the United Nations are concerned.

Territories taken from Britain in Malaya and Burma in 1943 would be returned, and damages were promised to citizens of these countries for losses suffered. The proclamation recalled the help given by Thai citizens to the Allies during the war and charged that the 1942 declarations of war had been unconstitutional.[21] Subsequently the Thai government offered to set up a war crimes committee to try Thai war criminals, and it decided to change the name of the country back to Siam in order to avert suspicion that it had designs on neighboring countries inhabited by Thai-speaking people. In addition, Pridi asked Seni Pramot in Washington to become Prime Minister during the crucial period of negotiations with Britain and the United States—negotiations that would determine whether Thailand would emerge from the war as an independent nation or as an occupied territory of the victorious powers.[22]

[21]*Department of State Bulletin*, August 19, 1945, pp. 261–2.

[22]Seni seemed well suited for the job during this critical period, because of his British education and his leadership of the Free Thai

The United States was prepared to accept the Thai government's position that it had been coerced by Japan into joining in an aggressive alliance. A statement by Secretary of State Byrnes, issued on August 20, 1945, said that "the American Government has always believed that the declaration [of war] did not represent the will of the Thai people." He recalled that the Thai minister in Washington had organized the Free Thai movement, which "contributed substantially to the allied cause"; and that the resistance movement within Thailand had been prepared to commence overt action against the Japanese, but had not done so because the British and American governments had "requested that such action be deferred" for operational reasons. This statement of policy concluded by asserting that the United States "regarded Thailand not as an enemy but as a country to be liberated from the enemy," and that it looked "to the resumption by Thailand of its former place in the community of nations as a free, sovereign, and independent country."[23] This declaration clearly put the British and other Allied powers on notice that the United States would oppose any effort to deprive Thailand of its independence.

The position of the British government was set forth on August 20 in a statement by the Foreign Secretary in the House of Commons. He said Britain's attitude toward Thailand would depend on future Thai action, namely, the outcome of negotiations with Britain for a peace treaty. With this divergence in policy between the principal Allied nations, the Thai government relied principally on the United States

movement. Also, he had been a professor of law at Thammasat University before going to Washington, D.C. Seni, however, was not enthusiastic about becoming a scapegoat if Britain imposed a humiliating treaty, and he consented to take the job only after Pridi made it a question of patriotism to his country.

[23]*Department of State Bulletin,* August 19, 1945, p. 261.

to help it obtain better terms from Britain than it might otherwise receive.

Early in September 1945 British military authorities summoned a Thai mission to their headquarters in Kandy, Ceylon, to arrange for the entry of Allied troops into Thailand. They presented the Thai delegation a list of twenty-one demands covering both economic and military points; it was implied by the British that these demands had been cleared with the United States. The terms were exacting, and an American O.S.S. officer reportedly asked Washington for confirmation that they had been cleared. When it was learned that the State Department apparently had not been informed, the Thai delegation refused to sign the document until it had more time to study its contents. It did, however, agree to the military demands, and Allied troops were then dispatched to Thailand. The economic demands were the subject of several months of negotiation between Thailand and Britain; and in order to show its interest, the United States sent an observer to these sessions. When British pressure for concessions became intense during October, the Thai government leaked a story to an American press representative to the effect that Britain was trying to impose economic control over Thailand. This produced some anti-British press comment in the United States, but the London government denied the stories and said that the United States had been fully informed on all aspects of the negotiations. The key point of dispute was the demand that Thailand supply without payment up to one and a half million tons of rice to neighboring countries under British control as restitution for having cooperated with the Japanese war effort. Despite American efforts to have this demand modified, the British stood fast.

Thailand signed a peace treaty with the United Kingdom

and India on January 1, 1946. Among the major points of
the treaty were: Thailand would return the Malay and Burmese territories acquired during the war, would turn over free
one and a half million tons of rice to the United Kingdom
(for distribution in Malaya, India, Burma, and Singapore),
would not build a canal across the Kra isthmus without
British approval, and would sell rubber, tin, rice, and tea in
accordance with prices fixed by an international committee.
In return, Britain and India agreed to support Thailand's
membership in the United Nations.[24] The harsh terms of this
treaty were not essentially different from the original twenty-
one demands presented at Kandy in September 1945; but the
British government made a major concession in May 1946,
when it agreed to pay Thailand a fixed price, albeit below
the world market price, for its rice in order not to cause the
collapse of the Thai economy. Also, Britain and the United
States agreed to set up a joint commission to assist Thailand
to increase its rice production. Thus, it appears that American efforts on Thailand's behalf did influence the British
to modify their heavy economic demands and to agree to
preserve Thailand's territorial integrity.

Although in January 1946 Thailand obtained the support
of both the United States and Britain for membership in
the United Nations, the approval of the other three permanent members of the Security Council—France, China, and
the Soviet Union—was also required. In each case Thailand
had to pay a price for joining the wrong side in 1941. Negotiations with the Soviet Union and China did not prove so
difficult as those with France, because neither of these countries had any territorial dispute with Thailand. The Soviet
Union's position was that it could not support Thailand's

[24]See Russell H. Fifield, *The Diplomacy of Southeast Asia, 1945–1958*
(New York, 1958), pp. 239–41.

membership in the United Nations until there were diplomatic relations between the two countries.[25] In addition, it demanded repeal of Thailand's anti-Communist law of 1933. Lack of formal diplomatic relations also delayed China's support of Thailand's membership. China also insisted on the repeal of certain Thai laws that restricted the local Chinese community and limited Chinese immigration into Thailand. Late in 1946 Thailand agreed to establish diplomatic relations with both of these powers and to repeal the legislation in question.

Negotiations with France were both long and acrimonious. When Pridi issued his proclamation on August 16, 1945, no mention was made of France or of returning to France territories in Laos and Cambodia that had been obtained by treaty in 1941. The reason was that Thailand did not consider itself at war with France; furthermore, it had acquired the disputed territories in Laos and Cambodia in accordance with a treaty with France in May 1941. However, France refused to recognize this treaty with Vichy France, arguing that it was not binding on the Free French government, and it refused to resume diplomatic relations until Thailand agreed to withdraw from the territories. Border incidents occurred in April and May 1946, many of which involved Thai support for Viet-Minh guerrillas, so the Thai government appealed to the United Nations, even though it was not a member. The matter did not come before the Security Council, because France agreed to submit the territorial dispute to the International Court of Justice. Before a decision was reached, however, a series of incidents occurred along the Cambodian border, and fighting then broke out

[25]Rama VI had not recognized the Bolshevik government, nor had the Thai constitutional government during the nineteen-thirties accorded recognition to the Soviet Union.

in Siemrat. France withdrew its offer to have the court arbitrate the dispute and informed the United Nations that it would deal directly with Bangkok. It also threatened to veto Thailand's request for membership in the United Nations unless all the disputed territories were returned immediately. The United States indirectly supported France by declaring that it did not recognize Thailand's acquisition of the Indochinese territories in 1941; but it proposed no solution to Thailand's dispute with France. Negotiations took place in Washington, D.C., in the autumn of 1946; and on November 17 an agreement was signed whereby Thailand agreed to return all disputed territories to France. The French government agreed to turn them over to Laos and Cambodia, which were still under French control. Thailand renounced its agreement with Vichy France of May 1941; a conciliation commission was to be set up to examine claims by both sides for frontier revision; and Thailand agreed to withdraw its complaint to the United Nations. Diplomatic relations between the two countries were to be resumed, and France then agreed not to oppose Thailand's request for membership in the United Nations.[26]

Thailand was admitted to the United Nations in December 1946. Although there was much public resentment in Bangkok in November 1946, when the government decided to acquiesce to the French demands for the return of the Laotian and Cambodian territories, Thai leaders could take some comfort in the fact that Thailand's postwar efforts to "work its way back" into the community of nations might have proved even more difficult without the restraining influence of the United States on its European allies. Without doubt, Thailand would have suffered considerably more if the Brit-

[26]Fifield, op. cit., pp. 242–5.

ish and the French had had their way, because of the indignities the Thais had inflicted on them in 1941 and 1942.

An Appraisal of Thai Diplomacy (1940–1946)

The Thais are among the best diplomats in the world, it is often said, because they managed to maintain their country's independence during a period when all other countries in South and Southeast Asia were forced to accept European colonialism. Thailand's foreign policy during World War II is cited as proof of the cunning and resourcefulness of its leaders: how many other countries emerged from the war as allies of the Germans or Japanese and were restored within eighteen months to their prewar status?

The author believes that Thailand's success in maintaining its independence during the nineteenth century and in emerging from World War II practically unscathed was the result of a combination of astute diplomacy, based on a realistic view of Thailand's relation to the great powers, and luck, in the form of the country's geographical position. After World War I, Thai leaders astutely used United States support as a lever to extract from the European powers concessions on the restrictive treaties and, eventually the restoration of full sovereignty. During World War II, however, Thai diplomacy overreached itself by going farther than was necessary to accommodate the Japanese. The sweeping Japanese victories of 1941 and 1942 in Southeast Asia caused Pibun to conclude that Thailand could become an important power in Southeast Asia by cooperating fully with Japan; he abandoned traditional Thai caution and pragmatism in foreign affairs and gambled on a Japanese victory. Had the Pibun government simply permitted the Japanese to occupy the country in 1941, as Denmark had done in the face of a German ultimatum in 1940, it would have retained some room to maneuver when it later became clear how the war would end. Nevertheless, when Pibun realized that he had made a mistake, he made no effort to prevent Pridi Panomyong from organizing a Thai underground in 1943 or from working closely with the Allies during the last year of his regime.

After the war it was rather luck than skillful diplomacy that saved Thailand from a humiliating fate. Fortunately for the Thais, United States postwar policy in Southeast Asia favored the emergence of free and independent nations rather than the restitution of colonial empires. The United States was not prepared to see Thailand become a protectorate; and because it possessed enormous influence in 1945, its views prevailed. It did not, however, prevent Britain from obtaining large economic concessions, or the French from demanding the return of all the territories Thailand had acquired in 1941; to this extent Thailand suffered as a result of its decision to ally itself with Japan. This decision also resulted in Pibun's political eclipse and in the emergence of his rival, Pridi, as the leading figure in postwar Thai politics.

Thailand emerged from World War II with a new sense of realism about its international position. Some Thais prided themselves on the fact that the nation had come through the war relatively unscathed, and it is undeniable that Thai diplomacy was very skillful in 1945; but the claim that some make that Thailand's success in extricating itself from the war was due primarily to its diplomatic skill is an overstatement. What saved Thailand in 1945 was largely the same set of factors that saved it in 1893 and 1894: it was not in the interests of the great powers to deprive the country of its independence.

Chapter 4

The Search for Security

THAILAND emerged from World War II as the only independent country in Southeast Asia, the same unique position
it had occupied for more than eighty years. Nevertheless in
the course of the war the world situation had changed considerably, and Thailand now found itself confronted with a
wholly new set of foreign policy considerations. Whereas the
European colonial powers—Britain, France, and the Nether-
lands—had ruled the other countries in Southeast Asia for
many years without regard for the aspirations of the peoples
involved, in the postwar period indigenous national movements were springing up, asserting their claims to independence from the colonial powers, and reinforcing these claims
with armed force. Only in the Philippines was there a smooth
transition from colonial status to independence, in accordance
with promises made by the United States before the war. The
new situation in Southeast Asia therefore presented postwar
Thai governments with a foreign policy problem: whether
to continue the prewar policy of dealing exclusively with the
European powers in matters affecting Southeast Asia, or to
cultivate close relations with the emerging nationalist forces
in Burma, Indochina, Malaya, and Indonesia. In the late
nineteen-forties, when the Cold War began to affect Asia,
Thailand was forced to choose; it decided to join with the

Western powers, even though this choice tended to alienate the new Asian nations which sought security in neutralism.

For two years following the collapse of Japan in 1945, Thai foreign policy was largely determined by Pridi Panomyong, who had emerged from the war as a national hero because of his leadership of the Thai underground, which had been so active on behalf of the Allies. Pridi had very definite ideas about the role that Thailand should play in Southeast Asian affairs. While maintaining good official relations with the victorious Allies, particularly with the United States, Pridi also was ambitious for Thailand to become the leader of independent nations in this strategic area of Asia. He foresaw that nationalist forces in Burma, Indonesia, and Indochina would one day force the weakened colonial powers to recognize the futility of trying to rule these areas in the prewar manner, and that it was only a matter of time until the powers were forced to grant them independence. Pridi believed that Thailand's long history of independence and political stability and its success in dealing with European powers made it a natural leader among these emergent nations. It was an ambitious vision, but Pridi was an extraordinary person who seemed to have unlimited faith in his ability to lead Thailand and Southeast Asia in the new postwar era.

The dilemma in Pridi's policy became apparent in Indochina, where French efforts to work out an agreement with Viet-Minh forces failed in 1946, and guerrilla warfare ensued. Pridi sought to mediate this conflict while negotiating with France in May 1947 over Thailand's border with Indochina. Pridi proposed that the two countries sponsor a Southeast Asian Union, which would include Laos, Cambodia, and Vietnam as free and independent states. If the plan succeeded, Pridi envisioned that other states in the area would join, and that a united Southeast Asia eventually could become an important factor in international affairs. In 1947 however, the French were more interested in crushing the Viet-Minh revolution than in recognizing its independence, and rejected the plan.[1]

Pridi then followed more vigorously a policy of support for the nationalist movements in neighboring countries: while maintaining correct relations with France, his government gave increasing aid to the rebel forces in Indochina. After the war some 50,000 Vietnamese refugees had settled in the northeastern area of Thailand; and now the Thai government did little to prevent them from infiltrating recruits and supplies into Indochina. After the Dutch launched military operations against the Indonesian nationalists in 1947, Pridi organized a Southeast Asia League in Bangkok. It included a number of his followers as well as exiled leaders from neighboring countries who wanted to expel the colonial powers from their homelands. By the autumn of 1947 Pridi was moving toward an anticolonialist policy in an effort to align Thailand with the emerging states of Southeast Asia.

Before Pridi could put this policy into effect, however, the Tamrong government, which supported his views, was ousted by an army *coup d'état* in November 1947; and Pridi went into exile. The Coup Group, which favored the return of Pibun Songkhram to power, tried to justify its action by accusing Pridi of plotting a rebellion in which he planned to depose the King, establish a republic, and place himself at the head of the state. Thereafter, it was charged, he wanted to make Thailand the cornerstone of a Southeast Asian union and to work for an accommodation with the Soviet bloc.[2] Although no proof of these charges was brought before the public, the record of Pridi's radical economic views, his repub-

[1] John Coast, *Some Aspects of Siamese Politics* (New York, 1953), p. 38.
[2] *Ibid.*, p. 42.

lican sentiments, and his failure to clear himself of charges in connection with the assassination of the King the previous year led many Thais to question his motives in 1947 and weakened his political position in respect to the army faction. The coup leaders did not immediately place Pibun in control of the government, because of the refusal of the Western powers to grant recognition; but when he finally became Prime Minister in April 1948, few Thais doubted that there would be a significant shift in foreign policy. No one knew, however, how far Pibun was prepared to go in aligning Thailand with the West or whether the United States and Britain would trust him after his wartime record of collaboration with the Japanese.

When Pibun formed his government in April 1948, Thailand was surrounded by conflict. Newly independent Burma was struggling for its life against Communist terrorists; British and Malayan forces were engaged in a war against Communist guerrillas; the French were trying to crush the Viet-Minh rebels; and the Dutch still hoped to restore their rule in Indonesia. It was remarkable, observes Fifield, that Thailand, "though literally surrounded by trouble, was able to remain at peace in Southeast Asia."[3] Even more ominous for Thailand's security was the steady advance of Communist forces in China against the Nationalist armies. Not only did the Thais fear having a powerful Communist China as a neighbor; they were obsessed with the possibility that the large number of Overseas Chinese in Thailand would be attracted to the new China and so become a powerful subversive force. Even before Pibun's return to power, the sentiment of the Chinese community was shifting from the Nationalists to the Communists. Pibun's appointment as

[3]Russell H. Fifield, *The Diplomacy of Southeast Asia: 1945–1958* (New York, 1958), p. 247.

Prime Minister signaled not only a change in foreign policy but also a program of repression of the Chinese community—a policy he had instituted in 1939, when he came to power for the first time. Skinner, in his comprehensive history of the Chinese in Thailand, states that when Pibun resumed government leadership, "the reaction of local Chinese was an almost visible, collective shudder."[4]

The Overseas Chinese and Thai Security

Thailand has the largest number of Overseas Chinese of any country of Southeast Asia; they number 3,000,000, or about 10 per cent of the total population. It is estimated that nearly half the inhabitants of Bangkok are Chinese or of Chinese origin, and as in most neighboring countries, the Chinese control the commerce of the capital while the indigenous population controls the government and the civil service. Until 1910, when King Chulalongkorn died, the government followed a policy of rapidly assimilating the Chinese immigrants who streamed into Thailand from the southern part of China, and there were few problems. In 1910, however, nationalistic manifestations on both sides broke the tranquility; from then until today the Chinese minority has been intimately linked to Thailand's security and is therefore a factor in its foreign policy.

In 1910, a few months before King Wachirawut ascended the throne, the Chinese secret societies in Bangkok organized a general strike. The local Chinese had been strongly influenced by the growing nationalism fostered by the Manchu dynasty during its last years, while the Siamese were becoming more nationalistic in the wake of the country's defeat by France a few years earlier. The people were also aroused by

[4]G. William Skinner, *Chinese Society in Thailand: An Analytical History* (Ithaca, N.Y., 1957), p. 289.

Siamese students returning from Europe with ideas of Western nationalism. By 1910 Siam was ripe for racial disturbances. Although the Chinese general strike was decisively dealt with by Siamese authorities and was a failure, it dramatized for the first time the economic power of the Chinese community as well as the potential threat of a mass Chinese uprising against the government. King Wachirawut, who was plainly concerned about the danger, embarked on an avowedly anti-Chinese campaign, which likened the Chinese to the Jews of Europe. This campaign intensified after the Chinese Revolution of 1911, which increased the nationalist sentiments among the Chinese in Siam; and the King warned that the government would tolerate no further disorders.[5] In 1913 the first Nationality Act was promulgated: it was directed against the Chinese community.

When Pibun Songkhram became Prime Minister in 1938, the Chinese community posed a problem because it was strongly anti-Japanese and also openly supported the Nationalist Chinese Government's war effort. As Pibun's policy was to accommodate the rising power of Japan, he could not tolerate a large Chinese opposition. Also, he had a general antipathy toward the large Chinese minority. In 1939 Pibun launched a series of sweeping anti-Chinese measures which greatly reduced the Chinese community's economic influence and also forced it to forgo much of its cultural separateness. Thai business firms were formed, assisted by government subsidy, in order to force Chinese companies to close; new taxes imposed on businessmen were designed to limit the profits of the Chinese; Chinese schools were closed; and most Chinese newspapers were forced to cease publication. So

[5] In 1914 King Wachirawut published under an assumed name a pamphlet entitled "The Jews of the East," a bitter denunciation of the Chinese.

drastic were these measures that the Nationalist government of China protested, and the colonial governments in Southeast Asia also became aroused because of the impact on their own Chinese communities. Later in 1939 Pibun moderated his policy somewhat, but he publicly advised the Thai people to avoid mixed marriages with the Chinese.[6]

During World War II, when Thailand was an ally of Japan, Pibun increased the restrictions on the Chinese minority. Many areas of the country were declared military zones, from which all alien Chinese were forced to leave on short notice. Chinese leaders who had cooperated with the Nationalists were imprisoned. During the last year of the war, after Pibun had resigned as Prime Minister and Khuang Apaiwong had taken over, many of the restrictions against the Chinese were relaxed. But the repression and the humiliation suffered during five years of the Pibun regime were not easily forgotten. By the end of the war, there was a surge of nationalist feeling among the Chinese, who were proud that China, but not Thailand, had fought with the Allies against Japan.

In September 1945, an incident in which the Chinese flag was flown together with those of the Big Five powers, and the Thai flag was not, touched off a riot in Bangkok between the Chinese community and Thai police. There were many casualties on both sides, and for several days anarchy reigned in the Chinese section of Bangkok. The Chungking government protested vigorously against the Thai treatment of the Chinese, and it was feared that China would veto Thailand's bid for membership in the United Nations. Finally, after ten days Thai and Chinese leaders restored order and cooperated to maintain peace in the city; but, as in 1910, an organized

[6]For a fuller description of these measures against the Chinese, see Skinner, *op. cit.*, pp. 261–8.

and militant Chinese minority caused deep anxiety among the Thai population. The Chinese and Thai governments soon found it to their mutual advantage to seek agreement on all outstanding issues, and normal diplomatic relations were established in September 1946. Thai authorities made many concessions to the local Chinese, restoring most of the rights they had enjoyed prior to 1939, and setting the immigration quota, a major issue, at 10,000 annually. Chinese schools were permitted to function again, and Chinese nationals were accorded the same freedoms enjoyed by any other aliens residing in Thailand. There followed a period of official amity between China and Thailand; and in the spring of 1947 the Thai-Chinese Friendship Society was established, of which Pridi was a prominent member.

It is significant that despite a long history of trade and commerce, the formal diplomatic relations were not established between Thailand and China until 1946. The Chinese had been making overtures for such relations since early in the twentieth century, but Thailand always declined for fear that such recognition would give the Chinese government a chance to interfere in its internal affairs. China's victory in World War II and Thailand's desire to rehabilitate itself after its wartime partnership with Japan were the principal causes of the change in Thailand's policy toward China. Nonetheless the deep-seated fear of the local Chinese remained an important fact of life for most Thais. When reports of rice smuggling and other scandals involving Chinese merchants became widespread during 1946 and 1947, these fears turned to hostility. Skinner believes that the Chinese merchants were in part responsible for the return of Pibun to power, because they contributed to corruption and inflation and helped to bring about "the downfall of the Thai administration which, of all administrations since the 1932 revolution, had been most consistently friendly to the Chinese."[7]

By the time Pibun became Prime Minister in April 1948, Communism had already made substantial gains in the Chinese community. Many Chinese teachers and members of Chinese-dominated labor unions were sympathetic to the Chinese Communists, and there was a marked increase in the amount of Communist propaganda appearing in the local Chinese-language press. Pibun's repressive policy was, however, directed not only against Communist influence among the Chinese but against the Chinese minority in general. Edwin Stanton, American ambassador to Thailand during this period, writes that

although the Prime Minister knew of the guerrilla campaigns being carried out in the countries surrounding Thailand and something of the Communist activities within his own country, he did not at that time take the matter seriously. ... He was thinking more of the threat posed by a large Chinese minority population in Thailand to the economy of his country and the livelihood of the people.[8]

Pibun's new policy affected Communist and Kuomintang groups alike: schools and associations were raided, and several hundred leaders were arrested; a new government-sponsored labor organization was set up to compete with Chinese labor groups; and the Chinese press was warned against promoting antigovernment themes. Although the Chinese immigration quota of 10,000 had already been lowered somewhat by the Tamrong government, Pibun went further and reduced it to the level of other nationalities, namely, 200 a year. By the end of 1948 the government had effectively limited overt

[7]Ibid., p. 288.
[8]Edwin Stanton, Brief Authority (London, 1957), p. 221.

Chinese influence in Thailand and had given every evidence of being in full control of the situation.

Soon after the Chinese Communists proclaimed their victory on mainland China in October 1949, Pibun warned the Chinese community in Thailand not to engage in political activity on behalf of either side in the Chinese war. He said that, whatever their political convictions might be, the Chinese should remember that they were living in Thailand as guests, and that the government would tolerate no violation of the law. He reminded them that Thailand had not recognized the new regime in China, and that it would not be proper to fly the red flag. Pibun was following a "wait and see" policy, and he did not want the local Chinese to embarrass his government in respect to either the Peking or the Taiwan regime until he had had time to assess the new international situation and decided what position Thailand should take. Pibun's policy received a severe jolt in January 1950, however, when Radio Peking broadcast a sharp attack against his government for oppressing the local Chinese and demanded assurances that Thai authorities would stop this policy. This broadcast was the signal for activating the entire network of political parties and mass organizations in China on behalf of the oppressed Chinese living in Thailand, and it alarmed Pibun so much that he began to alter his policy toward Communist China. Since at about the same time the United States began to re-evaluate its policy in the Far East, following the Communist conquest of China, it is likely that Pibun was encouraged into thinking that an anti-Communist policy would have the support of the most powerful nation in the Far East.

Except for the potential danger from the local Chinese and from the Vietnamese minority living in northeast Thailand, Marxism has never posed the problem for Thai governments that it has for other countries of Southeast Asia. The Thai population had been largely immune to foreign ideologies during the period of the country's accommodation to Western influences; as a result it escaped the Communist onslaught against Southeast Asia, which began in 1948, when the Cominform launched its program to subvert most of the countries in this area. The reasons for Thailand's relative immunity to Communism lie in its traditional independence from European colonialism and in the long history of monarchy and respect for authority which form an important part of Thai psychology. In a real sense Marxism could find no deep-seated grievances among the Thais, and it therefore had little appeal—even to the intellectuals.[9] Thus, when Pibun came to power in 1948, he was in a better position than any other leader in Southeast Asia to cope with Communist subversion. In dealing with the Chinese minority, he astutely made it an anti-Chinese rather than an anti-Communist campaign and so avoided the possibility of antagonizing one of the great powers, the Soviet Union. One writer has concluded that "by impartially clamping down on both the KMT and Communist Chinese he has not given valid cause for offense to the U.S.S.R."[10]

By 1950 Pibun and other government leaders were convinced that Communist China was a menace to all the countries of Southeast Asia, but they were undecided about how Thailand could best cope with it. Pibun inclined toward an association with the Western powers rather than toward a neutralist policy; but he was not prepared to join an anti-

[9]The factors that have worked against the rise of a Communist movement in Thailand are described in detail by David Wilson, in Frank Trager (ed.), *Marxism in Southeast Asia* (Stanford, Calif., 1959), pp. 59–101.

[10]Virginia Thompson and Richard Adloff, *The Left Wing in Southeast Asia* (New York, 1950), p. 68.

ments that it has for other countries of Southeast Asia. The Thai population had been largely immune to foreign ideologies during the period of the country's accommodation to Western influences; as a result it escaped the Communist onslaught against Southeast Asia, which began in 1948, when the Cominform launched its program to subvert most of the countries in this area. The reasons for Thailand's relative immunity to Communism lie in its traditional independence from European colonialism and in the long history of monarchy and respect for authority which form an important part of Thai psychology. In a real sense Marxism could find no deep-seated grievances among the Thais, and it therefore had little appeal—even to the intellectuals.[9] Thus, when Pibun came to power in 1948, he was in a better position than any other leader in Southeast Asia to cope with Communist subversion. In dealing with the Chinese minority, he astutely made it an anti-Chinese rather than an anti-Communist campaign and so avoided the possibility of antagonizing one of the great powers, the Soviet Union. One writer has concluded that "by impartially clamping down on both the KMT and Communist Chinese he has not given valid cause for offense to the U.S.S.R."[10]

By 1950 Pibun and other government leaders were convinced that Communist China was a menace to all the countries of Southeast Asia, but they were undecided about how Thailand could best cope with it. Pibun inclined toward an association with the Western powers rather than toward a neutralist policy; but he was not prepared to join an anti-

[9] The factors that have worked against the rise of a Communist movement in Thailand are described in detail by David Wilson, in Frank Trager (ed.), *Marxism in Southeast Asia* (Stanford, Calif., 1959), pp. 59–101.

[10] Virginia Thompson and Richard Adloff, *The Left Wing in Southeast Asia* (New York, 1950), p. 68.

Communist alliance until he was sure that it would have the full support of the United States. When in the summer of 1949 the Philippines proposed to join with Thailand, South Korea, and Nationalist China in an anti-Communist front, Pibun replied that Thailand would be interested only if other independent Asian countries joined also, and if the United States gave material support. In 1949 the United States had not yet formulated a new Far Eastern policy to replace the pro-Nationalist Chinese policy which was then crumbling. Although Britain and France continued to resist Communist insurgency in Malaya and in Indochina, it became increasingly clear to Thai leaders that unless the United States assumed an active role in Southeast Asia, it would be difficult for Thailand to resist the tide of Communism that threatened to engulf the area. The Thai government therefore waited to see how the United States would react to the new situation. Meanwhile, Pibun was fully prepared to cooperate with the British in Malaya to combat Communist terrorists who were using Thai territory as a haven in their guerrilla warfare against the British. Shortly after he became Prime Minister, Pibun took an active interest in the Malayan border situation, and his cooperation was a factor in influencing the British to grant his government recognition, despite Britain's strong feelings about Pibun's policy during World War II. In the case of the French in Indochina, however, Pibun was more cautious. For a time he continued to support the nationalist aspirations of the Laotian, Cambodian, and Vietnamese peoples, and he did not try to prevent arms from being smuggled across the Mekong River. In part, this policy was motivated by a deep anti-French feeling which persisted in official Thai circles after the war and was reinforced after France had threatened to veto Thailand's membership in the United Nations unless former French terri-

Communist alliance until he was sure that it would have the full support of the United States. When in the summer of 1949 the Philippines proposed to join with Thailand, South Korea, and Nationalist China in an anti-Communist front, Pibun replied that Thailand would be interested only if other independent Asian countries joined also, and if the United States gave material support. In 1949 the United States had not yet formulated a new Far Eastern policy to replace the pro-Nationalist Chinese policy which was then crumbling. Although Britain and France continued to resist Communist insurgency in Malaya and in Indochina, it became increasingly clear to Thai leaders that unless the United States assumed an active role in Southeast Asia, it would be difficult for Thailand to resist the tide of Communism that threatened to engulf the area. The Thai government therefore waited to see how the United States would react to the new situation. Meanwhile, Pibun was fully prepared to cooperate with the British in Malaya to combat Communist terrorists who were using Thai territory as a haven in their guerrilla warfare against the British. Shortly after he became Prime Minister, Pibun took an active interest in the Malayan border situation, and his cooperation was a factor in influencing the British to grant his government recognition, despite Britain's strong feelings about Pibun's policy during World War II. In the case of the French in Indochina, however, Pibun was more cautious. For a time he continued to support the nationalist aspirations of the Laotian, Cambodian, and Vietnamese peoples, and he did not try to prevent arms from being smuggled across the Mekong River. In part, this policy was motivated by a deep anti-French feeling which persisted in official Thai circles after the war and was reinforced after France had threatened to veto Thailand's membership in the United Nations unless former French territories in Laos and Cambodia were returned. Another factor was Pibun's suspicion that Viet-Minh forces under Ho Chi Minh might well defeat the French, and that it would be unwise to antagonize the Viet-Minh, at least until it was known that the United States and Britain were prepared to support the French in this war.

Thailand Moves toward the Western Camp (1950)

Early in 1950 the security situation in Asia crystallized, and the Thai government decided to join with the Western powers against the Communist bloc. Thai leaders were convinced that a Communist-dominated China would be antagonistic toward a Thailand ruled by Pibun, that it would give military aid to Vietnamese and Laotian Communists who were ready to assist the separatist elements in northeast Thailand, and that it would use the Vietnamese refugees there for subversive purposes. It also became clear during 1950 that the United States was not prepared to stand aside and permit the forces of Communism to sweep through Southeast Asia. Therefore Pibun felt safe in shifting his policy in the direction he instinctively favored, namely, a close association with the Western powers against Communist China. Pibun believed that a pro-Western policy would be accepted by most Thais—especially if it were accompanied by large amounts of economic and military aid; but there remained powerful voices who were not convinced that it was in Thailand's best interests to commit itself so decisively to one side in an international contest whose outcome was not certain. One of these dissenters was Foreign Minister Pote Sarasin.

The immediate issue in February 1950 was the war in Indochina. With the fall of the Chinese mainland to Communist forces a few months earlier and the material aid being channeled by the Chinese to the Viet-Minh forces, French efforts to ensure a free Vietnam became a major factor in American foreign policy. A conference of American ambassadors from the Far Eastern area took place in Bangkok in mid-February, and Ambassador-at-large Philip Jessup was sent by the Secretary of State to preside at the meeting. The group discussed the impact of Communist China on the countries of Southeast Asia and the means that could be adopted to prevent them from falling under Communist control. Technical assistance to countries of the area was considered important in raising standards of living and combating disease, and military assistance was also believed to be important as a means of countering subversion.[11]

Ambassador Jessup conferred at this time with Prime Minister Pibun and other members of the Thai government and urged that Thailand recognize the newly proclaimed independent Vietnam headed by Emperor Bao Dai. The United States and Britain, which had recently granted recognition to this regime, believed that if it were supported vigorously, the Viet-Minh forces could be stopped in their effort to take over Indochina. This matter caused a split in Pibun's government: the Prime Minister and the military leaders favored recognition, while the Foreign Minister, Pote Sarasin, strongly opposed it. The Foreign Minister counseled against hasty action, apparently in the belief that Bao Dai would not enjoy the support of the Vietnamese people, and he urged that Thailand should await further developments before it made so critical a decision in foreign policy.[12] Pibun, however, desperately wanted American protection of Thailand, and he believed that he could expect large amounts of aid from the United States in return for his pro-Western policy. Therefore, when after some days of debate the cabinet decided to leave the decision to the Prime Minister, he decided to delay no

[11]Stanton, *op. cit.,* pp. 234–5.   [12]*Ibid.,* p. 238.

longer. On February 28 the government announced its recognition of the Bao Dai government and of the newly established governments of Laos and Cambodia. The next day Pote Sarasin resigned. Pibun's decision incurred the strong displeasure of the Communist bloc and of many neutral nations as well as of many persons in Thailand who charged that he had become an American puppet. Nevertheless he believed that his course was correct, and he maintained his position against all opposition. Thereafter, Thai authorities took steps to isolate the Vietnamese minority living in Thailand and tried to curb Viet-Minh propaganda activities in Bangkok.

Pibun's recognition of the Bao Dai government was not an indication of support for French policy but was instead an attempt to gain the support of the United States. Pibun was being consistent with previous Thai foreign policy in acting in time of danger to align Thailand with the strongest power in Asia. Some Thais, however, were not convinced early in 1950 that the United States would use its vast power to defend Southeast Asia against Chinese imperialism. Even the British had doubts; and it became British policy, following the Communist conquest of China, to bring about a greater American involvement in the defense of Southeast Asia.[13]

The outbreak of the Korean War was a turning point for both the United States and Thailand, insofar as the military defense of Southeast Asia was concerned. Until that time American involvement in the area was largely economic and cultural; after June 1950 the military implications of Communist China's ambitions in Asia made United States military and economic assistance to Thailand of vital importance to both countries. Fifield contends that Southeast Asia was a power vacuum which both Communist and Western powers

[13]See the Chatham House study group report, *Collective Defense in South East Asia* (London, 1956), p. 16.

were eager to fill, a prize that East and West wished to deny the other, and that "obviously Thailand was a key country in the security policy of the United States in the area."[14] As a result, in September 1950, the Economic and Technical Co-operation Agreement was concluded between the United States and Thailand, and the following month a Military Assistance Agreement also was signed. In July an Educational Exchange Program (Fulbright Agreement) had been agreed to by the two governments; and soon Thai students were going to the United States on scholarships, and American professors were being attached to Thai educational institutions.

The Korean War also had a decisive effect on Thailand's foreign policy and tended to vindicate Pibun's earlier efforts to associate Thailand with a defensive arrangement among the Western powers in Southeast Asia. The Thai government was one of the first to respond to the United Nations' call for assistance in the Korean War, and Pibun dramatically offered 20,000 tons of rice and several thousand troops to assist the United Nations war effort. By offering to send Thai soldiers to fight beside British and American as well as other United Nations forces, Pibun felt he had a right to expect support from these countries in the defense of Thailand. Until June 1950 there was considerable opposition in Thailand to accepting military aid from the West, on the grounds that it might bring about retaliation by Communist nations; after the attack on Korea, however, these fears were largely dispelled, and there was little opposition to the equipping and training of the Thai armed forces by American military advisers. Still, the United States Military Assistance Agreement of 1950 did not go beyond equipment and training. It was made clear by the United States ambassador, at the time

[14]Fifield, *op. cit.*, p. 269.

this agreement was signed that no military alliance or bases were sought by either side, and that the United States had only responded to a request from the Thai government for military aid.[15] His statement indicated again that the United States was not prepared, even after the outbreak of the Korean War, to give Thailand a military guarantee, although Pibun and other Thai leaders wanted such an assurance. Military and economic aid soon began to flow into the country and brought increasing prosperity. By the end of 1950 Pibun had greatly strengthened his position in Thai politics and had gained the support of the United States and Britain, both of which had had strong reservations about his return to power in 1948. Whether or not one agreed with his ideas on government, it could not be denied that Pibun seemed to be a master politician who knew how to work with the major powers.

As the Korean War continued into 1951, and as United Nations forces were driven back by the Communist Chinese armies, opposition to Pibun's policy began to grow. Not only did the peace propaganda from Moscow and Peking cause some members of the press and the assembly to call for a halt to Thailand's contribution to the war effort, but various sections of the military, notably the navy, were unhappy over their small role in the political life of the country. In June 1951 the navy staged a revolt in an attempt to force the government to accede to its demands. Although this revolt was crushed by the army and the police, it showed that Pibun's position was not secure. The navy's daring action and the growing opposition to Pibun's policies caused the ruling army-police faction under Generals Sarit and Pao to carry out their "silent" coup in November 1951, so that they could deal more effectively with the internal threats to their position

[15]*Department of State Bulletin,* October 30, 1960, p. 703.

and could also pursue more vigorously the pro-Western policy.[16]

The year 1952 was a critical one for the Thai government's internal security policy. The Moscow and Peking propaganda campaign against Thailand had grown to huge proportions, and strong efforts were made to turn teachers, students, writers, and even Buddhist monks away from the government. It seemed obvious to Western observers that the Communists were making considerable progress in their campaign to turn a large segment of the Thai population away from Pibun's policy and toward neutralism. After the ceasefire was proclaimed in the Korean fighting, Peking was able to pose as both a peace-loving nation and an Asian power that had withstood the mighty United States and other Western nations in Korea. Such a two-pronged appeal had some effect in Thailand as well as in other Southeast Asian countries; and it caused some thoughtful Thais to wonder whether a close alignment with the United States was as wise a policy as it had appeared to be in the latter part of 1950.

For the Chinese community in Thailand, 1952 was also a crucial year. This minority group was now completely split between supporters of the Kuomintang and of the Peking government, and there was strong propaganda on both sides. General Pao and his police therefore decided to launch an assault on the Chinese community in order to immobilize it as a subversive force on either side. This campaign continued throughout 1952 and culminated in November in mass raids and arrests in the wake of the uncovering of an alleged widespread Communist plot to seize the government. Between November 1952 and January 1953, more than 250 Chinese were arrested, and over 150 Chinese firms were raided, in addition to the closing of many Chinese associations and

[16]See Chapter 3 for a fuller discussion of these events.

schools. The disclosure of this plot permitted the government to rush through the assembly a strong anti-Communist measure, which became known officially as the Un-Thai Activities Act of 1952. This legislation gave the government wide powers to arrest anyone who had any connection with a Communist organization, or who tried to propagandize for the Communist cause. If found guilty under the sweeping provisions, a person was liable to five to ten years in prison. This measure was directed primarily against the Chinese, and in the ensuing months General Pao used it to carry out the most thorough roundup of suspected subversives ever undertaken in Thailand.[17]

There is some dispute over the genuineness of the plot that sparked this massive government crackdown on leftists and Communists in 1952. Some observers have argued that Pibun and Pao were forced to invent a plot in order to arouse public opinion to accept the measures they planned against opposition elements. According to this theory, the police used the Communist "scare" of November 1952 as a pretext for rushing an anti-Communist bill through the assembly and obtaining public acquiescence in the subsequent police action. This view is not shared, however, by Ambassador Stanton, who credits British intelligence with bringing to the attention of Thai authorities evidence against a young Thai air force officer who had been on duty in London, and who allegedly had been won over by Soviet agents. Investigation of the case showed that this officer was involved in a military conspiracy to overthrow the Pibun government, depose the King, and establish a republic with the help of "liberation forces."[18] It is not unlikely that a plot against the government was being planned during 1952; such conspiracies were com-

---

[17]For details of this legislation, see Skinner, *op. cit.*, p. 335.
[18]Stanton, *op. cit.*, pp. 276–7.

mon in the early fifties, as the police and the army commanders increasingly dominated the political scene and thereby reaped the financial rewards of power. However, the
extent to which Communists were involved in this case is
unclear, although it is reasonable to assume that Communist
elements would have been eager to take advantage of any
opportunity to unseat the strongly pro-Western Pibun government. The essential element of this episode, insofar as the
security of Thailand was concerned, is that the Pibun regime,
believing that there was a serious threat of subversion in
Thailand at this time, took decisive steps to eliminate it
before it resulted in the government's overthrow.

The fears of the Pibun government seemed to be confirmed
by an announcement from Peking in January 1953 concerning the establishment of a Thai Autonomous People's Government in the province of Yunnan, where a sizable number
of Thai-speaking people live. In its propaganda Peking indicated that this Thai government would serve as a guide to
other Thai-speaking peoples in Southeast Asia who wanted
autonomy, and who wished to throw off the yoke of American
and Nationalist Chinese imperialism. The plan was "diabol-
ically cunning," says Stanton, and it "disturbed Thailand as
nothing else has done" because the Chinese had hit upon a
political theme cherished by Thais for many centuries—the
unity of all Thai-speaking people in Asia.[19] Pibun had
dreamed of a "Greater Thailand" in 1939 and 1940, and
Pridi had a similar policy in mind after World War II. Now
the Chinese had proposed the same plan, with the difference
that Peking rather than Bangkok would be its sponsor. Pridi's
emergence from obscurity in Peking in 1954 to denounce the
Pibun government and lend his prestige to the plan of unity
among Thai peoples confirmed the suspicion many Thais

[19]*Ibid.*, p. 278.

held that Communist China was working for Pridi's return to Thailand at the head of a government friendly to China.

The Thai leaders' fears of a Communist conspiracy coupled with outside assistance were further strengthened in the spring of 1953 when Viet-Minh forces moved into Laos for the first time and set up a so-called Free Laotian Government. Thailand feared that this was the prelude to an open appeal to the Thais living in the northeast provinces, who are ethnically and culturally related to the Lao people. In addition, some 50,000 Vietnamese refugees lived in this critical area along the Mekong River, and their loyalties were with Ho Chi Minh. It was a situation ripe for infiltration and subversion, and the Bangkok government was acutely aware of the danger presented by the marauding Viet-Minh troops directly across the river. A state of emergency was declared in the provinces adjacent to the border, and the army and police units stationed there were strengthened considerably in 1953 and 1954. In addition, Thailand appealed for more American military aid to counter the subversion, and such assistance was given. The high point in the Viet-Minh threat occurred in December 1953, when their forces captured the Lao town of Takhek which was strategically located on the Mekong. Another column invaded northern Laos early in 1954, and in April the Viet-Minh moved into Cambodia.

The Thai government was clearly alarmed at this threat to its security, and it found in the United States government at this time a great power that shared its alarm. Thailand appealed to the United Nations Security Council for an investigation, but the Soviet Union vetoed the request. Thailand then decided to make its appeal to the General Assembly. Before the matter was taken up in September 1954, however, the war in Indochina was ended, and the Geneva Agreements covering the three former Indochinese states were being implemented. Negotiations for the Manila Pact, inaugurating the Southeast Asia Treaty Organization (SEATO), were also in progress, so that Thailand did not press its charges. However, its previous action dramatized to the United Nations the threat to Thai security from Communist forces during the spring of 1954; in this respect it paved the way for Thailand's joining in a collective defense pact to protect itself in the future.

Thailand Joins SEATO (1954)

The conclusion of the Southeast Asia Collective Defense Treaty, also known as the Manila Pact, on September 8, 1954, marked the high point in Thailand's efforts to gain from the Western powers a guarantee of military assistance in case of an attack by Communist China or any other Communist force in the area. At the same time this treaty marked a departure from the United States policy of avoiding defense commitments on the mainland of Southeast Asia. Thailand had rejected neutrality and reliance solely on the United Nations for protection. In the face of a determined effort by Communist China to extend its influence southward, the United States in 1954 moved to fill the power vacuum in Southeast Asia created by the withdrawal of British and French power.

In the early spring of 1954 Secretary of State Dulles approached the Thai ambassador in Washington, Pote Sarasin, asking whether his government would be willing to participate in a collective defense arrangement for Southeast Asia. The ambassador relayed this message to Bangkok and within two days had a reply to the effect that Thailand would accept such an arrangement "unconditionally." Although some voices in the Thai government advocated caution and proposed that the matter be studied in some detail, Prime Minister Pibun decided that the situation on Thailand's eastern border was so desperate that his government could not afford to vacillate. Modelski believes that such an arrangement with the United States had been the goal of the Pibun government since 1950, and that the signing of the Manila Pact was the result of "a long period of skillful diplomatic activity" in which Thailand "succeeded in fashioning itself as the bastion of Western defence in South-East Asia."[20] The two countries negotiated during the spring and summer of 1954, and Bangkok worked closely with Washington in presenting its case to the United Nations and in bringing pressure to bear on the Communist powers to end the war in Indochina. So eager was Thailand to obtain a military guarantee from the United States that it offered in June 1954 to accept foreign troops on its soil if the Viet-Minh refused to agree to a peace treaty in Indochina.

In return for its strongly anti-Communist stand, however, the Pibun government wanted a commitment from the United States that was at least as firm as the one it had made in the North Atlantic Pact, namely, that the United States would immediately come to the assistance of any member nation attacked. When the foreign ministers of the eight nations establishing SEATO met in Manila in September 1954, the Thai Foreign Minister, Prince Wan Waityakorn, stated:

The Government and people of Thailand are anxious to have as strong a pact as possible. . . . While, in the matter of wording, there is a variety of models to choose from, it is the substance that counts; and, from this point of view, my Delegation would desire to see a commitment which in substance, is as near as possible to that of NATO.[21]

[20]George Modelski (ed.), *SEATO, Six Studies* (Melbourne, Australia, 1962), pp. 87, 88.

[21]Secretariat of the Manila Conference, *The Signing of the Southeast Asia Collective Defense Treaty* (Manila, September 8, 1954), p. 37.

Nonetheless the United States was not prepared to give the same guarantee to the SEATO nations that it did to the NATO nations, probably because it feared that the Senate might refuse to ratify a treaty that committed the United States to treat an attack on any member of the treaty as an attack on itself.[22] Therefore the treaty signed in Manila committed the signatories to meet a common danger in accordance with each member's "constitutional processes" (Article IV, paragraph 1).[23] Although on this and other occasions the United States made a number of verbal assurances that tended to increase the Pibun government's confidence in the American commitment, the Thai government was disappointed and feared that it would be criticized by its political opponents, who might argue that it had exposed the country to great risks from the Communist powers without obtaining an airtight guarantee of United States protection in case of a crisis. This doubt caused the Pibun government to have second thoughts about the treaty when the international situation improved in 1955 and 1956.

When the SEATO Ministerial Council met in Bangkok in February 1955, the Thai government made a strong plea for the establishment of a SEATO military command in Thailand and for the permanent stationing of SEATO forces in the treaty area. Pibun warned the day before the conference opened that the Chinese had massed 20,000 Thai-speaking troops in Yunnan, and that Thailand was in great danger of attack. Pibun hoped to counter some of the criticism of

[22]When the treaty was presented to the Senate for ratification, Secretary of State Dulles was careful to point out in his covering statement that the treaty did not automatically commit the United States to go to war in defense of the treaty nations. (*Department of State Bulletin,* November 29, 1954, p. 82.)

[23]For the text of the treaty and the protocol, see *Department of State Bulletin,* September 20, 1954, pp. 393–6.

the treaty within Thailand by demonstrating that it possessed forces that would immediately be used to defend Thailand in case the Communist powers moved against it. Secretary Dulles exploded this hope by rejecting the proposal on the grounds that it was not necessarily United States policy, in case of attack from a Communist state, to limit action to the area of Southeast Asia; a powerful mobile force capable of striking the enemy in various parts of the Far East was more in line with United States strategic thinking at that time. Thailand was partly mollified when treaty members agreed to establish the SEATO Council's headquarters in Bangkok and to appoint a Thai as Secretary General of the SEATO staff.

The diplomatic action taken by the United States in 1954 did contain Communist forces in Vietnam for the moment, without involving United States troops on the mainland of Southeast Asia; SEATO thus seemed to be an effective deterrent. American military and economic aid to Thailand increased substantially after the signing of this treaty. Economic assistance, for example, went up from $6 million in 1952–1953 to $11 million in 1953–1954; it then jumped to $38 million in 1954–1955. By the summer of 1955 the Pibun government could point with considerable pride to its success in securing protection of Thailand's territorial integrity in the face of a serious Communist threat, and also to the way that Thailand was benefiting from the increased economic assistance given by the United States as a result of this treaty. The Chatham House study concluded that the increased military and economic aid that the Pibun government received from the United States "has indirectly further consolidated its already strong internal position."[24]

Although there had been considerable criticism of Prime Minister Pibun in 1950 for his support of the French in

[24]Chatham House report, *op. cit.*, p. 25.

recognizing the Bao Dai government in Vietnam—which proved to be his initial step toward a defense pact with the Western powers—in 1954 there was little open criticism of Thailand's decision to accept the Manila Pact. In 1950 most Thais still considered the Viet-Minh forces to be essentially nationalists seeking to throw off the yoke of French colonial rule. By 1954 the situation had changed radically, and most Thais now saw the reality of their security problem. With a united and powerful China looming threateningly, the Thais wanted security; and the United States was the only nation powerful enough to grant it. Neutralism, therefore, did not seem to be a wise policy, although there continued to be some support for the Pridi view that Thailand should not become involved in the great power struggle. When the Pibun government was able to obtain a guarantee of Thailand's security from the United States, even though it was not as explicit as the government had desired, the public in general accepted this policy. Although economic and military aid no doubt was a consideration in Pibun's decision to join SEATO, this writer believes that it was not the overriding factor, because no amount of American aid would have been a substitute for the presence of American military power in Southeast Asia to protect Thailand.

The conclusion of the Manila Pact was also a personal achievement for Pibun: in the space of only six years he had redeemed the disgrace he had incurred by collaborating with Japan and had attained respectability as an ally of the West. When Pibun was invited to make a state visit to the United States and Britain in the spring of 1955, the respect and honor that both governments bestowed on him was a striking testimony to his political dexterity.

The Thai leader who had the principal task of negotiating the Manila Pact was Prince Wan Waityakorn, Thailand's

Foreign Minister in 1954 and former Thai ambassador in Washington. Although Prince Wan sought earnestly to obtain a stronger United States commitment to Thailand's defense, he acquiesced in the final wording of the Manila Treaty because he realized that in the final analysis the future actions of the United States in Southeast Asia would be determined primarily by the community of interests among it and the nations of that area. He and other leaders who supported the treaty appear to have believed that if Thailand proved to be a faithful ally the United States would strongly support its interests. Although there were some risks for Thailand in abandoning neutrality, in 1954 most Thai leaders were convinced that these dangers were outweighed by the advantages of an American commitment to the defense of mainland Southeast Asia and also of a large increase in American military and economic aid.

The security of the three new states of Indochina—Laos, Cambodia, and South Vietnam—figured prominently in the thinking of Thai officials during 1954, because they feared that any Communist threat to Thailand would come from this area. In addition, Thailand had historical interests in Laos and Cambodia which antedated the French occupation of Indochina, and which it was anxious to preserve against the pressures of the Viet-Minh and Chinese Communist forces. At Manila, Prince Wan urged that these states be included in a formal way in the treaty: "With regard to the treaty area, my Delegation is in favour of including Cambodia, Laos and the territory under the jurisdiction of the free Vietnamese Government. They deserve to be protected on their merits and, as a representative of Thailand, I should also say, as neighbours to my country."[25]

The United States and the Philippines supported the Thai

[25]Secretariat of the Manila Conference, *op. cit.*, p. 37.

position, and a protocol was finally attached to the treaty in which the parties designated "for purposes of Article IV of the Treaty the States of Cambodia and Laos and the free territory under the jurisdiction of the State of Vietnam."[26] The significance of this statement was that in the case of outright aggression against one of these states, any other treaty member whose peace and security were threatened could come to its aid in accordance with Paragraph 1 of Article IV, provided such aid was requested by the protocol state. In the event, however, that the danger arose from subversion or internal conflicts within the country, Paragraph 2 would apply, in which case "the Parties shall consult immediately in order to agree on the measures which should be taken for the common defense."

The threat of subversion in Laos, Cambodia, and South Vietnam was a key reason for this treaty, inasmuch as all the signatories were aware that the real problem in the area in the immediate future was Communist subversion rather than outright aggression. What would happen if a Communist faction came to power in one of these three countries without any act of overt aggression and then aligned the country with Peking? The Chatham House report observed, "it may be, therefore, that, however much the signatories may wish to cast a mantle of protection against subversion over the designated states, and so to include them firmly in the orbit of the Treaty Powers, they cannot in fact hope to do so." The next best course, concluded the report, was "to secure the general acceptance of a genuinely neutral status for them and so to prevent them from falling irretrievably into the Chinese Communist orbit."[27] Here lay the crucial factor insofar as Thailand was concerned; for Thai leaders were convinced

[26]*Department of State Bulletin*, September 20, 1954, p. 395.
[27]Chatham House report, *op. cit.*, pp. 146–7.

that, owing to its unstable political situation, a neutral Laos would become a Communist Laos. Thai officials ruled out the possibility that Laos could have a truly independent and neutral government, capable of resisting Communist pressures, without the active military and economic support of the Western powers. This issue plagued SEATO for the next decade and eventually caused Thailand to question the advisability of remaining in the organization.[28]

The Thai government was also aware that there was not complete agreement between the two strongest members of SEATO, the United States and Britain, on the objectives of the treaty. Because Britain was mainly concerned with protecting the Malay Peninsula and its colonies in Singapore and Borneo, it was much less interested in the defense of the Indochina states than was the United States, which, strongly supported by Thailand and the Philippines, was determined to resist further penetration southward by the Chinese Communists and the Viet-Minh. While the United States was convinced that weakness or appeasement anywhere in Southeast Asia would eventually lead to Communist domination of the whole area, Britain believed that no protective guarantee would work effectively in the area unless it had the support of the Colombo Powers, namely, India, Pakistan, Burma, Ceylon, and Indonesia. With the exception of Pakistan, however, these nations were more interested in following a neutral policy in the Cold War and were opposed to military alliances. In the end only Pakistan joined SEATO, and the organization therefore achieved much less acceptance among the Asian states than Britain had hoped. For Thailand, whose geographic position made it the pivotal nation in the alliance, the crucial question was whether the Communist advance

[28]See Chapter 5 for Thailand's reaction in the Laotian crisis of 1960–1961.

would be stopped in Laos and Vietnam *before* it reached Thailand's borders. In 1954 Thailand was not convinced that Britain would fight to defend the former Indochina states; but it *was* convinced that the United States would do so. And because American power was overwhelming in Asia at that time, the Thai government believed that American determination to use its power in the designated states would prevent the advance of Communism to the Mekong.

The "Spirit of Bandung" and Thai Attitudes toward SEATO

By the spring of 1955 it was clear that a thaw was taking place in the Cold War and that Moscow and Peking were prepared to relax the pressure in Asia in favor of a policy of "peaceful coexistence." In the West a summit conference was scheduled in Geneva, and in Asia the Colombo powers were preparing for a conference of Asian-African nations to seek a way of bringing a "third force" to bear on the international scene in order to reduce the possibility of nuclear war. Both in Europe and in Asia, governments were thankful for the retreat from the prospect of global war that had seemed imminent in Korea, in Indochina, and in Berlin; and they were now seeking new means of bridging the gulf between the Soviet and the Western powers. The Bandung Conference in Indonesia was an effort by the neutral nations of Asia to counter what many of them believed to be the neocolonial aspects of the SEATO and the Baghdad pacts, and to offer an alternative to military alliances in maintaining peace in Asia. Significantly, the new Soviet "peace offensive" took full advantage of the neutralist and anticolonialist sentiments of these newly developing nations and sought to use their suspicions of Western policies to its own advantage. Brimmell goes so far as to say that Soviet and Chinese leaders had decided, well before SEATO was founded, that the Cold

War should be abandoned in favor of a policy of peaceful coexistence, because in the long run the Communist powers had more to gain by capturing the leadership of the nationalist forces in Asia and Africa than they had in pursuing a belligerent policy toward the West.[29]

In June 1954 Chinese Premier Chou En-lai visited New Delhi and conferred with Prime Minister Nehru; subsequently they reiterated the Five Principles of Peaceful Coexistence that had been agreed upon two months earlier as the basis for Sino-Indian relations. The Chinese Premier then visited Rangoon and concluded a similar agreement with Burmese Prime Minister U Nu. Later in the year the Indian and the Burmese leaders paid return visits to Peking. A new spirit of cordiality between China and the neutral nations of Asia was well under way.

After some hesitation Thailand decided to attend the Bandung Conference, which convened in April 1955, and was represented by its Foreign Minister, Prince Wan. During the conference he and Chou En-lai discussed relations between their countries, and the Chinese Premier invited Prince Wan to visit China. During informal discussions Chou also sought to reassure him that China had no aggressive designs on Thailand, that the autonomous Thai government in Yunnan had no significance outside China, that Pridi Panomyong was not engaged in subversive activities against Thailand, and that China was willing to negotiate the question of citizenship for the Chinese minority in Thailand along the lines of the agreement previously concluded with Indonesia. The Chinese were willing to enter into such negotiations with the Thais even though diplomatic relations did not exist between

[29] J. H. Brimmell, *Communism in South East Asia* (London, 1959), p. 286.

them.[30] Thailand did not accept the Chinese offer to send an official delegation to negotiate in Peking, but the reasonableness of Chou En-lai at Bandung impressed the Thai government and people and contributed to the easing of the fears that had been so prevalent one year earlier. Although the Thai leaders were wise enough to know that Bandung did not reduce the long-term danger that Chinese power posed for its neighbors to the south, the Bandung Conference did have the effect of making that danger seem less imminent. With a reduction in world tensions, moreover, the Thai government found it increasingly difficult to justify the repressive measures that for several years had been in effect against the Chinese minority and leftist political groups; and it also found itself being criticized more strongly, from both within and without, for having aligned the nation so closely with the Western powers as to alienate its neutral Asian neighbors. Just as some NATO countries found it difficult in the "Geneva spirit" period to justify a high military budget and a strong anti-Communist policy, so Thailand found that the "spirit of Bandung" created internal political problems.

The new international climate also had an effect on Thai attitudes toward SEATO. Thailand's dilemma was that its SEATO policy was based to a large extent on an anti-Chinese attitude. As Modelski put it, "The viability of Thailand's stand depends vitally on the United States position. If that position were suddenly reversed and accommodation reached with China, Thailand would be left out on a limb."[31] By the summer of 1955 the Thai government began to fear that it might indeed be left on a limb because, not only had China scored a significant diplomatic triumph at Bandung by appearing to harbor only peaceful intentions toward its Asian

[30]Fifield, op. cit., p. 264.
[31]Modelski, op. cit., p. 110.

neighbors, but the United States had commenced, in August 1955, informal discussions in Geneva with representatives of the Peking government. It was widely believed in Bangkok that these talks portended a *rapprochement* between the United States and Communist China; and despite strong reassurances by Secretary of State Dulles that the United States would not downgrade SEATO, Thai leaders deeply regretted that such important discussions took place without prior consultation with all SEATO nations. Because these talks commenced only six months after Thailand had sought unsuccessfully at the Bangkok Conference to obtain United States agreement on the establishment of a SEATO military command and on the stationing of permanent military forces in the treaty area, many Thai leaders came to doubt the sincerity of the United States in concluding the treaty at all. What some officials had privately warned against in 1954— namely, that the Manila Pact did not commit the United States strongly enough to Thailand's defense in case of emergency—now began to assume major proportions as a factor in the government's attitude toward SEATO. Prime Minister Pibun had committed his country to the United States in the expectation that the latter's policy would be strongly opposed to the Communist Chinese regime; but within one year it began to appear that he had bought an already outdated pact and had in the process strained Thailand's relations with most of its Asian neighbors. Pibun's real difficulty was that he could not predict the course of United States policy in Southeast Asia; and as he began to see the ramifications of the new political situation resulting from the easing of world tensions, he decided it would be safer to shift his position in order to give Thai foreign policy more flexibility. One writer termed this the "peace-time variant of the 'Pibun Songgram system,' tried out in Thailand against the Japanese." According to

this system, the government maintains an official policy toward the alliance partner while it quietly seeks alternative
arrangements with the opposing camp. In this way Thailand
could adjust its policy to meet a new situation without having
to incur the wrath of a potential power—in this case, China.[32]
Whether or not Pibun consciously pursued such a double
policy in 1955 and 1956, the effect of the changes he instituted
following his return from a world tour in 1955 seemed to
tend toward closer relations with Peking.

The most striking example of the change in policy was the
new attitude toward the Chinese minority. During the critical Cold War years of 1952 to 1954 the government abandoned the policy of showing no favor to either faction within
the Chinese community—Kuomintang or Communist. After
the mass arrests of suspected Communist plotters in November 1952, the government's policy was hostile toward Peking
and friendly toward Taiwan, with which it continued to have
diplomatic relations. Within the Chinese community the
Kuomintang faction then enjoyed the most cordial relations
with the government; and KMT sympathizers came to dominate the various Chinese societies and associations, while
Communist sympathizers were arrested or intimidated into
inaction. As late as the spring of 1955 "most of the politically
conscious Chinese in Thailand were in some degree opposed
to Communism and the Peking regime," reports Skinner,
because the Peking regime had been effectively isolated by
American power in the Far East, and because Thailand had
consistently opposed recognition of Peking or its admission to
the United Nations. The Bandung Conference proved to be
an eye opener for the Chinese community, however, because
"the general acceptance of Chou En-lai as a sane and moderate

[32]D. Insor, *Thailand, A Political, Social and Economic Analysis* (London, 1963), p. 126.

statesman of a great Asian power put the mainland regime in something of a new light."[33] News that Prince Wan and the Chinese Premier had actually conferred about matters of mutual interest, particularly the status of the Chinese community in Thailand, set off a flurry of rumor and speculation in Bangkok regarding future relations between the two nations.

Other developments within Thailand combined to ease the restrictions on the Chinese community and to cause a definite shift in attitude—apparently with the approval of the Pibun government. In March 1955 the alleged Communist conspirators in the November 1952 plot were brought to trial, and it became obvious that many more Thais than Chinese were involved. General Pao's efforts to blame the Chinese proved ridiculous in light of the evidence. A few months later he was stripped by Pibun of several of his posts and lost responsibility over Chinese affairs. Another factor that permitted the local Chinese to shift their anti-Communist line was the lifting of press censorship and the legalizing of political organizations in 1955. Also, mainland Chinese goods were flowing into Thailand in ever-increasing quantities, and in the summer of 1956 the government reversed its previous policy and permitted merchants to carry on nonstrategic trade with the China mainland. Unofficial visits also took place during this period; the most notable was the visit to Peking of a delegation of important leftists, led by the Assemblyman and well-known Pridi supporter Tep Chotinuchit. This group had no official sanction for its trip; and when it returned full of praises for the Peking regime and for the great opportunities for trade between the two countries, its members were arrested and held for a short period. It was widely assumed, however, that the group could not have made this trip unless the government had quietly acquiesced.

[33]Skinner, *op. cit.*, pp. 340, 341.

Thereafter a number of other groups visited the Chinese mainland and were given maximum publicity by the increasingly vocal leftist newspapers in Bangkok. Meanwhile, the Kuomintang faction, which had enjoyed the government's blessing for four years, found itself out of favor and constantly harassed by the police for its activities in behalf of the Taiwan government. The Chinese Nationalist regime, fearing that Thailand was moving toward accommodation with Peking, made great efforts in 1955 and 1956 to stiffen the attitude of the Pibun government and to check the growing number of contacts between the Chinese community and Peking. But in the wake of an official policy favoring an increase in trade and contacts with the Chinese mainland, there was little the Kuomintang faction or the Taiwan government could do. By the end of 1956, only a year and a half after the Bandung Conference, attitudes of the Chinese community had shifted toward neutralism and a pro-Peking policy. Another sign of the times was that, although the Thai government had previously taken a strong position against recognition of the Peking government and against seating it in the United Nations, Foreign Minister Prince Wan declared in June 1956 that Thailand realized the Peking regime controlled the large majority of the Chinese people and most of the territory; therefore, he said, Thailand's attitude on recognition of China would depend on the United Nations decision to admit China to the international organization.

The new policy toward the local Chinese and toward the Peking regime was coupled with increasing attacks in the press on the United States and on SEATO. The press and many public speakers began to complain that the United States was giving economic aid to neutral countries such as India and Cambodia, which often were hostile to American foreign policy, while Thailand, a close ally, was receiving much less aid than it needed and expected. There were also complaints that too many American advisers, both military and economic, were stationed in the country. Many other grievances against the United States were aired in the Bangkok press, now free, and the government seemed unperturbed. The criticism against SEATO was even stronger. It was charged that membership in this alliance had caused Thailand to be branded among Asian nations as the "puppet" of the United States and had caused the nation to abandon valuable markets and good relations with its historically friendly neighbor, China. The examples of Burma, Indonesia, and Cambodia were frequently cited to show that neutralism paid off handsomely. In the light of the changed international atmosphere in 1955 and 1956, this kind of criticism had some impact on the Thai population, although less than the volume of material in the left-wing press indicated. With general elections impending, it seemed that the Pibun government was taking a considerable risk in not effectively counteracting this propaganda, because it had little choice but to stand on its record in the election campaign. The official policy continued to support SEATO and the United States, although with much less vigor than previously. Modelski observed that by the end of 1956 "official spokesmen were almost apologetic" in their support of the American alliance and remained on the defensive until Marshal Sarit staged his *coup d'état* in September 1957.[34]

All of this new freedom to criticize the government's foreign policy and to advocate neutralism inevitably had an impact on the internal political situation. During 1955 and 1956 a number of leftist political parties were formed whose programs included anti-Americanism, neutralism, recognition of Communist China, major domestic reforms, and eco-

[34]Modelski, *op. cit.*, p. 117.

nomic development of the rural areas of Thailand—particularly the northeast provinces where these parties had their
strongest appeal. Just before the February 1957 elections four
of these leftist parties joined forces in the Socialist Unity
Front under the leadership of Tep Chotinuchit, who had
been released from jail after being detained because of his
trip to Communist China. Although the socialist label is mis-
leading,[35] the Socialist Unity Front made much propaganda
during the election campaign. Its objective was complete
independence and peace for Thailand, a genuine people's
democracy, an improved standard of living, elimination of
the anti-Communist act, neutralism, and the Five Principles
of Peaceful Coexistence. "The Front, in fact, was doing the
work of a legal Communist Party," Brimmell concluded; and
along with several other anti-Western parties, it was sowing
the seeds of Communist subversion. "Thus were the ideas of
Maoism filtering into Siam by a sort of osmotic process, and
expressing themselves whenever permitted."[36] During 1957
spokesmen for these groups advocated Pridi's return from
exile in China, and it was apparent that these parties would
be the nucleus of a popular leftist appeal for a new government headed by the former Free Thai leader.

In less than two years, therefore, the security situation
within Thailand and the nation's attitude toward Communist
China had undergone a significant change, clearly opening
up the possibility of a neutralist foreign policy. One can only
speculate about the motivation of the Pibun government, for

[35]Brimmell reports that when an Indonesian Socialist leader visited
Bangkok in the spring of 1957 and talked with leaders of the so-called
socialist parties, "he disputed that claim, and advised the parties to
learn what socialism really meant." Their idea of socialism, states Brimmell, was anti-Westernism, which they had derived from listening to
Communist propaganda. (*Op. cit.*, p. 350.)

[36]*Ibid.*, pp. 350–51.

it is certain that such a shift could not take place without its consent. It seems likely that one reason for Pibun's policy of *détente* toward Peking was uncertainty whether the government's strong anti-Communist policy of the 1952–1954 period could be maintained during a period of friendliness with Communist China. The Pibun government may have been influenced also by a growing feeling that membership in SEATO tended to have more disadvantages than advantages during a period of peaceful coexistence.

There is little doubt that the Thai government expected to receive much greater economic aid from the United States than it actually obtained after joining SEATO. There was a sizable increase in military assistance to help the army strengthen Thai defenses, and to the police to curb subversion; but certain Thai officials in the spring of 1955 were disappointed by the refusal of the United States to support some of their more ambitious projects for economic development. Government leaders were keenly aware that neutralist leaders such as Sukarno, U Nu, and Sihanouk were able to obtain economic assistance from the United States and from the Soviet Union without involving their countries in military pacts. Thus, the anti-SEATO and anti-American publicity may have been a means of exerting pressure on the United States to give more attention and aid to its SEATO ally; and it tended also to relieve some of the political tension that had been building up within Thailand as the international *détente* made an anti-Communist policy at home seem unrealistic. However, the events of 1957 showed that Pibun had misjudged his ability to play this risky double game successfully. When the Pibun-Pao group attempted to steal the elections of February 1957, it found itself swept out of power on a wave of popular indignation. In the crisis of September 1957, the army, as in 1947, was the decisive factor in maintaining public order and in supplying a new leadership clique headed by the Commander in Chief, Field Marshal Sarit Tanarat.

Renewed Thai Support for SEATO (1957–1960)

When Marshal Sarit carried out his bloodless coup against the Pibun government on September 17, 1957, many Thai and Western observers seriously questioned where he stood on such questions as SEATO and relations with the United States. The reasons for these doubts were that during the previous two years Sarit had exhibited an increasingly nationalistic attitude in foreign affairs and had been critical of United States policy toward Thailand. The source of Sarit's antagonism toward the United States during 1956 and 1957 is not entirely clear, but according to one informed observer, he was resentful of what he believed was United States support for his rival, General Pao, in his effort to oust Sarit from command of the army and take over the job for himself. Although the army under Sarit had also been trained and equipped by the United States through the Military Assistance Program, Sarit reportedly felt the United States had given far too much assistance to General Pao's police and thereby permitted Pao to challenge Sarit's own political power.[37] During the election campaign two newspapers that supported Sarit were sharply critical of the United States and SEATO and advocated neutralism for Thailand and recognition of Communist China. Following the February elections, which Sarit branded as "dirty," he accused "a foreign power" of complicity with the Pibun regime and drew considerable support from the students and left-wing groups for his nation-

[37]Darrell Berrigan, "Thailand: New Cast, Same Play," *The Reporter*, November 28, 1957, pp. 12–14.

alistic statements.[38] As his power struggle with the Pibun-Pao faction intensified during the summer of 1957, Sarit moved farther to the left in seeking to rally support for his own position, and this included strong criticism of the government's foreign policy.

Once Sarit had removed Pibun and Pao from power, however, he took immediate steps to reassure the United States and other SEATO nations that there would be no change in Thailand's foreign policy. He sent his personal aide to the British and American embassies to reassure the ambassadors; and to make his policy even firmer, he asked the Secretary General of SEATO, Pote Sarasin,[39] to form a caretaker government to serve until new elections could be held in December 1957. Pote quickly announced that Thailand would continue to support SEATO strongly and to accept American military and economic aid. However, the national police was sharply reduced in size and power and placed under Sarit's personal control. By the end of 1957, then, the Sarit-backed government had made its peace with the United States, SEATO was once again given strong support, and the left-wing supporters of Sarit were clearly without a leader. It was not without significance, however, that American economic aid increased substantially after the new regime had taken over. A Development Loan Fund agreement in 1958 raised the total economic aid to $46.5 million for the year 1958–1959, compared with a 1957–1958 figure of $24 million—an increase of nearly 100 per cent.

When the new government, headed by Sarit's trusted subordinate, General Tanom Kittikachorn (January to October

[38]Albert Pickerell and Daniel Moore, "Elections in Thailand," *Far Eastern Survey,* July-August 1957, pp. 92–6, 103–11.

[39]He had previously been Foreign Minister under Pibun and had thereafter served as ambassador in Washington.

1958), took office, it continued the firm support of United States policy and of SEATO, although there was a noticeable change in the tone of Thai statements regarding American economic aid. Modelski describes this as "a tendency towards greater assertiveness," attributable on the one hand to "the trend towards greater nationalism noticeable in the Sarit regime and the emergence of younger officials who are discarding the cautious manner characteristic of earlier Thai diplomatic behaviour." The new tone also reflected "the pressure of articulate Thai opinion for greater aid as 'compensation' for being in SEATO and as a right to which Thailand is entitled because of its association with the West."[40] This assertiveness became particularly pronounced when Tanat Khoman was brought back early in 1959 by Sarit from his assignment as ambassador to the United States and was appointed Minister of Foreign Affairs. He represented a "new look" in Thai diplomacy which sought to bring Thai foreign policy more into accord with the views of other Asian nations and to avoid the charge made by some neutral nations that Thailand was a satellite of the United States. In this respect Sarit's policy seemed to be more appealing to the Thai educated class than was the Pibun policy from 1950 to 1954.[41]

General Tanom served as interim Prime Minister until October 1958 while Marshal Sarit went to the United States and Britain for medical treatment. During the first six months the internal security situation of Thailand improved significantly. Tanom succeeded in reducing Communist influence in the Bangkok press; he was able to remove Communists from entrenched positions in the two major universities; and

[40]Modelski, op. cit., p. 104.
[41]For a fuller discussion of Sarit's success in maintaining his position, see Donald E. Nuechterlein, "Thailand after Sarit," Asian Survey, May 1964, pp. 842–50.

his government succeeded in reducing the neutralist appeal of the Communists and the leftists. This was accomplished by constitutional means, as the assembly, the press, and various associations continued to exercise the freedom that Pibun had begun to permit in the summer of 1955. Nevertheless there was increasing speculation in 1958 that key leftist groups were quietly plotting the return of Pridi from China to head a neutralist and leftist-oriented government. To what extent a real threat to the Tanom government existed in the summer and autumn of 1958 is not altogether clear; it is certain that the political situation during this period was increasingly unstable, owing to the government's inability to deal effectively with the economic situation and with the growing amount of corruption among politicians and government officials. Many observers saw in this situation the ingredients of a new grab for power by opportunist elements. When Sarit returned suddenly in October and abolished the constitution and the assembly and took over as virtual dictator, he justified this drastic action on the basis of a threatened Communist coup. "It seemed fairly obvious that the 'revolution' was not really directed against the Communist threat," wrote one observer, but "it offered the opportunity to clean up a large number of those who were active Communists or were receiving money and favors from them."[42]

Following Sarit's "coup against himself," as the revolution of October 1958 is sometimes described, there was a general clamp-down by the government on all opposition groups, especially known Communists and supporters of Communist-front organizations. Hundreds of persons were jailed, newspapers were closed, labor unions were abolished, political organizations and parties were banned, and political leaders

[42]Darrell Berrigan, "Tidying Up in Thailand," *The Reporter,* November 27, 1958, p. 29.

were warned to remain quiet. In effect, Sarit had returned to the Pibun policy of 1952–1954; he dealt harshly with all opposition to his foreign policy of aligning Thailand closely with the United States and SEATO. However, one significant difference from the Pibun period was Sarit's handling of the Chinese minority. Although Sarit banned all trade with Communist China and took strong measures to stop the travel of Thais to Peking, he did not reimpose the general repression of Chinese activities. Instead, his policy was directed against Communist subversives of any nationality; many Chinese were detained by the police, but they were not singled out for special treatment. Sarit favored the rapid assimilation of the Chinese minority in order to reduce the possibility of their succumbing to Communist subversion. He also worked closely with the leaders of the Chinese associations and the Chinese Chamber of Commerce to ensure their support for his policies. Chinese schools were restricted in their numbers and were forced to teach the Thai language; but there was little of the blatant anti-Chinese campaign that characterized Pibun's policy from 1952 to 1954. The Chinese Nationalist embassy again enjoyed a privileged position. News of the Chinese "communes" and the terrible hardships suffered by the peasantry, which filtered out of China in 1957 and 1958, had a sobering effect on the Chinese community. Also, the Chinese invasion of Tibet shocked both Thais and Chinese. By 1959 much of the appeal of the Peking regime in 1955 and 1956 had worn off, and a new note of realism had permeated the Chinese community, just as the reality of Thailand's position in the face of a renewed hostility by China had affected Sarit's attitude toward the United States and SEATO.

By 1960 Thailand seemed to have recovered from the effects of the political storm of 1957–1958, and to have emerged a stronger ally of the United States than before. The change of policy by Communist China in 1957 and 1958 from coexistence to hostility produced a renewed solidarity of Thailand with the West. China's growing support for the Viet-Minh effort in Vietnam and the increasingly hostile tone of its propaganda contributed to the renewed value that Thais began to place on their membership in SEATO. At the same time American determination to resist China's attempts to wrest control of Taiwan and of the Offshore Islands from the Nationalists, as well as American steadfastness in Berlin and elsewhere in the face of Soviet blandishments, gave Thai leaders renewed confidence in the United States. The period 1959–1960, therefore, may be considered a high-water mark in Thai-American relations. It is against this setting that the subsequent events in Laos, which seriously affected these relations, must be judged.

Chapter 5

Impact of Events in Laos

IN 1960 no country in Southeast Asia held such historical and strategic importance for Thailand as did the tiny kingdom of Laos. Many Laotian states were for several centuries under some type of tutelage arrangement with Siam, and the Thais have always looked upon the Lao people as cousins. Culturally the Thais and the Laos share a similar language and religion, as well as similar customs. Until 1893 Siam considered Laos part of greater Siam and viewed it, along with the western Cambodian provinces that Siam also administered, as buffer zones between the kingdom of Siam and the powerful Vietnamese kingdom of Annam. Following the French conquest of Indochina and Siam's humiliating defeat in 1893, Thai leaders continued to think of Laos as a part of Siam's legitimate sphere of influence. Their determination to re-establish this influence was a major factor in the Pibun government's decision in 1940 and 1941 to reach an accommodation with Japan and to take advantage of France's weakness to re-establish Siamese hegemony over Laos and Cambodia. In the postwar period Pridi Panomyong sought to create a Thai sphere of influence through a Southeast Asia League, designed in part to make Thailand the champion of the Laotian and Cambodian peoples in their efforts to throw off the French colonial yoke. After Pibun returned to power in 1948, however, this policy was subordinated to a new one: resistance to the Communist pressure on Indochina that was being exerted by Viet-Minh forces in concert with a new power in Asia—Communist China.

During the nineteen-fifties Thailand's policy toward Laos changed from a desire to re-establish Thai control to a determination to prevent Laos from falling prey to any hostile country. Thailand was convinced by 1954 that the greatest threat to its security was from Communist China and North Vietnam. Laos, which stretched for hundreds of miles along Thailand's northern and eastern borders, was the obvious route for Communist penetration toward Thailand and the Malay Peninsula; it was, therefore, imperative for Thailand that Laos be preserved as a buffer zone between the Communist and the non-Communist areas of Southeast Asia. The Thai government was not opposed to a neutral Laos that maintained friendly relations with Thailand, but it would look with great apprehension on a neutral Laos that maintained friendly relations with Moscow, Peking, and Hanoi. To the pragmatic Thai mind, friendship with both Communist and anti-Communist neighbors was basically dishonest; and in the case of Laos, friendly ties with Communist powers were viewed as hostility toward Thailand. By 1960 the Sarit government had come to the conclusion that unless Laos had a pro-Western government, it would eventually come under the influence of Hanoi and Peking; then Thailand would be "on the firing line." It was therefore in Thailand's interest to preserve the Laos buffer at any cost—including military intervention in that kingdom to ensure the continuation in power of a friendly government.[1]

[1] A fuller discussion of Thailand's deep interest in developments in Laos and their effect on Thai attitudes may be found in David A. Wilson, "Bangkok's Dim View to the East," *Asian Survey*, June 1961, pp. 13–16.

When Thailand joined SEATO in 1954, a major concern of the Pibun government was the security of Laos and Cambodia. Viet-Minh forces had invaded Laos in 1953 and again in 1954, when they had penetrated also into Cambodia. Therefore, Thailand urged that these two countries plus South Vietnam should be included in the area under the protection of the treaty powers, even though Britain and France were not enthusiastic about guaranteeing the security of these weak and exposed Indochinese states. The Thai government was also fully aware that outright aggression was not the only or even the principal threat posed by the Communist powers. At the Manila conference in September 1954, Foreign Minister Prince Wan stated, "The danger from which we are to defend ourselves is two-fold: that of aggression and that of subversion." Asserting that Thailand had been threatened by both forms of intimidation, he urged that the question of subversion be thoroughly studied and stated, "My delegation will, therefore, insist on the matter of subversion being dealt with in the treaty."[2]

The matter of subversion was discussed at some length by the signatories to the Manila Pact; but the final treaty was so carefully worded on this point that it later made SEATO seemingly powerless to act in 1960 when the Laotian problem became critical. Article IV, paragraph 2 of the treaty makes this dilemma clear:

If, in the opinion of any of the Parties, the inviolability or the integrity of the territory or the sovereignty or political independence of any Party in the treaty area or of any other State or territory to which the provisions of paragraph 1 of this Article from time to time apply is threatened in any way other than by armed attack or is affected or threatened by any fact or situation

[2]Secretariat of the Manila Conference, *The Signing of The Southeast Asia Collective Defense Treaty* (Manila, September 8, 1954), p. 37.

which might endanger the peace of the area, the Parties shall consult immediately in order to agree on the measures which should be taken for the common defense.[3]

The treaty further specified (Article IV, paragraph 3) that no action on the territory of any state covered by the treaty could be taken "except at the invitation or with the consent of the government concerned."[4] According to the Manila Treaty, therefore, SEATO could take action against subversion in Laos only if all the treaty nations were in agreement, and then only if the Laotian government approved of such action. The wording of the treaty was unfortunate and disappointing for Thailand and provided one reason for the Pibun government's disenchantment with the alliance in 1955 and 1956.

The first test of SEATO over Laos occurred in the summer of 1955, when fighting flared in northern Laos between government troops and the Pathet Lao forces. Thailand urged SEATO to declare its concern, but as this proposal was not favored by other members, no action was taken. Thus, as Modelski pointed out, this first attempt to mobilize SEATO showed "the influence of British and French views upon the organization, and imparted an early lesson in the difficulties of bringing the SEATO machinery into action."[5]

After the conclusion of the Geneva Agreements of 1954, the Laos question was more political than military owing largely to a provision in the treaty on Laos which stated that Pathet Lao forces would temporarily administer the two northern provinces that they held at the time of the cessation

[3]*Department of State Bulletin,* September 20, 1954, p. 394.

[4]This provision proved a serious stumbling block to Thailand's efforts, particularly in 1960, to have SEATO intervene in Laos when the latter's government did not want SEATO's protection.

[5]George Modelski (ed.), *SEATO, Six Studies* (Melbourne, Australia, 1962), p. 9.

of hostilities—namely, Pong Saly and Sam Neua—pending their reintegration. Communist negotiators at Geneva carefully insisted on this point, because it gave the Pathet Lao legal status, and it provided them with an important bargaining point in subsequent negotiations with the Laotian government. It also provided the Communists with a safe haven inside Laos from which guerrilla activities against the whole country could be organized when and if conditions called for them. When negotiations took place early in 1955 between the Pathet Lao and the royal Lao government headed by Prince Souvanna Pouma, the Laotian Communists found many excuses for refusing to integrate their two provinces and their several thousand troops under the government in Vientiane.[6] Instead, they began to use their advantageous position to infiltrate other parts of the kingdom and to undermine the government's position. It was obvious that the Pathet Lao was acting in concert with the North Vietnamese Communists and trying to better its bargaining position in order to force its way into the Laotian government.[7]

Efforts at Reconciliation with the Pathet Lao

In the face of mounting political pressure from the Pathet Lao and because of his inability to negotiate a settlement with them, Prime Minister Souvanna Pouma decided to go to the sources of his problem, Hanoi and Peking, to see whether he could reach an agreement with the Communist

[6]The conventional spelling rather than the actual pronunciation, Wiengchan, is used hereafter.

[7]Russell H. Fifield states that by 1956 Pathet Lao had enlisted 3,000 new recruits in Pong Saly and Sam Neua provinces, thus permitting the release of experienced partisans for work in other parts of the kingdom. Subversion was carried on in every province during this period, particularly in those bordering on North Vietnam. (*Southeast Asia in United States Policy*, [New York, 1963], p. 182.)

chiefs in Asia. The new "spirit of Bandung" as well as efforts toward *détente* in Europe had caused Prince Souvanna to believe that Chinese Communist leaders might be induced to demonstrate their belief in peaceful coexistence by agreeing to a solution of the problem of the Pathet Lao minority. As one of the members of his staff put it: "To Prince Souvanna Phouma, who was Premier at that time, and who had taken upon himself the noble task of restoring peace to the torn kingdom, no sacrifice was too great, no concession too difficult if it helped achieve his goal. He was even ready to 'go to Canossa'—Peking—to bear witness to his peaceful intentions."[8] Souvanna made his trip in August 1956 and was royally received in the Chinese and North Vietnamese capitals. Communist leaders took every opportunity to assure him of their desire for peaceful coexistence and of their friendship with Laos. However, in private conversations they made it clear to the Laotian delegation that they expected eventually to be masters of all of Southeast Asia, and that Laos would find it profitable to cooperate. Souvanna did not go to China and Vietnam expecting the Communists to sign a definitive agreement that would permanently solve the Pathet Lao problem. Rather, he wanted "to create a favorable climate for pending negotiations with the Pathet Lao." He believed that he had accomplished this objective because all the Chinese and Vietnamese declarations of respect for the principle of noninterference in internal affairs of neighboring countries left the Pathet Lao "theoretically isolated in its dealings with the legal government."[9]

Although Prince Souvanna was convinced that he had achieved a strong bargaining position in his dealings with the Pathet Lao, the Thai government was not impressed. In

[8]Sisouk Na Champassak, *Storm over Laos* (New York, 1961), p. 40.
[9]*Ibid.*, pp. 49–50.

fact Souvanna's trip tended to confirm Thai suspicions that he was sympathetic toward the Communists and could be persuaded to make agreements with the Pathet Lao that would prove disastrous to both Laos and Thailand. These fears were confirmed a few months later when Souvanna negotiated an agreement with the Pathet Lao whereby his cabinet would be expanded to include several Pathet Lao leaders and would be known as the National Union Government. According to this agreement, the Pathet Lao would become a political party, and the two Pathet Lao provinces would be integrated into the kingdom—after the new government was formed. This agreement produced a storm of protest both in Laos and in Thailand, and it was not ratified by the Laotian national assembly. The government sought to amend the terms and asked the Pathet Lao to disband their forces *before* a new government was formed. The Pathet Lao countered with a demand that Laos agree to accept economic assistance from China as well as from the United States. The breakdown in negotiations caused a political crisis in Vientiane in May 1957; and when Souvanna failed to receive a clear vote of confidence from the assembly for his policy of bringing the Pathet Lao into the cabinet, he resigned. Most Laotian leaders did not desire a resumption of hostilities; but neither did they want to accept a dangerous arrangement with the Pathet Lao, which many believed would be the prelude to a political takeover.

After several months of futile efforts to find an alternative government, the assembly finally agreed by a narrow margin to ask Souvanna to continue as Prime Minister and to seek an honorable agreement with the Pathet Lao. By September 1957 it had become clear to most Laotians that he was the only leader who could command a majority in the national assembly and lead the country during this critical period.

Under the agreement signed on November 12, 1957, a coalition government was formed which included two leaders of the Pathet Lao.[10] On the day of the formation of this government, the Pathet Lao would restore the two provinces of Pong Saly and Sam Neua to government control, and Pathet Lao military forces would thereafter be integrated into the Royal Laotian Army or demobilized. The Pathet Lao movement would be replaced by a new political party named *Neo Lao Hak Sat* (Lao Patriotic Front), which would function openly in Vientiane and in other parts of the country. All war matériel was to be turned over to the government, and no foreign alliances or foreign military bases were to be granted to any power. Following this agreement, some 6,000 Pathet Lao troops were demobilized, and 1,500 of the best guerrilla fighters were officially integrated into the Royal Lao Army. However, less than 5,000 weapons were turned over to the government.[11]

The November agreement was reached just two months after Marshal Sarit had staged his *coup d'état* against the Pibun government, and it caused considerable disquiet in Bangkok. The Thai government reacted by closing the border with Laos—an action that could have brought serious economic dislocation to Laos because most of its trade with the outside world transits Thailand. In 1957 this was a gesture to show Thailand's displeasure and was not enforced for any length of time; however, it was a threat that could be employed whenever Thailand was unhappy with events in the neighboring country.

The Laotian supplemental elections of May 4, 1958, to elect twenty-one additional members of the national assembly,

[10]One of these was Prince Soupanouvong, younger half-brother of Souvanna Pouma.
[11]Fifield, *op. cit.,* p. 183.

thereby increasing its membership to fifty-nine, marked a turning point in Thailand's and in the United States' policy toward Laos. The *Neo Lao Hak Sat* had campaigned vigorously and effectively, while the non-Communist forces were divided and quarreling among themselves. The result was that Communist forces captured nine of the twenty-one contested seats and thereby exploded the optimistic view expressed the previous November that the Pathet Lao could be "contained" if they were brought into the government. Although the non-Communist parties still held a comfortable majority in the assembly, these elections had the beneficial effect of shocking them out of their complacency and resulted in the formation of the Rally of the Lao People, which united most of the non-Communist members of the assembly into an anti-Communist front. This group chose as its leader Prince Souvanna Pouma, who had had second thoughts about the *Neo Lao Hak Sat* threat. However, a group of younger civil servants, businessmen, and army officers was dissatisfied with the way the older politicians had bungled the elections and had permitted the Communists to make such startling gains. This energetic group, known as the Young Ones, formed a political organization called the Committee for the Defense of the National Interest (CDIN), whose program was to root out corruption in government and fight Communism vigorously. Obviously, the Young Ones wished to offer a political alternative both to the People's Rally and to the *Neo Lao Hak Sat* in the postelection period.

In the wake of the May 1958 elections and with the growing fear of Communist influence in the government, the position of Souvanna became untenable; he resigned in August 1958. A major factor in the demise of his government was the unwillingness of the United States to continue to subsidize the Laotian government and the armed forces while Communists participated in the cabinet. Souvanna was replaced by the staunchly anti-Communist Poui Sananikone, who had long been active in Laotian politics. His government was broadly based among non-Communist factions and included four members of the CDIN, even though the latter was at odds with Poui on many points of domestic policy. The cabinet, however, was united on a strongly anti-Communist policy, and it soon made this apparent by establishing closer relations with South Vietnam and with Thailand. It also established diplomatic relations with the Nationalist Chinese government on Taiwan. By the end of 1958, therefore, Laos had discarded the coalition experiment with the Communists and had replaced Souvanna Pouma's neutralist policy with one of close cooperation with the West. This was a serious reverse for the Pathet Lao, which had expected the November 1957 agreement to pave the way for their assumption of power by political rather than military means. Although the nine members of the *Neo Lao Hak Sat* continued to hold their seats in the assembly and did everything in their power to discredit the Poui government, they were successfully outmaneuvered at every turn; and their influence diminished steadily.

Matters did not remain quiet in Laos for long. In January 1959, Viet-Minh forces crossed the border into southern Laos and occupied a number of villages. Despite protests from the Laotian government, these forces refused to leave, and the North Vietnamese regime called for negotiations to end the "dispute." It seemed clear that the Communists were again resorting to military pressure to force political concessions from the government, and the latter therefore appealed to the United Nations to obtain the withdrawal of the Viet-Minh troops from its territory. At the same time Prime Minister Poui asked the national assembly to grant him full powers for one year to deal with the serious internal and external problems of the nation; this request was granted despite the strong opposition of the nine Communist members. Poui reshuffled his cabinet to include three military men—among them Colonel Poumi Nosavan, a member of the CDIN, as Defense Minister. It appeared from these various actions that the government was preparing for a military as well as a political onslaught from the Viet-Minh and the Pathet Lao, which seemed imminent at the beginning of 1959. Thailand was also greatly alarmed by this new Viet-Minh threat, because the latter's incursion into Laos was at a point only slightly more than a hundred miles from the Thai border. The Sarit government urged SEATO to look into the situation, but no action was forthcoming. Nevertheless the United States shared Thailand's concern and kept a close watch on the situation.

Crisis of 1959

The Laotian crisis began in July 1959, when Pathet Lao forces, resurrected as a fighting unit two months earlier, launched a determined attack in Sam Neua province and succeeded in taking a large part of it before the government could rush reinforcements to its defense. The government also informed the United Nations Secretary General of the danger. In August there was a lull in the Pathet Lao attacks, but on August 30, Viet-Minh units crossed the border into Laos and openly assisted the Pathet Lao in a new drive to gain control of Sam Neua province. The Laotian government immediately addressed an urgent request to the United Nations to send an emergency force to Laos to stop the aggression. To show its concern, the United States issued a warning to the Communist powers that further support of the invading force would raise the question of greatly increased free world support for the Laotian government.[12] Although the Laotian government did not request assistance from SEATO, the council representatives, under Thailand's prodding, met three times in emergency session during the first two weeks of September 1959. On September 26, SEATO issued a strong warning, which was in marked contrast with its previous views on Laos: "In the event of its becoming necessary to defend the integrity of Laos against outside intervention, SEATO has made preparations so as to be able to act promptly within the framework of the Manila Treaty."[13]

At the United Nations, the three SEATO Western powers —Britain, France, and the United States—combined to push through the Security Council a resolution calling for the appointment of a committee of inquiry to go to Laos to study the situation and report back to the council at the earliest possible date. Although the Soviet Union voted against the proposal, its vote did not constitute a veto because the council held that the matter was procedural rather than substantive. A committee of inquiry was dispatched to Vientiane early in September, and almost simultaneously the fighting in Sam Neua province stopped. By the time the United Nations subcommittee reached the area of battle, Viet-Minh forces had vanished across the North Vietnamese border. In its report the United Nations group concluded that although there was evidence of North Vietnamese support for the Pathet Lao in the form of arms, ammunition, supplies, and help from political cadres, it could not clearly establish whether regular troops of the North Vietnamese government had crossed the border. The report seemed to conclude that the Laotian government's claims of large-scale aggression were exaggerated; but the prompt dispatch of the United Nations group to Laos

[12]*Department of State Bulletin,* September 21, 1959, p. 414.
[13]Quoted in Modelski, *op. cit.,* p. 11.

undoubtedly had a beneficial effect in restoring order in the northern areas of the country.[14] Despite disagreement over the extent of Viet-Minh intervention in Laos, the Secretary General of the United Nations, Dag Hammarskjold, visited Vientiane in November in an effort further to stabilize the situation. After he conferred with Prime Minister Poui, the latter issued a statement pledging Laos to remain neutral and asserting that he would not permit the country to become a base for any foreign power bloc. The Secretary General thereafter dispatched a personal representative to Laos to maintain a United Nations presence there, and he also arranged for a United Nations technical assistance team to be assigned to Laos. By thus establishing the United Nations' influence in Laos, the Secretary General hoped to keep the country from becoming a battleground between the SEATO countries and the Communist powers.

The summer crisis of 1959 thus ended satisfactorily for the SEATO nations and for the government of Poui Sananikone. Following the determined stand by the three great SEATO powers and the swift action of the United Nations Security Council, the Viet-Minh military threat quickly receded, and Laos returned again to a state of relative stability. For Thailand the outcome was reassuring, because it indicated that SEATO would honor its pledge to defend the territorial integrity of Laos and to prevent it from becoming a Communist base of operations against Thailand.

Unfortunately the 1959 crisis also brought into the open

[14] In his account of the events of August-September 1959, Sisouk Na Champassak describes the extent of Viet-Minh intervention in the Laotian fighting and how these forces quickly dispersed when word was received that the United Nations fact-finding subcommittee would make an on-the-spot inquiry into the government's charges. Sisouk deplored the efforts of some governments and many press correspondents to call the aggression a hoax. (Op. cit., pp. 99–100.)

a growing cleavage between the United States and France regarding methods of strengthening the internal stability of Laos. The French were authorized by the Geneva Agreements of 1954 to maintain military advisers in Laos to train the Royal Laotian Army, but the equipment and most of the supplies were paid for by the United States. The Americans and French did not always agree on the division of responsibility, and the French suspected that American military advisers were quietly trying to oust them from their positions. As a result of the 1959 summer crisis, American military and economic aid to Laos was greatly increased; and although France still retained its over-all training responsibility and increased its own efforts to build up the Laotian army, there was growing resentment in the autumn over the desire of the United States to play a role in these matters commensurate with the size of its financial contribution. The French government agreed to the show of strength both in SEATO and in the United Nations during the crisis; but it was apparent to observers in Vientiane and in Bangkok that French officials were not convinced there was a real threat of invasion from the Viet-Minh, and that they believed the crisis had been manufactured by the Laotians in order to obtain greater American military and economic aid. Increased American influence in Laos would inevitably diminish French influence, a possibility that greatly distressed French officials on the scene.[15] The British took a position between France and the United States, holding that there was a threat to Laos but that it was more political than military. The British believed strongly that Laos could not reasonably follow any policy other than strict neutrality without provoking the North Vietnamese and Chinese Communist governments. Therefore, they agreed with the French that the Lao government

[15]Sisouk, *op. cit.,* pp. 105–7. See also Fifield, *op. cit.,* p. 191.

ran considerable risks if it became too closely identified with the Western powers, especially with the United States. On the other hand, the British were prepared to oppose any effort by the Communists to use force to take over Laos or to impose an anti-Western policy on it.

In this growing divergence among the SEATO nations over policy in Laos, Thailand was the most belligerent. The Sarit government was convinced that the Viet-Minh intervention in August 1959 was clear notice that the Communists had abandoned peaceful coexistence in regard to Laos and, since subversion had failed, were determined to force a change in that country's policy through outside military pressure. Thailand strongly urged SEATO's intervention in Laos in September and had even designated certain Thai army units for duty there. Thailand sent a military mission to Laos to observe the situation, and statements of Thai military leaders indicated that the government was ready to aid the Vientiane government if it asked for SEATO's help. However, the Sarit regime gave no indication of willingness to intervene in Laos without the participation of SEATO. But it was clear after September 1959 that Sarit would not be content to see a neutral government in Laos of the nature of the late 1957 coalition; such an arrangement, according to the Thai view, would permit the Communists slowly to take over Laos from within. Thus the only alternative, the Thais believed, was to support a strongly anti-Communist government—one that would maintain close relations with Thailand and with SEATO, even if it were officially neutral. Some militants in the Thai government were in favor of making Laos a forward area of SEATO strength in Asia in order to move the Communist threat as far as possible from the Thai border. Unfortunately such a view entailed serious risks of Chinese and Viet-Minh retaliation and was wholly dependent on the willingness of SEATO, particularly the United States, to support such a bold policy in Southeast Asia.

In December 1959 the internal political situation in Laos once again erupted, and the result seemed to confirm British and French fears that Laos was being turned into a Western ally instead of remaining a neutral state. When Poui Sananikone sought to reshuffle his cabinet to eliminate the Minister of Foreign Affairs, who was a member of the CDIN and a strong anti-Communist, the CDIN strongly supported the Foreign Minister; Poui countered by ousting all of the CDIN ministers. This precipitated the crisis of December 25, in which the army, led by the recently promoted General Poumi Nosavan, demanded that the government resign. When Poui refused, the army took over Vientiane in the night of December 30–31, and the government was placed in the hands of five generals who called themselves the High Command. The King appointed an interim government under the leadership of Kou Abhay, and general elections were scheduled for April 24, 1960.

The *coup d'état* was highly successful, and there seemed to be no opposition among the people of Vientiane. Nevertheless the coup caused great anxiety in foreign capitals and produced a storm of protest from the Communist powers, which charged that the United States and SEATO were turning Laos into a military base to launch aggression against China and North Vietnam. The fact that General Poumi was a cousin of Marshal Sarit and was strongly pro-American lent credence to the fears that Laos was abandoning its neutrality. Bangkok greeted the news with satisfaction; but Washington and other Western capitals felt the coup might have repercussions on the maintenance of peace in Southeast Asia. The Laotian government was in the hands of young and aggressive men who, it was feared, lacked the caution and judgment of the older politicians and might blunder into a situation with the Communist neighbors of Laos that could involve SEATO in a large war. The British and French, for their part, were greatly worried that Western policy would overreach itself in Laos by supporting a government closely associated with SEATO.

The elections of April 24, 1960 seemed to substantiate the trend. The Laotian government ensured that there would be no repetition of the *Neo Lao Hak Sat* victory of 1958 by redistricting the country to the Communists' disadvantage and by making the eligibility requirements for voting too high for most of the semiliterate Pathet Lao followers to qualify. In addition, the *Neo Lao Hak Sat* leaders, including Prince Soupanouvong, had been in jail since the previous summer—when Pathet Lao attacks resumed in Sam Neua— and the party therefore had few eloquent speakers and organizers. But the crucial factor in the election campaign was the army, which supervised the elections and often campaigned in favor of CDIN candidates. The leader of the army, General Poumi Nosavan, was quickly becoming the strong man of Laotian politics. The election results produced a striking victory for the CDIN and the elimination of the *Neo Lao Hak Sat* from the national assembly. Out of fifty-nine seats, the CDIN received thirty-two; and the RLP (Rally of the Lao People), twenty-seven.[16] That the army had figured prominently in the victory of the CDIN was admitted by a leader of this group: "Its victory was, of course, shared by the Army, which had made every effort to back CDIN candidates before and during the election. Effective as this support had been, it meant that the majority of the new deputies were now indebted to the Army."[17]

[16]These totals include candidates who ran independently but were allied with one or the other of these two parties.

[17]Sisouk, *op. cit.*, p. 145.

The trend toward military rule in Laos alarmed the three great SEATO powers—Britain, France, and the United States. Their fears apparently were heeded to some extent when General Poumi, the leader of the majority group in the new national assembly, was passed over for Prime Minister; instead, the King selected an older politician who was on friendly terms with most political groups and was respected by the diplomatic community—Chao (Prince) Somsanit (often spelled Tiao Somsanith). General Poumi retained the post he had held in the previous government as Minister of Defense. In the new cabinet he was clearly the dominant personality because he headed a new political party formed after the elections, which included all CDIN members as well as sympathizers, and was thus in a strong position to control the Laotian government. With the support of the growing and well-equipped army, he set about to achieve the government's major objective—to unite the whole country and to improve the living conditions of the remote areas that had been infested for years by Pathet Lao forces.

Between April and August 1960 the internal situation in Laos remained quiet, and many observers began to believe that Laos might yet become a united and stable country, not posing a military threat to any of its neighbors. The Thai government was highly pleased to have a regime in power in Vientiane which in many ways resembled its own—strongly anti-Communist and largely run by military men. General Poumi frequently conferred with Marshal Sarit, and Thailand gave the Lao government its full support. Except for the daring escape from jail in May of Prince Soupanouvong and his fellow Pathet Lao prisoners, and their flight to Sam Neua, the political situation remained calm until the explosion of August 9.

Crisis of 1960

In the early morning hours of August 9, 1960, an obscure parachute battalion commander named Captain Kong Lae moved his troops into Vientiane; and by daybreak they had occupied all the strategic positions in the administrative capital. Kong Lae had planned his *coup d'état* well and had executed it at a most opportune time: the entire cabinet was away in the royal capital of Luang Prabang to make funeral arrangements for the former King, who had died some months earlier. The only high official still in Vientiane who might have acted against the rebellious troops was the Commander in Chief of the Army; but his house was quickly surrounded by the paratroopers, and he was placed under house arrest. Thus, in a matter of hours the whole political situation in Laos was upset; and a crisis was brought about, for Laos and for the whole of Southeast Asia, whose solution occupied SEATO and all the great powers for several years.[18]

The motives of Kong Lae in staging this coup have been a matter of some dispute among political observers. Charges were made that he was pro-Communist, that he was a tool used by the Pathet Lao and perhaps by North Vietnam to precipitate a crisis that would permit the Laotian Communists to return to power in another coalition government under Souvanna Pouma. In view of the way in which the Laotian crisis of 1960 developed, there would seem to be some reason to suspect that Kong Lae had acted according to a larger conspiracy. In the opinion of this writer, however, Kong Lae was a factor in one of those quirks of history in which someone supplies a spark at a critical moment and then finds himself the captive of political forces that have

[18]These events are described in detail in Arthur J. Dommen, *Conflict in Laos* (New York, 1964), pp. 144–148.

been waiting for just such an opportunity to shape the course of events. Kong Lae was probably the best troop commander in the Laotian army, he was thoroughly honest and dedicated to his country, and he instilled a sense of personal loyalty among his troops that was rare in the Laotian army. He hated corruption among political and military leaders, and he attributed their high living to American military and economic aid, which he believed was being used to keep Laos in a state of civil war. His battalion had an excellent record in fighting against Pathet Lao forces in various parts of the country, and it was constantly being moved from one point in the kingdom to another to put down Pathet Lao disorders. Eventually Kong Lae could no longer endure the sight of Lao killing Lao, with no end in prospect, and concluded that neutralism in foreign policy and cooperation with the Pathet Lao was the only way his country could avoid further bloodshed and restore peace. By staging a revolt and disposing of the pro-Western government, he thought he could end the fighting and rid the country of foreign interference. Such were the motives of the man who nearly caused a great war in Southeast Asia.

Once the coup had taken place, a new government had to be formed. Kong Lae looked for a well-known leader to head it and first approached Prince Boon Oum, a respected nationalist leader who had fought the French for many years but had retired from politics after the events of 1954. The prince declined the offer; probably he was aware of the possible consequences of the coup and did not want to head a government with so little legal standing. Kong Lae then turned to Prince Souvanna Pouma, leader of the opposition RLP and also president of the national assembly. Souvanna accepted the premiership on condition that the assembly give him a vote of confidence. Souvanna, like Boon Oum, could see the crisis that was looming, but he believed that he was better qualified than any other Laotian leader to guide his country during this period and prevent it from becoming a battlefield for the great powers. Souvanna was even more convinced in 1960 than he had been in 1957 that for Laos the only real possibility for survival was in a neutral foreign policy that would reassure both the Western and the Communist powers that Laos would not become a base of operations for any country. While Kong Lae and Souvanna discussed these matters, however, pro-Communist agitators were infiltrated into Vientiane and began to organize the students and leftist elements in the population into a pressure group capable of forcing the government to heed its demands. It was soon apparent that these groups also controlled the radio station in Vientiane and were broadcasting anti-Western and pro-Communist propaganda. As a result Thailand was convinced that Kong Lae was turning the government over to the Pathet Lao, and that SEATO should act swiftly to restore the legal government to power before it was too late.

When news of the coup reached Luang Prabang, where the cabinet was in session, there was great reluctance among many cabinet ministers to return to Vientiane lest they be arrested by Kong Lae's troops. Rather than fight for the restoration of his government, Somsanit decided to resign. This action complicated efforts to restore a rightist government in Vientiane and provided Prince Souvanna with an opportunity to be invested as the lawful Prime Minister. Poumi Nosavan did not return to Vientiane but instead flew to Savannakhet in the south, where he began to organize the Royal Laotian Army for an assault on Vientiane. He was joined there by several other cabinet members and also by some members of the assembly who were sympathetic to his views. Poumi was also in close contact with the Thai government, which strongly supported his position and urged the United States and SEATO to supply him with the equipment to march on Vientiane and oust Kong Lae.

Thus, within a week of the August 9 coup, the lines were being firmly drawn in a struggle for power that was to last nearly two years. In Vientiane there was a new neutralist government headed by Prince Souvanna Pouma and supported by Kong Lae's paratroops, as well as by a growing number of Pathet Lao sympathizers who were infiltrating the city; and in the south there was the remnant of the ousted pro-Western government, led by General Poumi Nosavan and supported by the bulk of the Royal Laotian Army. The real question was: which side would the United States support?

To appreciate the complexity of the decision that had to be made by the American government, it is necessary to take into consideration the views of the foreign powers that were involved in Laos as well as those of the political divisions within Laos. On the one hand, Thailand strongly urged that the United States and SEATO support Poumi with whatever power was needed to oust Kong Lae and Souvanna from Vientiane as quickly as possible—before the Pathet Lao could take advantage of the confused situation in the capital to entrench themselves and turn Laos into a satellite of Hanoi and Peking. Marshal Sarit and other Thai leaders thought that the Kong Lae coup could have disastrous consequences for the security of all Southeast Asia unless it was crushed immediately and a friendly government restored. Thailand was ready to send its forces into Laos as soon as SEATO agreed on a policy.

The Thai leaders distrusted Prince Souvanna Pouma because of his previous dealings with the Pathet Lao and especially for bringing them into his cabinet in 1957. Although few believed that Souvanna was a Communist, most

Thai leaders thought he was a weak and somewhat naive intellectual whom the Communists could use for their purposes. They felt that Souvanna's half brother Prince Soupanouvong, who was the nominal leader of the Pathet Lao movement, had considerable influence on Souvanna and caused him to lean far to the left in trying to solve Laos' internal political problems. To the Thai government, United States policy in this critical situation was a test of American determination to resist further encroachments of Communism in Southeast Asia. If the United States failed to support General Poumi in his effort to restore a pro-Western government in Vientiane, Thailand would seriously question whether the United States would be firm in the event that the Communists menaced it. In August 1960, therefore, Laos was a critical test of American intentions in Southeast Asia, insofar as the interests of the most directly affected SEATO country, Thailand, were concerned.

On the other side of the argument were the two European SEATO powers, Britain and France, and also the personal views of the special representative in Laos of the Secretary General of the United Nations. Their positions were that Souvanna Pouma was probably the only leader who could at this critical juncture unite all factions behind the government and prevent the country from being turned into a battleground between East and West—one that might precipitate World War III. The British and the French were alarmed at how close Laos had been to civil war and foreign intervention during the crisis of 1959; and they were first of all interested in preventing Laos from becoming the spark that would set off a great war in Asia. As they viewed the strategic and political problem of Laos, they found it imperative to retain this small kingdom as a true buffer zone between China and Western power based in Thailand and in South Vietnam; in order to accomplish this aim, a truly neutralist policy, carried out by a broad-based Laotian coalition government, was essential. They believed that, of all the Laotian politicians, Souvanna was the most capable of providing the necessary leadership, and that he was perhaps the only Lao leader who would be acceptable to both the pro-Western and the pro-Communist factions within the country. Since the British and the French believed that it was highly dangerous for SEATO to try to turn Laos into a forward base in Asia, they had been deeply concerned by the military coup of December 1959 which had put General Poumi in the commanding position in Lao politics. So obvious an effort to turn Laos into an ally of the West, they thought, would surely result in a counterthrust from the Communist powers, which were no more willing than was Thailand to have Laos become a hostile neighbor. Therefore, the British and French argued, SEATO should support Souvanna Pouma's efforts to build a coalition government made up of all non-Communist forces, which General Poumi and the Laotian army must be prevailed upon to join. They argued that SEATO intervention to support General Poumi would be not only sheer folly, but also illegal because SEATO was prohibited from intervening in the country unless the government requested such assistance. Obviously Souvanna Pouma would not make such a request.[19]

In August 1960, the United States was faced with three alternatives in dealing with the Laos crisis. It could accept Thailand's position and strongly support General Poumi in his effort to take Vientiane by military force and could then negotiate regarding a new and broader-based government. Or it could agree with the British and the French and strongly

[19]Article IV, paragraph 3, of the Manila Pact states that no action can be taken on the territory of any state "except at the invitation or with the consent of the government concerned."

support Souvanna Pouma's efforts to establish his authority in Vientiane; it could also help him to negotiate the withdrawal of Kong Lae's battalion from the city and then assist Souvanna to build a strong non-Communist neutral coalition government that could unite the country, without frightening either the Communists or the Thais into counter action. Finally, the United States could follow a middle course by supporting both General Poumi and Prince Souvanna and trying to obtain their agreement to cooperate in keeping the Communists out of Laos. The United States government was sharply divided on this crucial policy question and found it difficult to arrive at a clear decision during the first weeks after the August 9 coup.[20]

Therefore the United States initially followed the third alternative, namely, to seek an agreement between the two key men, Poumi and Souvanna Pouma, whereby they would cooperate to restore order in Vientiane, persuade Kong Lae to reintegrate his forces into the Royal Lao Army, and then support a government program for building national unity without bringing the Pathet Lao into the government. It was believed that if these two leaders could unite in a common effort, the Pathet Lao would have little influence, and the government could proceed to deal with the urgent economic and social problems in the country. Under peaceful conditions a policy of fence-straddling might have been successful; but with the political pressures then building up in Laos, this policy was probably doomed to failure almost from the start.

[20]It is not without significance that the Laotian crisis of 1960 occurred during the American presidential election campaign. It occurred also after the death of Secretary of State John Foster Dulles, when the Department of State did not influence foreign policy formulation as much as it had during Dulles' time.

In late August, Souvanna and Poumi met at Seno Airbase in southern Laos and negotiated a provisional agreement under which they would cooperate against the growing influence of the Pathet Lao. It was agreed that Poumi would visit Vientiane for political talks about the formation of a coalition government. In this hopeful atmosphere the King called a meeting of both political factions in Luang Prabang on August 30, and an agreement was reached whereby a new government would be headed by Prince Souvanna and would include General Poumi as Deputy Prime Minister and Minister of Interior. Other cabinet positions would be divided between the Vientiane and the Savannakhet groups. This agreement among the non-Communist leaders was then approved by the King. It seemed to be a turning point in the three-week-old crisis.

Unfortunately the Luang Prabang agreement was never implemented. Kong Lae was reported to have threatened to arrest General Poumi if he tried to return to Vientiane. By this time Kong Lae was being influenced to an ever greater extent by Communist agitators in Vientiane; and while Prince Souvanna was away from the city, Kong Lae apparently succumbed to their arguments that the Luang Prabang agreement was a sellout of his revolution, that he had been ignored in the negotiations, and that he would be arrested if General Poumi took over as Minister of Interior. Since Kong Lae's troops firmly controlled Vientiane, no government could function there without his consent. Therefore the carefully negotiated truce to the political crisis was exploded, and Prince Souvanna returned to Vientiane as leader of a government supported by Kong Lae's troops and by a growing number of Pathet Lao supporters, rather than by General Poumi and the rightist faction in Savannakhet. Poumi refused to go to Vientiane but returned to Savannakhet, where he began to prepare for military action against Vientiane. Thailand branded the Souvanna Pouma government illegal and charged that it was preparing to bring the Pathet Lao into the cabinet as a prelude to the assumption of complete control by the Communists.

Although intensive efforts were made during September to bring about a reconciliation between the opposing forces, the presence of Kong Lae's troops in Vientiane proved to be the crucial factor in determining the course of events in Laos. Some persons charged that Prince Souvanna secretly maneuvered to keep the paratroopers in the city as a counterweight to Poumi's military force. Many observers were convinced, however, that Souvanna was a prisoner of Kong Lae's forces—now supplemented daily by Pathet Lao sympathizers—and that he could neither exercise any freedom of action nor make any agreement with Poumi without the blessing of Kong Lae. Thus, at the beginning of September, it was increasingly clear that time was running out on efforts to bring about a non-Communist coalition in Laos, unless the United States strongly supported Souvanna and persuaded Poumi to use his army to support him also. Such a policy was not, however, forthcoming from Washington; and the situation in Vientiane continued to deteriorate.

While the Western powers were divided in their attitude toward the Laos crisis, the Communist powers and their Pathet Lao allies seemed to be cooperating closely to achieve a political victory. Although there is little evidence to show that the Laotian crisis of August 1960 was planned and executed by the Communists, they were quick to exploit the confusion produced by Kong Lae's revolt and to press their advantage to the fullest before the Western powers and General Poumi's faction could set a counterattack in motion. The pro-Pathet Lao group in Vientiane quickly seized control of the radio station and began to broadcast pro-Communist propaganda. They also organized the students and all dissident elements in the city into a vocal, popular demonstration group which was called upon frequently to pressure Souvanna Pouma into taking actions he might otherwise not have taken. Most important, the Communist apparatus in Vientiane sought to shape the policies and statements of Captain Kong Lae, whose troops continued to be the decisive power factor in the capital and who seemed to be susceptible to anti-American propaganda. Only three weeks after the August 9 coup the Communists had manipulated the political situation in Vientiane to the point where they could prevent the implementation of the Luang Prabang agreement on a coalition government. They then began a strong propaganda campaign designed to bring about a leftist coalition government between Souvanna and his half brother, the Pathet Lao leader, Soupanouvong. By early September the Communists seemed well on their way to recouping the position they had lost in 1958, when they were forced out of the government by Poui Sananikone.

Reaction of Thailand

Thai press and public reaction to the events in Laos during August supported the government's official line. It was evident how sensitive the Thais had become to political events in this neighboring country, and considerable anxiety was expressed about the statements by Kong Lae that he intended to eliminate all foreign military advisers from the kingdom and adopt a neutralist policy. Many editorials referred to Laos as Thailand's "buffer" against Communist power in Asia and said that if Laos were to change its friendly policy toward Thailand, it would be a severe blow to the latter's efforts to resist the Communist menace. There was little press criticism of Prince Souvanna Pouma during the first weeks, while he sought to establish a coalition government to include General Poumi and the Savannakhet group. When, however, Radio Vientiane began its sharp attacks on Thailand and the United States, and as Souvanna encountered difficulties in keeping Kong Lae's forces under control, the Thai press became apprehensive and then openly hostile. The turning point in the Thai attitude was Kong Lae's denunciation of the Souvanna-Poumi coalition agreement of August 30 and Souvanna's subsequent decision to form a government without representation from Savannakhet. Thereafter Thai official and press opinion came out strongly in support of Poumi and was increasingly critical of Souvanna for collaborating with the Communists. Prime Minister Sarit's newspaper *Sarn Seri* summed up what was undoubtedly the government's view in an editorial charging that Kong Lae's coup group held all the power in Vientiane and was compelling the Prime Minister to do its bidding. Communism, the paper said, was the issue that divided Prince Souvanna and General Poumi, and it accused Souvanna of "doing everything he can to help his younger brother, Prince Soupanouvong, the leader of the Lao Communist movement, and his supporters." The editorial seemed to reject any possibility that a coalition government could be established among non-Communist factions in Laos, stating: "Water and oil can never mix, and similarly the policies of Prince Souvanna Phouma and of General Phoumi can never become aligned and coordinated."[21]

As the political situation in Laos continued to deteriorate during September, the Thai press began to question SEATO's role in Laos. In August the Secretary General of SEATO, Pote Sarasin, had stated categorically that SEATO would not

[21]*Sarn Seri,* September 7, 1960. *Thai Press Comment* (translations), U.S.I.S., Bangkok.

interfere in the internal affairs of Laos. He said that a neutral policy for Laos would be a good thing from SEATO's point of view, and that SEATO's responsibility was to protect countries from aggression rather than to try to settle local conflicts.[22] Members of SEATO, with the exception of Thailand, did not consider that struggles between political factions in Laos came under the jurisdiction of the treaty, and there was no evidence that foreign military forces had intervened in this Laotian conflict—unlike the situation a year earlier, when there was reason to suspect that Viet-Minh forces had entered Laos. The unwillingness of SEATO to take any official interest in the Laotian crisis of 1960, and the efforts of the British and French to win support for a neutral government headed by Souvanna Pouma, proved very frustrating to the Thai government. When it became clear that Souvanna and Poumi would not join a coalition, and that Souvanna was obliged to lean heavily on the leftist elements in Vientiane for political support, Thai spokesmen and the Thai press began to ask what value SEATO had for Thailand if it could not prevent Laos from falling under Communist control. *Siam Rath,* the most influential paper in Bangkok, stated in an editorial:

If SEATO continues to remain inactive, the situation in Laos will become increasingly dangerous to Thailand. . . . The proposal made to SEATO by the Thai government [to have SEATO mediate the political dispute in Laos] ought to arouse its interest and ought to make it realize that danger occurring in any country naturally causes grave concern and anxiety to neighboring countries.[23]

Another paper, *Kiattisak,* speculated that the Western

[22]Modelski, *op. cit.,* p. 12.
[23]*Siam Rath,* September 23, 1960. *Thai Press Comment* (translations), U.S.I.S., Bangkok.

powers were not concerned about Laos because they were too involved in the Congo. Urging SEATO to take action to prevent a Communist takeover in Laos, the paper said: "Laos is the weakest point in the line of defense of the Free World in this part of the world. If the Communists are able to penetrate it, they will be able to destroy peace in this region. Once the Communists have seized the whole of Laos, a dread fate will face Asia."[24]

In late September, Prime Minister Sarit issued an unusually strong statement on the Laos situation which set the tone for the Thai government's attitude during the crucial developments that followed. He began by asserting that events since August 9 had shown clearly that the new government in Laos was pro-Communist and that the Communists were well on their way to taking over the whole country from within. The Thai government had extensive means, he said, for finding out the true situation and had reliable evidence that the Communists had Vientiane in their grip. "It is certainly without the slightest doubt [sic] that if this situation persists in this manner, the Kingdom of Laos would entirely fall into Communist hands." Sarit asserted that his government had no wish or intention to interfere in the internal affairs of Laos. However, he admitted that the relationship between Thailand and Laos was "of a special character." Any trouble in Laos, he said, would inevitably have serious repercussions in Thailand, and there was no way of avoiding it. Sarit deplored Communist accusations that the Thai government was aiding Poumi Nosavan to unseat Souvanna Pouma, and that Thai forces had fired mortar shells across the Mekong River into Laotian territory. He also expressed concern over the sudden increase in antigovernment agitation in Thailand and

[24]*Kiattisak,* September 17, 1960. *Thai Press Comment* (translations), U.S.I.S., Bangkok.

asked: "If the Kingdom of Laos were to fall completely under the control of the Communists, how much danger would befall Thailand?" After promising that his government would not "entertain any ambitious plans to expand power and influence over neighboring countries," Sarit declared that if the situation in Laos developed to the point where Thailand was threatened, "I shall have to fight in defense of it." In that case Sarit expected "to receive the assistance and cooperation from friendly nations of the Free World, because fighting against the Communists is a fight for the welfare of the whole free world." Even if such assistance were not forthcoming, he asserted, Thailand would fight the Communist menace alone:

To regard ourselves as having little power, so that, if there is no one to help us, we would have to stay with folded arms [sic] and leave the nation in danger, is impossible, because if we do not fight against the danger that comes to our country, we shall have to die in the end. Let us die fighting; let us die like a man. It is better than to have to die like a coward.

Finally Sarit called on all political leaders in Laos to join in an effort to free the country of Communist domination. If this could not be done, he said, and there were circumstances that constituted aggression upon Thailand, "Thailand will have to decide for itself, and defend the nation in every possible way without consideration whether there will be help from any source or not."[25]

Sarit's impassioned plea for action in Laos was a warning to Thailand's allies that his government would not stand idle while Communists and pro-Communists took over con-

[25]For the text of Sarit's statement on Laos, see Thailand's Ministry of Foreign Affairs special publication, *Statement of His Excellency the Prime Minister on the Situation in the Kingdom of Laos,* September 21, 1960. The text is also printed in both French and Thai.

trol of Laos. Frustrated with SEATO inaction, with the efforts of the British and French to encourage support for Souvanna Pouma, and with American vacillation, Sarit wanted it clearly understood that Thailand felt free to take whatever action in Laos it deemed necessary to protect its national interests. His words also revealed the emotional feelings that Thais have concerning the security of Laos. The growing anti-Thai campaign of Radio Vientiane and the anti-Thai reports appearing in the Western press were bitterly resented in Bangkok, and Sarit's statement demonstrated this resentment. But the major objective of Sarit's statement was to jolt the United States into action on Laos before the situation was beyond salvage. Although Sarit did not say so, there was little doubt that he wanted the United States to support General Poumi in his plan to unseat the Souvanna government and replace it with one more friendly to the West.

Up to now the United States had given no indication that it would support Poumi in an effort to oust Souvanna's government. United States military assistance was still being given to Poumi's troops in Savannakhet and also to Kong Lae's neutralist forces in Vientiane. American economic assistance had as yet not been denied to the Souvanna government, because the United States still believed that it was possible to form a coalition government among all non-Communist elements. By the end of September, however, this likelihood was becoming ever more remote, and Thailand was urging Washington to make a choice between Souvanna and Poumi. General Poumi sought to expedite matters in mid-September by forming a Revolutionary Committee in Savannakhet, with Prince Boon Oum as President and with members of the former Somsanit cabinet as prominent participants. Poumi's move was a prelude to formation of a revolutionary government for the purpose of overthrowing the

Souvanna government and claiming recognition from friendly foreign countries. The United States discouraged these moves, but by October developments in Vientiane were making it increasingly difficult for the United States to avoid making a choice.

Thailand had refused to grant recognition to the Vientiane government, and it maintained a virtual blockade on Laotian foreign commerce by closing the border at Nongkai, thereby preventing goods transported across Thailand from entering Laos. At the same time Thailand expressed a strong preference for Poumi and the Savannakhet Revolutionary Committee. Meanwhile it openly expressed displeasure with SEATO and became increasingly annoyed with the United States for continuing to give financial and political support to the Vientiane government. Sarit's paper, *Sarn Seri,* stated editorially that SEATO was established primarily to prevent Communist aggression in Southeast Asia, and that Thailand joined the organization because it felt that its security would be better protected if it were allied with other nations in a common defense.

Since the outbreak of incidents in Laos [the paper continued] nobody knows for certain what action SEATO will take should the Communists be able to seize and rule over the whole of Laos. This has made people who formerly felt full confidence in SEATO now feel anxiety because it does not seem to be showing concern over the situation in Laos, although it is clear that the Communists are intervening in that country in every possible way.[26]

In another issue of the same paper, the situation in Laos was compared to a fire that had broken out in the house of a neighbor. "Some neighbors watch it with indifference because it is a long distance from them, while others say they cannot

[26]*Sarn Seri,* September 27, 1960. *Thai Press Comment* (translations), U.S.I.S., Bangkok.

interfere because no request for help has been made; and still others hope that the fire will die out by itself." Thailand was likened to the next-door neighbor "which naturally feels alarm and fear that the fire will spread to his house. He is therefore compelled to take measures to protect his own house."[27]

Early in October the political situation in Vientiane reached a point that eventually caused the United States to agree with Thailand's position. Being pushed further to the left by the Pathet Lao groups that were now heavily infiltrating the capital, and beginning to feel the effects of Thailand's economic pressure, Prince Souvanna decided to establish diplomatic relations with the Soviet Union. When the Soviet ambassador to Pnom Penh arrived in Vientiane to open discussions with Souvanna, the local Communists organized an elaborate welcome, and Kong Lae's paratroopers put on a spectacular military exhibition to commemorate the occasion. This demonstration was embarrassing to Souvanna because the Soviet ambassador's arrival nearly coincided with the visit of the United States Assistant Secretary of State for Far Eastern Affairs, who had traveled to Laos to determine whether his government should continue to give economic and military assistance to Souvanna's regime. The effusive welcome for the Soviet ambassador was a disquieting omen of the direction that Souvanna's policy was taking, and it caused grave concern in the United States. He stopped short of establishing diplomatic ties with all Communist states, however, and opened relations only with those that had been admitted to the United Nations. Although this excluded the Peking and Hanoi governments, the presence of a Soviet embassy staff in Vientiane, working in harmony with local Communist groups, had a profound impact on official think-

[27]*Ibid.*, September 25, 1960.

ing in the United States during this crucial period and eventually caused the termination of United States economic assistance to the Souvanna government.

Prince Souvanna's decision to open diplomatic relations with the Soviet Union and his subsequent request for a Soviet airlift of rice and fuel, as well as for other badly needed supplies, to Vientiane, was partially the result of Thailand's refusal to permit the transport of these goods across its soil. The Thai government never officially refused the requests of the Vientiane government to permit food to flow freely across the Mekong, but it found a number of pretexts to avoid reopening the border, which had been closed since the August 9 coup. By October, Vientiane was in serious economic trouble, for the areas around the capital were controlled by General Poumi and therefore did not send food into the city. Oil and rice were needed desperately; and when Thailand refused to permit the movement of these staples, Souvanna asked the United States government to airlift them into Laos. This would have been a costly operation, and the United States did not approve it; but the refusal gave Souvanna grounds for asking for such assistance from the Soviet Union, which agreed to fly in supplies via Hanoi. In addition, the Soviet government decided to make this a gesture of friendship for Laos and would not accept payment from the Vientiane government. By agreeing to Souvanna's request, the Soviet Union scored a major psychological victory over the West and also gained the opportunity to supply military equipment later on when civil war broke out.

Whether Souvanna Pouma would have turned to the Soviet Union even if the United States had acceded to his request for supplies is debatable. Some observers believe that Souvanna was forced into this decision because he had no other place to turn to preserve his regime. The Thai government

in cooperation with General Poumi, it is argued, was tightening an economic stranglehold on Vientiane in an effort to
topple Souvanna's government, and the United States was
unwilling to bring pressure on Thailand to reopen the border
or to undertake an airlift itself; therefore, Souvanna had no
alternative but to ask for Soviet aid. On the other hand, it
may be argued that in October 1960 Souvanna was no longer
in control in Vientiane, that the combination of Kong Lae
and the Pathet Lao was forcing him to move ever farther to
the left, and that it would have been impossible for the
United States to stop this trend with an airlift of rice and oil.
Furthermore, it would have put the United States in the
strange position of bypassing the virtual economic blockade
of its ally, Thailand, to help a government that was clearly
anti-West in its propaganda and was moving steadily toward
a pro-Communist policy. The conclusion seems to be that by
mid-October 1960 the political situation in Laos was so pre-
carious that military rather than political considerations were
becoming paramount in the formulation of United States
policy. The questions whether Souvanna Pouma was a real
neutralist and whether he sincerely wished to retain good relations with the United States and Thailand were fast becoming academic.

Rightist Military Assault on Vientiane (December 1960)

Early in December 1960, General Poumi Nosavan moved
his troops toward Vientiane and prepared for an all-out assault
on the city. By then his forces were well equipped with American arms and were in what was believed to be fighting condition. In addition, Poumi had obtained the support of several
military garrisons in other parts of Laos, notably in the royal
capital of Luang Prabang; and shortly before the battle for
Vientiane began, one of the army units that had remained

loyal to Souvanna Pouma defected to Poumi after failing to drive Kong Lae's forces out of the capital. It had been Poumi's hope that the capital would fall to his superior forces without a major battle; but when Kong Lae demonstrated his determination to defend Vientiane, Poumi had no choice but to commence an attack on the city. At this point Prince Souvanna decided to flee to Cambodia with several of his ministers and to set up a government in exile. He officially remained head of the government, but he left his chief of staff, General Suntorn, in Vientiane as acting Prime Minister.

The battle for Vientiane began on December 13 and ended on December 16, when Kong Lae's forces withdrew from the city and moved north about eighty miles to Vang Vieng. This battle was costly in both lives and property, and it proved that Poumi could not intimidate Kong Lae's troops with an overwhelming superiority in men and fire power. Kong Lae's paratroopers proved to be tough adversaries, and they did not finally abandon the capital until they had inflicted considerable damage on Poumi's army. To those Laotians who had assumed that their passive Buddhist countrymen were incapable of violence and bloodshed, the three-day battle was a shocking example of what was in prospect if the civil war continued. Sisouk writes that "no one would have believed that Laotian soldiers—members of the same army and sometimes even of the same unit, who knew each other like brothers—would fight and kill each other so savagely. . . . Where are the peaceful and placid Lao of bygone days?"[28]

On December 18, Prince Boon Oum, president of the Revolutionary Committee of Savannakhet, General Poumi Nosavan, and other members of the committee entered Vientiane and assumed control of the government. It now appeared that, after more than four months of political maneu-

[28]Sisouk, op. cit., p. 169.

vering, the rightist forces had re-established their control in Vientiane and were determined to pacify the country with the help of an expanded and fully equipped army. Once the Revolutionary Committee set up its government in Vientiane, however, the momentum generated during the previous two weeks suddenly ended: as the Boon Oum government paused to survey the situation, Kong Lae's forces joined up with the Pathet Lao north of Vientiane and presented an entirely new threat to the security of Laos.

The last two weeks of December were crucial to future developments in Laos. Significantly, the failure of the Revolutionary Committee to do two things had a profound effect on the future course of events. First, it did not take steps immediately to convene the national assembly—most of whose members were sympathetic to the new regime—and obtain a vote of confidence. By failing to legitimatize immediately its seizure of power, the Boon Oum government remained vulnerable for several weeks to the charge that it was illegal and lent substance to Prince Souvanna's claim that he was the only legal head of the Laotian government—even though he was temporarily residing in Pnom Penh. This also complicated the position of the SEATO nations, particularly the United States, because they were unwilling to extend diplomatic recognition to the new regime until it had been approved by the assembly and by the King. It placed the United States in the somewhat embarrassing position of giving political and military support to a government that was not yet legal, and it presented the Soviet Union and other Communist states with an excuse to continue to recognize Souvanna Pouma's as the only government of Laos. Perhaps Boon Oum and Poumi were not aware of, or not concerned with, the niceties of international practice at this time; or they may have hoped that Souvanna Pouma would return to Vientiane, after peace had been restored, and participate in a new government. Whatever the reason, the two-week delay in establishing its legality cost the Boon Oum government considerable international prestige and contributed to the widening gulf between the Revolutionary Committee and the Souvanna Pouma group.

The second failure of the new regime—specifically, the failure of the Royal Laotian Army to follow up its victory in the capital with a vigorous pursuit of Kong Lae's forces—was even more damaging and resulted in a wholly different military picture in Laos from what had been anticipated when the Revolutionary Committee captured Vientiane. It was expected that Poumi's troops would move on through Vientiane and continue their offensive until Kong Lae was defeated or surrendered. If Poumi's troops had maintained their offensive during the last two weeks of December, there was a good possibility that they could have routed Kong Lae's greatly outnumbered force before it could link up with the Pathet Lao in the north. Without Kong Lae's support the Pathet Lao would have found it more difficult to claim they were helping to re-establish Souvanna Pouma's government in Vientiane; and thus it would have been more difficult for the Soviet Union to justify its airlift of supplies to the Pathet Lao. But Poumi's troops remained in Vientiane for nearly two weeks—enough time for Kong Lae to regroup at Vang Vieng and eventually to move into the Plaine des Jarres and into full cooperation with the Pathet Lao.

The reasons for the Royal Laotian Army's failure to pursue Kong Lae's paratroopers immediately are not difficult to find. For one thing, Poumi's men had been told that their goal was the capture of the capital city; they therefore assumed that once the city was taken, they would be able to enjoy the fruits of victory. The prospect of moving out of the city

immediately and continuing the fighting did not appeal to
Poumi's soldiers. Also, this was the first taste of real fighting
and bloodshed that most Laotian soldiers had experienced,
and the stubborn defense put up by Kong Lae's troops did
not make them eager to engage in battle again—even though
the odds in their favor were great. This failure to pursue
Kong Lae showed for the first time that Poumi did not have
complete control over his forces. His position as a military
commander was in marked contrast to that of Kong Lae, who
was able to maintain discipline over his troops even in defeat.
This lesson was not lost on Western military observers or on
the Communist powers.

The restoration of the rightist regime in Vientiane, which
received immediate endorsement from the United States government, was greeted with considerable satisfaction by the
Sarit government and silenced for the moment those voices
in Bangkok that had been asking whether an alliance with
the United States was of any value to Thailand. During
November, when Souvanna Pouma was moving ever closer
to the Pathet Lao domestically and to the Communist powers
internationally, Sarit and other members of his government
made little effort to conceal their displeasure with American
hesitancy in facing up to what they believed to be the realities
of the Laotian situation. Sarit went so far as to discuss with
the Soviet ambassador the possibility of an agreement between
Thailand and the Soviet Union to expand trade and to establish cultural exchanges between the two countries. Although
nothing came of these discussions, the publicity given them by
the government made it seem that Thailand would not remain quiet if its SEATO allies permitted Laos to come under
Communist control. When Foreign Minister Tanat Khoman
returned from the United Nations General Assembly meeting,
he showed considerable annoyance that Thailand's position

was so poorly appreciated, even among its allies. "The feeling is growing very strong," he said, "that we are treated less favorably than those nations that are uncommitted. There is less attention to our needs, our requirements, and our security than if we had been by ourselves."[29]

When SEATO's military advisers met in Bangkok late in November, Thai spokesmen made it abundantly clear that if SEATO could not agree on a policy to prevent the deterioration of the political situation in Vientiane, Thailand wanted the unanimity rule amended so that member nations wishing to take action would be free to do so. This demand was directed primarily against Britain and France, which were reported to be opposed to any action that would unseat the Souvanna Pouma government. This debate was suspended temporarily when the Lao rightist forces were successful in overthrowing Souvanna and establishing their control in Vientiane; but the debate remained suspended only so long as there was no strong counteraction from the Communist side in the war. And herein lay the factor that distinguished the Laotian crisis of 1960 from the one of 1959.

The key question in the crisis of August-December 1960 was whether the Communist powers would permit the neutralist government of Souvanna Pouma to be ousted by rightist military action, once that government had established itself legally and opened friendly relations with the Communist as well as the Western powers. In 1959 this question did not arise, because the Poui Sananikone government was not overthrown; also, the threat of Pathet Lao and Viet-Minh military incursions into the northern Lao provinces had been met so swiftly by the United Nations and by SEATO diplomatic action that the Communist powers had little opportunity to

[29]See Darrell Berrigan, "Thailand Is on the Spot," *The Reporter,* January 19, 1961, pp. 29–31.

take a stand. In 1960, however, the situation was far different, because a neutralist-leftist government was actually in power; also, SEATO was sharply divided in its approach to the problem. By establishing diplomatic relations with the Souvanna Pouma government and by agreeing to supply it with essential food and fuel, the Soviet Union undertook an obligation to Souvanna's government that it could not forsake without losing considerable prestige among all the nations of Southeast Asia. When General Poumi used force to oust the Souvanna government, many observers doubted seriously whether the Soviet Union would be willing to accept such a defeat without some kind of retaliation; thus, there were serious risks of escalation in Poumi's decision to use military force against the Soviet-supported government of Souvanna Pouma.

For the Thai government, however, the issue was entirely clear: the Western allies, by failing to act decisively in August to quash the Kong Lae *coup d'état,* had permitted a pro-Communist group to gain control of the political situation in Vientiane and then to push the government along the road to Communist domination. Thai leaders felt that in August there would have been few risks in giving Poumi's forces all the support they needed to march on Vientiane and oust Kong Lae's rebellious paratroopers—as the latter were then looked upon as rebels by all concerned. But SEATO's inaction, the Thais argued, permitted the Souvanna government to entrench itself, so that by November the risks involved in overthrowing it were much greater. By this time, however, Thailand was so convinced that Laos was succumbing to Communist subversion that it was willing to run many risks to avoid having the Communist menace face it along the length of the Mekong. Therefore, Thai leaders were fully in favor of supporting General Poumi's military action against Vientiane.

As the year 1960 came to a close, the first chapter in the Laotian crisis of 1960 and 1961 had ended with Vientiane once again in the hands of pro-Thai and pro-Western leaders. If the risk of Soviet intervention seemed large at this point, Thai leaders felt more comfortable facing such a clear-cut threat than they did the more subtle menace of Communist subversion and political warfare directed by a hostile Laotian government.

Chapter 6

Crisis in the Alliance

THE year 1961 presented the United States with a crucial test of its policy in Laos; and as a result American determination to defend Thailand and other parts of Southeast Asia was called into serious question. Although the change in administrations in the United States in January 1961 caused a reappraisal of American policy toward Laos and Vietnam, the critical problem in Laos was the inability of the right-wing forces of Prince Boon Oum and General Poumi Nosavan to consolidate their victory of December 1960 and extend their control throughout Laos before the Communists and the Neutralists—who constituted a specific faction from January 1961 on—could launch a counteroffensive with the help of Soviet arms. Whereas in the autumn of 1960 the question for American policy makers was whether to support Poumi's forces to re-establish a pro-Western government, in the spring of 1961 the military situation in Laos was so critical that they had to decide whether to send in American troops to hold the line indefinitely. When the United States decided not to risk a major escalation of the fighting by committing its own forces to Laos, the alternative was to seek a negotiated settlement with the Soviet Union. This decision had the most profound implications for the Thais; they feared that if the United States, upon which they had placed full confidence for maintaining the security of Southeast Asia, was unwilling to risk war to preserve Laos as a non-Communist state, what assurance was there that it would risk war to defend Thailand if the latter was threatened by internal subversion supported by external Communist forces?

The likelihood of escalation in the Laotian fighting was evident in mid-December, when the Soviet Union began flying arms and Vietnamese military personnel into Laos in an effort to bolster the Pathet Lao and the Neutralist forces of Kong Lae.[1] This action made it clear to all concerned that the Soviet Union was prepared to undertake a major supply effort of military equipment and personnel to prevent the Pathet Lao and the Neutralists from being crushed by the American-supported army of General Poumi, following the latter's capture of Vientiane. This bold move so strengthened the Pathet Lao forces that when Poumi's troops finally proceeded north, they were unable to capture the strategic town of Xieng Khouang and its adjacent airfield in the Plaine des Jarres which the Soviets were using for their supply effort. It was at the Plaine des Jarres also that Kong Lae and the Pathet Lao later joined forces and, with the assistance of Soviet arms and Vietnamese "advisers," began an offensive that eventually led to the defeat of Poumi's army both in central and in southern Laos. By the beginning of 1961, therefore, the Soviet Union had taken a clear stand in support of the Pathet Lao, thus putting an entirely new complexion on the war in Laos. It was now left to the United States to decide whether to escalate the situation or to try to find a compromise solution. In either case the Soviet action had made it unmistakably

[1]The State Department charged that at least 180 sorties had been flown by Soviet and North Vietnamese aircraft during the last two weeks of December. *(Department of State Bulletin,* January 23, 1961, p. 114.)

clear that the Pathet Lao was a political force to be reckoned with in the future of Laos. It was a nasty and very dangerous situation that President Kennedy inherited when he took office.

During the last days of the Eisenhower administration the United States decided to make a show of force in Southeast Asia in an effort to dissuade the Soviet Union from continuing its airlift of military supplies into Laos. United States forces in the Pacific were alerted, and an urgent meeting of the SEATO Council was called in Bangkok to take up the question of Soviet intervention in the Laotian war. The State Department issued a lengthy statement on Laos, which served as the basis for any subsequent action the United States might take there. Stating that "it is obvious to all that Laos is not a military threat to any of its neighbors, least of all to the strong military regimes in north Viet-Nam and Communist China," this paper declared that the United States was not engaged in building any military base in Laos and that it had never sought to persuade Laos to enter into a military alliance. Asserting that the real problem in Laos was the determination of the Communists to take over control of the country, the State Department listed three ways in which the United States might contribute toward a solution: first, by exposing "the true nature of communist intentions and actions in Laos"; second, by "continuing clearly to show that it has no intention and no desire to establish a Western military position in Laos"; and third, by "joining with other free nations to support and maintain the independence of Laos through whatever measures seem most promising."[2] The SEATO Council met on January 4, 1961, and issued a communiqué that indicated its concern over the deteriorating situation caused by the Soviet airlift and declared that "the continu-

²*Department of State Bulletin,* January 23, 1961, pp. 115–17.

ance of such intervention could only serve to promote diversion and civil war in Laos and lead to a situation which would imperil not only the integrity of the Kingdom of Laos but also the security of neighboring countries." The council called for a solution to the Laotian problem by peaceful means but warned that "all SEATO member countries remained determined to continue to develop and maintain their readiness to fulfill anywhere in the treaty area their obligations under the Manila Pact."[3]

In early January 1961, therefore, the United States had taken the preliminary steps to prepare for more decisive action in Laos if the situation continued to deteriorate. The government of Thailand strongly concurred in these moves, for it was convinced that the Boon Oum government offered the best insurance of keeping the Communist menace away from its own border.

Despite strong American support of the Boon Oum government, it was clear in January 1961 that there was a deep division within SEATO on this matter, and that the Soviet Union found considerable sympathy among the uncommitted nations for its support of a government headed by Prince Souvanna Pouma. When the government of Laos approached the Secretary General of SEATO about the possibility of sending a SEATO observation team to determine the extent of Communist intervention in Laos, only the United States and Thailand supported the proposal. Although several other members later gave their approval, the two European powers —Britain and France—opposed it, so nothing further came of this first modest effort to establish SEATO presence in Laos.[4] The stumbling block to American efforts to find a

[3]*Ibid.*

[4]L. P. Singh, "Thai Foreign Policy: The Current Phase," *Asian Survey,* November 1963, pp. 536-7.

peaceful solution to the Laotian problem was that all its proposals for a neutral, independent, and peaceful Laos were predicated on a continuation of the Boon Oum government in power. There was so little support, however, for it among the neutral nations and among the European allies of the United States that this political position was difficult for the American government to maintain. As one writer has stated, "So long as the United States stood isolated in support of the Laotian right-wing, there was little need for the Communist bloc to compromise."[5]

Approach to the Brink of War

When John F. Kennedy became President, the situation in Laos was the most pressing international problem, and he had discussed it with President Eisenhower thoroughly. He was faced with three alternatives: abandoning Laos; risking a larger war by furnishing massive American aid—including the use of American troops; or seeking a settlement through negotiations with the Soviet Union and other interested powers. Because President Kennedy was more inclined than his predecessor to seek a solution based on genuine neutrality for Laos,[6] his administration sought first to coordinate American policy with the policies of its SEATO allies and thereafter to seek a peaceful solution among the various factions within Laos. Meanwhile, the Pathet Lao and the Neutralist forces continued their slow military advance into key areas of central and southern Laos, being careful not to provoke the United States into counter action by threatening the principal cities along the Mekong. The Communists' strategy was

[5]Oliver E. Clubb, Jr., *The United States and the Sino-Soviet Bloc in Southeast Asia* (Washington, D.C., 1962), p. 65.

[6]Russell H. Fifield, *Southeast Asia in United States Policy* (New York, 1963), p. 197.

to use military pressure to achieve their political ends, namely, the establishment of a coalition government in which the Pathet Lao would be represented, and through which they could eventually take over control of the government.

In line with President Kennedy's view that a solution should be found on the basis of a neutral and independent Laos, strong efforts were made during the early part of 1961 to bring about a compromise in the internal political situation that would be acceptable to all non-Communist factions. In February, Laotian King Savang Vattana made a speech from the throne in which he called for a truly neutral and independent Laos not tied to any bloc or receiving military aid from any foreign source. He called for national reconciliation at home and voiced support for Prime Minister Boon Oum's efforts to bring other political groups into the government. He asked foreign countries to stop interfering in Laotian affairs and requested that Cambodia, Malaya, and Burma send a mission to Laos to investigate reports of foreign intervention. This was clearly an effort to bring about a *rapprochement* between the Boon Oum government and Prince Souvanna Pouma, who was then residing in Cambodia but still claimed to be the legal head of the Laotian government.

General Poumi journeyed to Pnom Penh in mid-March to confer with Souvanna, and they agreed that King Savang's call for a neutral Laos and for the withdrawal of all foreign forces could serve as the basis of restoring peace and unity to Laos. Souvanna agreed to act as mediator with the Pathet Lao, and further meetings were envisioned. Finally, they agreed that Prince Sihanouk's recent call for an international conference to guarantee the neutrality of Laos would be acceptable if agreement could be reached to stop the fighting and bring about a coalition government. This preliminary agreement came to nothing because of Pathet Lao opposition.

Within a few days the latter, with strong Viet-Minh support, launched a heavy offensive against the Laotian government forces. The United States, in the face of the continued Soviet airlift of arms to the Pathet Lao troops and in anticipation of renewed fighting, had also greatly increased its supply of arms and equipment to General Poumi's forces. Despite their large numerical superiority and excellent equipment, however, Poumi's troops were no match for the Communist forces. When the Pathet Lao and the Neutralists launched their offensive, Poumi's forces retreated all along the line without offering real resistance. The consensus was, even among Thai leaders, that Poumi Nosavan's troops were not willing to fight the Communists, and that the Boon Oum government could not be counted on to resist Pathet Lao pressure without foreign intervention. This was the hard fact of the situation in Laos at the end of March 1961.

As the military situation began to deteriorate, President Kennedy was forced to consider armed intervention to stabilize it. It was clear that the Soviet Union, which at that time appeared to be the decisive influence on the Communist side, was willing to enter into negotiations for a settlement in Laos only on the basis of Souvanna Pouma's return to the premiership and of a coalition government that would include the Pathet Lao. Since the United States was not prepared to accept such a solution, a military confrontation seemed inevitable. On March 23, President Kennedy addressed a televised news conference and spelled out the dangers in the Laotian situation. He strongly reaffirmed that the United States wanted a "neutral and independent Laos, tied to no outside power or group of powers, threatening no one, and free from any domination." In order to dispel any possible doubt about the policy of his administration, the President said that "if in the past there has been any possible ground for misunderstanding of our support for a truly neutral Laos, there should be none now." But, Mr. Kennedy asserted, a peaceful solution could not come about until the armed attacks, supported externally by the North Vietnamese Communists, had ceased. "If these attacks do not stop, those who support a genuinely neutral Laos will have to consider their response." This matter would be carefully considered, he said, at the SEATO ministerial council meeting in Bangkok the following week. The President favored negotiations among various powers to find a peaceful solution to the Laotian problem, but he insisted that negotiations could not take place while military action was in progress. "No one should doubt our own resolution on this point," he declared. "We are faced with a clear threat of a change in the internationally agreed position of Laos," he said, and the threat of military operations directed from outside Laos had to stop if peace was to be maintained in Southeast Asia. The President concluded by expressing confidence that "every American will want his country to honor its obligations to the point that freedom and security of the free world and ourselves may be achieved."[7]

This statement was understood in Bangkok, and in most other world capitals, as a sharp warning to the Soviet Union to stop the Pathet Lao advance and start negotiations to settle the conflict, or to risk American and SEATO military action to preserve the position of the Boon Oum government. To back up his words, the President ordered all United States forces in the Pacific on the alert and began a build-up of American military strength in the area of Southeast Asia. Also, two days after this statement some 250 United States Marines were dispatched by air to Udorn in northeast Thailand near the Laotian border to set up a helicopter maintenance facility for ferrying supplies to rightist forces in Laos.

[7]*Department of State Bulletin,* April 17, 1961, pp. 543–4.

Although this movement was given little publicity, it was taken as a clear sign by Thai officials that the United States was preparing for more active involvement in Laos.

Meanwhile the British government took the intiative on the diplomatic front. As co-chairman with the Soviet Union of the 1954 Geneva Conference which brought about an end to the Indochina war, Britain on March 23 sent the Soviet government an *aide-mémoire* in which it accepted previous Soviet proposals that an international conference be called to consider a solution to the Laotian problem, and that the International Control Commission, set up by the Geneva Conference, be reinstituted. Britain refused, however, to accept the Soviet assertion that Souvanna Pouma was the only legal head of the Laotian government and proposed instead that various Laotian factions resume the discussions that were begun in Pnom Penh "with a view to agreeing on a national government which could represent Laos at the proposed conference." If the Laotian factions could not agree among themselves on a government, the British replied, the international conference would have to "address itself as its first task to helping the parties of Laos to reach agreement on this point." The British were firm that no negotiations could be held unless there was "an immediate cessation of all active military operations in Laos," and it suggested to the Soviet Union that the two nations issue an immediate request for a *de facto* ceasefire.[8] The American and British governments were working in concert at this critical moment, as was evident in the visit of Prime Minister Macmillan to the United States and his full exchange of views on the Laotian situation with President Kennedy on the eve of the SEATO Council of Ministers meeting in Bangkok. At the conclusion of their meeting the two government leaders issued a joint communiqué in

[8]*Department of State Bulletin,* April 17, 1961, p. 545.

which they agreed that "the situation in Laos cannot be allowed to deteriorate," and that the recent British note to the Soviet Union contained proposals that could end the war and "pave the way for Laos to become the truly neutral country, which it is their joint wish to see." They also hoped that the Soviet government would make "a positive and constructive reply to these proposals."[9]

On the eve of the SEATO Council meeting (March 26–27) in Bangkok, the military situation in Laos was deteriorating rapidly as General Poumi's troops continued their broad retreat. On the diplomatic front the British proposal for a ceasefire had not yet drawn a reply from the Soviet Union. Meanwhile the United States Seventh Fleet and the United States army and air force were being readied for action. The Laotian situation was, therefore, the most urgent item of business before the SEATO meeting.

Marshal Sarit opened the SEATO conference with a warning that another Dienbienphu might occur in Indochina, and that another section of free world territory might be lost or partitioned unless SEATO could find the means of preventing it. Despite the outward show of solidarity, the discussions showed that sharp differences of opinion existed among the member nations over what action the organization should take to preserve the independence of Laos. Thailand, the nation most directly affected, Pakistan, and the Philippines were strongly in favor of military intervention. On the other side was France, which flatly opposed intervention and favored Souvanna Pouma's return to power. Great Britain favored armed action only as a last resort and was anxiously awaiting the Soviet Union's reply to its ceasefire proposal. The United States position was between the extremes: it did not wish to antagonize the Soviet Union before determining

[9]*Ibid.*, p. 544.

what the latter was prepared to offer; at the same time it feared that the military situation in Laos might deteriorate to a point where the Communists would hold all the cards at the conference table. Although the final communiqué of the Bangkok Conference was considerably weaker than Thailand and the Philippines wished, it probably represented the maximum agreement that could be achieved under SEATO's rule of unanimity. The position of the United States was crucial. Fifield believes that "if Washington had at that time determined upon military intervention in Laos, it is likely that Thailand, the Philippines, Pakistan, and Australia would have gone along, possibly joined by Great Britain and New Zealand."[10] However, the United States was more interested in preserving the unity of SEATO and therefore settled for a mild warning, to the effect that if efforts to reach a ceasefire and peaceful negotiations should fail, "and there continues to be an active military attempt to obtain control of Laos, members of SEATO are prepared, within the terms of the treaty, to take whatever action may be appropriate in the circumstances."[11] Although the United States was determined to prevent a Communist military victory in Laos, the SEATO meeting showed that it was prepared to wait a little longer to see whether the Soviet Union would use its controlling influence in the Laotian situation to halt the Pathet Lao attacks.

The real problem in the Laotian crisis at the beginning of April 1961 was the inability of General Poumi's army to hold any defensive line against the numerically inferior Pathet Lao and Neutralist forces, who were bolstered by Viet-Minh cadres. Had the government's forces been able to stop the Communist advance for any length of time, it is likely that a ceasefire could have been arranged promptly, and negotia-

[10]Fifield, *op. cit.,* p. 199.
[11]*Department of State Bulletin,* April 17, 1961, p. 549.

tions started to bring about a solution to the Laotian problem. However, so long as the Communist forces were winning nearly every engagement and met very little resistance from Poumi's soldiers, there was little incentive for the Communist powers to negotiate. Indeed, if the Soviet Union had agreed to a ceasefire while the Pathet Lao and Neutralists were steadily advancing, other Communist countries would have greatly resented it. Thus Western efforts to bring about a political solution were constantly thwarted by the inability of the Laotian government to stabilize the military situation. As time went on, it seemed increasingly clear that circumstances would force the United States to intervene militarily in Laos, if it hoped to negotiate with the Communists from a position that would make negotiations meaningful.

On April 1 the Soviet Union replied to the British *aide-mémoire* of March 23 and agreed to an international conference and to a ceasefire in Laos. The Soviet note suggested, however, that the interested parties in Laos negotiate on questions connected with the ceasefire. It also agreed to the convening of the International Control Commission for observation and control in Laos. Referring to the British suggestion that a neutral government of national unity be established, the Soviet government said that this was an internal affair to be solved by the Laotians themselves. The note said that "in Laos there exists the legal government of His Highness Prince Souvanna Phouma, which stands on a platform of strict neutrality and restoration of unity of internal forces, and has the support of a majority of the population of the country." It claimed that a coup against this government, supported from the outside, was organized "precisely for the purpose of ending the neutrality of Laos in international affairs." Finally, the Soviet note said that efforts at peaceful negotiations on Laos demanded a favorable international situation and that threats of interference by SEATO and the tactic of saber rattling "not only does not promote this, but can seriously complicate the entire matter of settlement of the Laos problem."[12] Although President Kennedy expressed the view that the Soviet reply appeared to be a "useful step" toward a peaceful settlement of the potentially dangerous situation in Laos, no date was established for a ceasefire, and there was no indication that the Soviets would settle for anything less than a return to power of Souvanna Pouma at the head of a coalition government including the Pathet Lao.

By mid-April the military situation in Laos was desperate: the major cities of Luang Prabang, Vientiane, and Savannakhet were threatened by Pathet Lao and Neutralist forces. Despite strenuous efforts by the British to arrange a halt to the Communist advance, the Soviets continued to delay. Thailand was frantically calling for American intervention to save the Laotian government from collapsing. The United States now had to make the critical decision of whether to send its own troops into Laos to prevent a complete disaster.

Thailand's Expectations

After Poumi Nosavan's troops drove Kong Lae out of Vientiane in December 1960, the Thai government showed much satisfaction that a friendly government had been restored in Laos, and that the Laotian buffer against Communist China and North Vietnam had been re-established. When the Soviet Union began to airlift arms and equipment to bolster the Pathet Lao, Thailand became worried and appealed to SEATO. Except for the United States, the Philippines, and Pakistan, other SEATO countries were opposed to armed action in Laos and could not agree at the end of January even to send a SEATO observer team to that country. SEATO's

[12]*Ibid.*, p. 546.

inaction was discouraging to the Thai government, but it was no surprise because SEATO had similarly refused to be drawn into the Laotian crisis a few months earlier when Thailand urged it to intervene to prevent the Pathet Lao from seizing control of the government. By January 1961, Thailand had come to the conclusion that only the United States could preserve the Boon Oum government in Laos. Thai policy was therefore designed to ensure that the United States continue its strong stand in Laos and use whatever force was required to prevent the Communists from upsetting the new government.

A new phase in Thailand's relations with the United States began with the Kennedy administration. Thai leaders had come to respect the Eisenhower administration's determination to resist Communist encroachments throughout the world, particularly in the Taiwan Straits and in Laos in 1958 and 1959. Although the Sarit government was exasperated that the United States wavered in the summer and autumn of 1960 on the question of assisting Poumi Nosavan to restore a rightist regime in Vientiane, these criticisms had subsided with Poumi's successful effort in December to oust Souvanna Pouma and replace him with Boon Oum. The Sarit government was convinced that neutralism was a dangerous policy for any nation—particularly Laos—to adopt in the Cold War. As the Republican administration came to an end, Thai leaders were anxious to learn whether President Kennedy would be as firm in Laos as President Eisenhower had been. An early indication of the new policy came late in January when President Kennedy stated that the United States wanted to see a peaceful, independent, and uncommitted Laos that would not be a threat to any of its neighbors. The President's statement was made at about the same time that Prince Sihanouk of Cambodia proposed that Laos and Cambodia should form a neutral buffer between the Communist and free world countries of Southeast Asia. In Bangkok shortly thereafter, Wichit Watakarn, assistant to the Thai Prime Minister and a spokesman for the government on certain foreign policy matters, stated in an interview that "the Thai government desires Laos to be independent with peace and progress. . . . Therefore, there is no objection to Laos being neutral, if neutrality is beneficial to happiness in Laos. However, Laotian neutrality should be genuine neutrality, not pro-communist neutralism." Asked about Thailand's position if Laos adopted a neutral policy, Wichit said that there would have to be a guarantee by both the Communist and the Western powers that "Laos would not become communist," and that Thailand should be one of the guarantors. He firmly rejected any suggestion that Laos be partitioned.[13]

In February, while other countries were trying to achieve a political settlement of the Laotian question, the Thai government remained quiet but followed developments closely. It did not oppose suggestions that a coalition government be formed to unite non-Communist elements, including Prince Souvanna Pouma, but its approval of a coalition was conditional on Prince Boon Oum remaining as Prime Minister and Poumi Nosavan as Defense Minister. Thai Foreign Minister Tanat Khoman remarked that a coalition government might be beneficial for Laos "if it can be named without a change in administration and also without coming under the direction of a foreign power." Tanat believed that a genuine neutrality policy carried out by a coalition government in Laos would "be a good thing to maintain the security and peace of Laos."[14] Thailand was favorable to the Laotian King's call for a neutral Laos, but it was skeptical of the

[13]*Bangkok Post,* February 1, 1961, p. 1.
[14]*Bangkok World,* February 21, 1961, p. 1.

talks between Poumi Nosavan and Prince Souvanna in early March that looked toward a coalition government of rightist and neutralist groups. Several newspapers, including Marshal Sarit's *Sarn Seri*, believed that it was unwise for the Laotian government to make large concessions to Souvanna Pouma in order to bring him into a coalition government. When the Pathet Lao emphasized their opposition by launching a large-scale offensive against government forces in mid-March, the Thais concluded that the Pathet Lao would refuse to accept any agreement for a settlement of the war unless they were a party to it and were included in the government.

As the Communists continued their military pressure in Laos, the Thai government became suspicious of Western efforts to find a political solution to the problem. Many editorials expressed the fear that Communist tactics were forcing the Western powers to accept a partitioned Laos or a united Laos dominated by the Communists. There was wide approval of President Kennedy's March 23 warning; but there was concern that British efforts to seek negotiations with the Soviets would delay any American military move and give the Pathet Lao an opportunity to extend their control ever farther before a ceasefire was finally effected. The real fear of Thai leaders was that the Communists would be able to establish themselves before the ceasefire along the Mekong at strategic points which they could then use as staging areas for infiltrating Thailand. For all these reasons Thai leaders looked to the meeting of the SEATO Council in Bangkok at the end of March as a decisive indicator of SEATO's, and especially of American, intentions in Laos. Foreign Minister Tanat Khoman stated the question clearly in his opening statement to the SEATO meeting on March 27:

After all, it is not only a question of whether a nation should be allowed to continue to enjoy a free and independent existence, which is of paramount importance by itself, but fundamentally a question of whether or not we are capable of withstanding the forces of disruption and enslavement. If, by lack of determination and unity of purpose, our strength is so weakened that we should yield to the superior force of destruction, the collective security system on which this organization is based shall prove to be a failure.[15]

The Thai government officially expressed satisfaction over the outcome of the SEATO meeting and its decision to take appropriate action if efforts at arranging a ceasefire in Laos were not successful. Unofficially, however, there was much concern over the failure both of SEATO to take a much stronger position and of the United States to indicate its willingness to act without the approval of other SEATO members if the military situation in Laos deteriorated further. The Thai government was well aware, from the discussions that had taken place both during and outside the meeting, that there was a deep gulf between the French and the British positions, on the one hand, and the Thai and the Philippine view, on the other. Thai leaders were not opposed in principle to British efforts to seek a basis with the Soviet Union for ending the fighting in Laos; what worried them increasingly was that these negotiations might lead to a coalition government which included the Pathet Lao and in which Prince Souvanna would be a weak Prime Minister, relying principally on Communist support. With publication on April 1 of the Soviet reply to the British aide-mémoire, these fears seemed to be confirmed. Thai leaders viewed this important document as meaning that the Soviet Union insisted that Souvanna Pouma be recognized as the legal head of the Laotian government; that if interested parties in Laos—including

[15]Collection of Principal Speeches of Foreign Minister Tanat Khoman, Bangkok, Ministry of Foreign Affairs, December 1961.

the Pathet Lao—could not agree on a coalition government, the international conference would seek to impose a solution —that is, a government that included the Pathet Lao; and that no ceasefire would be arranged until the United States and Thailand stopped threatening to intervene. The Thai government concluded that the only way of reaching a reasonable solution in Laos—namely, a non-Communist coalition government—was to have the United States and any other interested SEATO nations station troops along the Mekong in Laos.

The Thai government's anxiety was expressed by Wichit Watakarn, who was obviously speaking with the Prime Minister's authority. Commenting on the Soviet note, he said that if negotiations were held on Laos before a ceasefire went into effect, Vientiane and Luang Prabang might well be lost before the Communists halted their drive. Wichit believed that the proposed fourteen-nation conference on Laos would be a defeat for the anti-Communist nations because seven of the countries that were to be invited did not recognize the Boon Oum government in Laos. He said that Thailand probably would not accept an invitation to attend such a conference, and that the vote would undoubtedly be seven nations against six in favor of accepting Prince Souvanna Pouma as the legal head of the Laotian government. The end result of the conference, Wichit predicted, would be to force Thailand to accept Souvanna Pouma as Prime Minister of Laos; therefore, "if they hold the conference, we will lose in the first round."[16] On April 10, while Pathet Lao forces pushed dangerously close to the Mekong at Takhek and thereby threatened to divide Laos, Prime Minister Sarit called together his key military and civilian advisers to discuss the situation. After the meeting Sarit made a statement to the press: "We

[16]*Bangkok World,* April 5, 1961, p. 1.

are most concerned with developments in Laos. There is no cease-fire. The Laotian government may go at any time." He said he was not so much concerned about the Communists capturing Vientiane, which he thought Poumi Nosavan could hold, as he was about Takhek, whose capture would pose a real threat to Thailand. "If it is captured by the Communists, we are in trouble," he declared. Asked his opinion about a coalition government in Laos, Sarit said he believed it would lead to "the eventual takeover by the Communists." Sarit also revealed that he had sent a personal letter to President Kennedy expressing Thailand's view of how the Laotian problem should be settled.[17]

By April 20, Communist forces had approached to within ten miles of Takhek, and Sarit declared that Thailand's armed forces were prepared to go into action immediately if the city was attacked. Sarit declined to elaborate on when and where Thai forces would be used, but he left the impression that a Communist attack on Takhek would be considered a direct threat to Thailand's security, and that he might then take military action regardless of what other SEATO countries were prepared to do.[18] The week of April 17, therefore, saw the acid test of the SEATO alliance, insofar as the long Laotian crisis was concerned. By this time it was clear to nearly all observers that the Pathet Lao were capable of toppling the Boon Oum government and imposing a settlement by military force unless strong counter action was taken by SEATO, particularly by the United States. British efforts to bring about an early ceasefire had produced no agreement with the Soviet Union, which seemed content to delay a ceasefire as long as the Pathet Lao were gaining more territory. The Thai government was convinced that SEATO would

[17]*Bangkok Post,* April 11, 1961, p. 1.
[18]*Bangkok World,* April 21, 1961, p. 1.

not agree on joint action to defend Laos, because of the unanimity rule and because of French and possibly British opposition to any intervention. Thailand therefore looked to the United States as the only nation that had the military power to preserve the independence of Laos against Communist domination.

It is significant that when President Kennedy was forced to make the critical decision whether to support the Thai view and send American troops into Laos, he was preoccupied with an entirely different crisis much closer to home—in Cuba; for the week of April 17 was also the week when the Bay of Pigs invasion by Cuban exiles failed so miserably and brought down on the new administration in Washington much world criticism for supporting it. When President Kennedy turned to the difficult problem of Laos, he was not inclined to risk another political and military failure in an area much farther from home. Instead, the United States decided to support British efforts to work out the best arrangement possible with the Soviets to end the fighting.

When the Thai leaders became aware of America's decision not to intervene, they were astonished and even angry because they could not believe that the United States would adopt such a course in Southeast Asia after the previous strong stand of the Eisenhower government and also after the recent warning of President Kennedy to the Soviet Union to help stop the fighting. This decision, the Thais thought, effectively immobilized the SEATO alliance and opened up all of Southeast Asia to Communist subversion and military pressure. If the United States was not prepared to accept its responsibilities by defending Laos against a Communist takeover, Thai leaders concluded, what reason was there to believe that it would be any more prepared to defend Thailand when it was faced with a similar threat? This was a moment of truth for the Thai government, and it is not surprising that its leaders began talking privately about a change in foreign policy and even about abandoning SEATO. Their disillusionment was not expressed publicly at this time, but editorials in various newspapers indicated how disturbed the leadership was over the new situation. The paper *Thai Rath* probably reflected the prevailing view when it stated that a major change had occurred in American policy toward Southeast Asia, that Laos was no longer considered a line of defense against Communist penetration of the area.

The present American government is endeavoring to emphasize that Cuba is of greater importance than Laos. If war has to be risked to prevent either of these two countries falling into the hands of the communists, America prefers running the risk for Cuba. This might mean that Laos will have to be sacrificed to the communists.[19]

Retreat from the Brink

Once the President had decided not to use American troops to achieve a solution to the Laotian problem, the alternative was to negotiate. Secretary of State Rusk summed up the situation in a news conference on May 4, 1961. In answer to a question whether the United States and other SEATO powers lacked the will to take military action in Laos or in Vietnam to prevent Communist advances, Mr. Rusk said that since early January the administration had been proceeding along a "double track" in its policy toward Laos. On the one hand, it had supported British efforts to work out a cease-fire in cooperation with the Soviet Union and to convene an international conference to try to find a peaceful solution to the Laotian problem. On the other hand, if negotiations failed, he said, the SEATO powers were prepared to take

[19]Thai Press Comment (translations), April 25, 1961, U.S.I.S., Bangkok.

appropriate measures to prevent a Communist takeover. Admitting that there might be differences of opinion among various SEATO governments "when a particular track runs out and when another track has to be adopted," the Secretary concluded with this statement: "But the present effort on the part of all those who are deeply involved in this is to settle this question without a major escalation of the fighting if possible."[20]

The United States decision to seek a negotiated settlement in Laos represented a significant shift in its policy in Southeast Asia. Implicit in the acceptance of negotiations was a withdrawal of the SEATO shield from Laos and acceptance of the Pathet Lao as a major political force in that country. Therefore, no settlement could deny the demands of the Pathet Lao, led by Prince Soupanouvong, that it be included in any government formed, and also that all foreign military assistance programs be withdrawn from the kingdom. The proposed international conference to deal with the Laotian question would include Communist China and North Vietnam, in addition to the Soviet Union and Poland; and the International Control Commission, made up of Canada, India, and Poland—which proved to be so frustrating to American efforts to promote a non-Communist Laotian government during the nineteen-fifties—would again be the watchdog of a ceasefire and of any political settlement. Finally, when the United States decided to negotiate, fighting was still raging in Laos, and Communist forces were continuing to advance all along the line against the ineffective army of General Poumi Nosavan. In reality, the United States had come close to the brink of war during the first three months of 1961 and had then drawn back in the face of the risks involved in

[20]*Department of State Bulletin,* May 22, 1961, p. 759.

bringing its full power to bear in this remote area on the border of Communist China.

On April 24 the British and Soviet governments, as co-chairmen of the 1954 Geneva Conference, called for an immediate ceasefire in Laos and invited twelve other countries to participate in an international conference beginning May 12 in Geneva. The Anglo-Soviet appeal for a ceasefire stated that if the situation continued to deteriorate, "the position of Laos may become a serious threat to peace and security in Southeast Asia." On the other hand, the co-chairmen believed that "real conditions exist for normalizing the situation in Laos in accordance with the national interests of the Laotian people, on the basis of the Geneva Agreements of 1954." Therefore, they asked all Laotian factions to meet and to work out a ceasefire arrangement and to cooperate with the International Control Commission when it arrived in Laos. The United States replied that it "welcomes this development which we hope will bring about a peaceful settlement in Laos." However, it attached two conditions to its acceptance of the invitation to the international conference: that a ceasefire be effected before the conference convened, and that the role of the International Control Commission be limited to verifying the ceasefire. The statement concluded by saying that if a verified ceasefire could be effected, the United States "hopes to see emerge from the conference the peaceful, united, and unaligned Laos of which President Kennedy spoke on March 23."[21] Unlike the President's statement of March 23, however, the State Department's response did not carry any threat of military action in case a ceasefire was not in effect when the Geneva Conference was scheduled to convene. Although sporadic fighting continued for some weeks,

[21]For texts of these messages, see *Department of State Bulletin*, May 15, 1961, pp. 710–11.

the International Control Commission was able to report that a *de facto* ceasefire was effective on May 12. By that time, however, the Pathet Lao and Kong Lae's Neutralist forces, supported by strong Viet-Minh cadres, had captured strategic points in northern and central Laos; and, more significantly, they had captured key areas in southern Laos through which supplies and guerrilla forces could be infiltrated from North Vietnam into South Vietnam to take part in the new assault on the South Vietnamese government. In May the Laotian Communists controlled over half of the land area of Laos, in contrast to their small areas of control prior to the Kong Lae coup of August 1960: they were now in an excellent position to seize control of the whole country if negotiations failed and military action was reinstituted. In many ways, the military situation in Laos in the spring of 1961 was similar to that in Vietnam in 1954: the Communists held the superior negotiating position at the conference table because of their gains on the battlefield. For the United States the prospect was not encouraging.

The International Conference for the Settlement of the Laotian Question opened in Geneva on May 16, 1961; and from the outset the participants were involved in acrimonious and complicated discussions about an effective ceasefire, which group should represent Laos, the responsibilities of the International Control Commission, and the practical ways in which neutrality and independence could be secured in Laos.[22] The United States sought to ensure that an effective ceasefire was established before serious negotiations began, and it favored seating the Boon Oum representative. However, it seemed clear from the beginning of the conference that most of the

[22] The fourteen nations invited to this conference were: Burma, Cambodia, Canada, Communist China, North Vietnam, France, India, Laos, Poland, South Vietnam, Thailand, the Soviet Union, the United Kingdom, and the United States.

countries represented favored a coalition government headed by Prince Souvanna Pouma and including both the rightist faction of Poumi Nosavan and the Communist faction of Prince Soupanouvong. As the conference progressed, the real question was whether this solution could be brought about without endangering the ceasefire.

The key to the outcome of the Geneva Conference was the attitudes of the two major powers involved in the Laotian problem—the Soviet Union and the United States. If between them an understanding could be reached to remove Laos as an area of confrontation, it was believed that peace could soon be established in this hapless kingdom. The British were convinced that the Soviets did not want a war over Laos, and that they would settle for something less than a complete victory there. The United States had indicated on many occasions since President Kennedy assumed office that it was prepared to negotiate if the fighting stopped. Therefore, when it was announced that Chairman Khrushchev and President Kennedy would meet in Vienna in June, it was assumed that Laos would be one of the questions they would take up. By this time the Geneva Conference had reached an impasse, and all the representatives now waited for word from Vienna before resuming discussions. On June 4 a joint communiqué from Vienna indicated that the American and the Soviet leaders had agreed that Laos should be neutralized under an international agreement, and that an effective ceasefire was essential. The short statement read:

The President and the Chairman reaffirmed their support of a neutral and independent Laos under a government chosen by the Laotians themselves, and of international agreements for insuring that neutrality and independence, and in this connection they have recognized the importance of an effective cease-fire.[23]

[23]*Department of State Bulletin,* June 26, 1961, p. 999.

In his subsequent report to the American people, President Kennedy emphasized the "critical importance" of a ceasefire to the success of the Geneva Conference and said that he hoped his agreement with the Soviet leader would be translated into progress at Geneva within a few days. The implication of this statement was that the President had obtained a commitment from Khrushchev that the fighting would stop permanently in Laos, and that the country would be neutralized by international agreement. But the question of what had been agreed to regarding the composition of the Laotian government was not answered in the public statements, except that a government should be "chosen by the Laotians themselves." The Thai government and many others took this to mean a government headed by Prince Souvanna and including both rightist and Pathet Lao representatives. When the Geneva Conference resumed a short time later, the agreement reached at Vienna seemed to clear the way for final negotiations covering the future of Laos. The major problem remaining was how to persuade the three Laotian factions to form a coalition government so that the international agreement could be ratified. Bringing the Laotian factions together consumed a whole year of effort on the part of the great powers; but once the American and Soviet leaders had reached their understanding at Vienna, it became only a matter of time until they agreed on a coalition government headed by Souvanna Pouma.

An important aspect of the Geneva Conference of 1961 was the relative harmony in which the three Western powers in SEATO worked. The British and the French had been opposed to United States intervention in Laos during the Bangkok meeting of the SEATO Council; but once the United States decided to negotiate, these two governments strongly supported it on the matter of an effective ceasefire and on most other points of conflict with the Communist powers. The Soviet Union and Communist China also appeared to work in harmony, despite much speculation that Soviet intervention with an airlift to support the Pathet Lao was motivated by the fear that if the Chinese controlled the situation, they might let it get out of hand. Fifield discounts this view, saying that although there was at this time some rivalry between Khrushchev and Mao over spheres of influence, it should not be exaggerated. "Peking and Moscow operated as a team" at the Geneva Conference, and "the Soviet airlift was certainly facilitated by Chinese cooperation." Moreover, he states, the Soviet role in Laos was consistent with Communist doctrine on support of wars of national liberation.[24]

A major problem faced by the United States, once it had decided not to risk war in Laos, was how to obtain the acquiescence of its Asian allies to a negotiated settlement which probably would be viewed as a reversal of previous United States policy in Southeast Asia. Not only was Thailand, but the Philippines, South Vietnam, Nationalist China, and Pakistan were all shocked by what they believed to be a significant sign of American weakness in the face of Communist pressure in Asia. It was therefore imperative that the Kennedy administration take immediate steps to reassure its Asian allies that it was not withdrawing American power from Southeast Asia but was merely trying to extricate itself from an impossible situation in Laos—which was not a member of SEATO and was not considered vital to the defense of Southeast Asia. For this difficult assignment President Kennedy selected Vice-President Lyndon Johnson. While Secretary of State Rusk and Ambassador-at-large Harriman went to Geneva in May to try to salvage what they could at the conference table, Mr. Johnson visited Saigon, Manila,

[24]Fifield, op. cit., p. 195.

Taipei, Bangkok, New Delhi, and Karachi on a mission to sell the American policy in Laos to a disillusioned and frustrated group of Asian leaders (excepting Nehru) who could not understand and greatly feared the change in United States policy. Mr. Johnson's trip was helpful in restoring confidence in American steadfastness; but even with all his persuasive skills, the Vice-President was not able to dispel the growing concern among Asian leaders that the United States' mantle of protection—which had secured the safety of their countries for nearly seven years—was now about to be slowly withdrawn. This fear haunted those governments of Asia that had placed so much faith in the policy pronouncements of Washington during the nineteen-fifties and, to a lesser extent, those governments that had chosen neutralism in the Cold War. American presence and determination to use its power to prevent Communist advances in Southeast Asia was the best guarantee these nations had of retaining their newly won independence. Now they doubted whether the United States would be willing to exert its vast power and influence to keep Southeast Asia free.

Disillusionment in Thailand

When during the latter part of April the Thai government understood that the United States was not prepared to risk war in Laos by moving American troops into that country, its leaders privately expressed much unhappiness. Publicly, however, the Thai government was careful not to criticize the United States, for it still had some hope that the latter might be firm enough at the conference table to bring about a solution that it could accept: a solution that would prevent the Communists from gaining control over all of Laos. The critical question was whether the Communists would agree to a genuine ceasefire before the Pathet Lao forces had occupied many strategic locations, which they could use for future operations against the government forces. Therefore, when the British and Soviet ambassadors in Bangkok presented the Foreign Minister with a copy of their ceasefire agreement, Tanat Khoman expressed hope that the cessation of hostilities would be effective soon and that it would be a permanent arrangement. Also, when Thailand was invited to attend the fourteen-nation meeting in Geneva, the initial reaction was favorable. However, the government made it clear that it was opposed to any partition of Laos as well as to a coalition government in which the Pathet Lao participated because it believed this would be a prelude to an eventual takeover of the country by the Communists. By the end of April, when it was obvious that the Pathet Lao forces were pressing their military advantage and had not yet agreed to a ceasefire, the Thai government issued a statement declaring that it would not participate in the Geneva Conference unless there was a verified ceasefire, and unless a stop was put to the supplying of arms to the Pathet Lao forces. The Foreign Ministry's statement reflected the government's deep anxiety over the drift of events in Laos:

It is, therefore, clear that the communists' main objective is to expand their area of occupation in Laos with a view to gaining political advantage and tightening their political stand at the forthcoming 14-nation conference. A parallel may be drawn from the communists' vital victory seven years ago at Dien Bien Phu, which was achieved just one day before the Geneva Conference of 1954 began.[25]

When the Pathet Lao finally agreed to a ceasefire early in May, the attention of the Thai government turned to the ground rules of the Geneva Conference. It was deeply afraid that the conference would be dominated by the Communists,

[25]*Bangkok World*, April 29, 1961, pp. 1, 14.

because half the nations that were invited to attend the meeting were Communist or Neutralist. Therefore the Thai government sought to increase the number of participants and to include two more Asian nations having an interest in the Laotian question—namely, Indonesia and Malaya. The question of the Laotian representation was also important to the Thai government; and when it appeared that the three Laotian factions would not be able to agree on a new government and send one representative to Geneva, Thailand was strongly opposed to any arrangement under which the Pathet Lao representative would sit at the conference table. Thai leaders expressed support for a proposal that the Lao King form a provisional government and send his representative to the conference. It was in this charged atmosphere that Vice-President Johnson arrived in Bangkok in mid-May for talks with Prime Minister Sarit.

Prime Minister Sarit greeted the Vice-President on May 16 with the statement that his visit at this time could not fail to have a deep significance. He obviously hoped to obtain a commitment from the Vice-President that Laos would not be partitioned, and that the United States would not agree to a coalition government that included the Pathet Lao. Mr. Johnson carefully avoided being drawn into a commitment on Laos, but he reaffirmed in strong terms American determination to protect Thailand. He also offered greater United States military and economic assistance to Thailand to help it to strengthen itself to meet the increased danger of Communist subversion. But nowhere in the joint communiqué issued at the conclusion of the discussions was there any mention of Laos. The closest these leaders came to this was a statement that "the Vice-President and the Prime Minister rededicated themselves to work for an honorable peace in Southeast Asia." The whole emphasis was on the defense of Thailand:

"The United States Government expressed its determination to honor its treaty commitments to support Thailand—its ally and historic friend—in defense against subversion and communist aggression." Also both governments "reiterated their determination to fulfill their SEATO commitments" and to work in close partnership.[26] During the conference, a press report stated that the Vice-President had offered American troops to Thailand to help defend the country, but that Marshal Sarit had turned down this suggestion. This report was denied; but some days later, when a newsman asked Sarit about it, he said that the suggestion had been made by several persons, but that "we don't want to agree to that because the Thai people will not like it." He asserted, "We support the sending of SEATO troops into Laos if the Geneva conference fails, but we do not want troops based in our country."[27]

Although the Thai government welcomed the Vice-President's visit and his reassurance of American support, it was disappointed that he was not specific about American intentions in Laos. At the conclusion of the talks Marshal Sarit told the press that he was only partially satisfied with the outcome. He was pleased, he said, that the United States fully guaranteed Thailand's territorial integrity, but he was disappointed that a similar guarantee was not given in the case of Laos, which Thailand considered very important to its own security. It seemed clear that Thai leaders, on the eve of the Foreign Minister's departure for Geneva, were still deeply concerned over what would happen to Laos as a result of that conference.

Foreign Minister Tanat Khoman arrived late at the Geneva Conference and was the last of the representatives to present his country's views. In his speech to the meeting he forcefully

[26]*Department of State Bulletin,* June 19, 1961, pp. 958–9.
[27]*Bangkok Post,* May 31, 1961, p. 1.

presented Thailand's position on the Laotian question. After calling for an end of violations to the ceasefire agreement, he strongly recommended that only the representative of the Laotian government be seated at the conference. Tanat declared that Thailand could not accept any decision of the conference to admit representatives from other Laotian factions, and he said that the meeting had "started on the wrong foot" by making concessions to the Communists on this point. The Foreign Minister said that Thailand had a deep historical interest in Laos, and that "Our sole desire has been to see a free, united and independent Laos, because on those conditions alone can Thailand feel secure from any threat to her own freedom and independence from that direction." Tanat proposed that Indonesia and Malaya be represented at the conference and participate in the work of the International Control Commission. Thailand was strongly in favor of a neutral Laos, he asserted, but it wished to be sure that this neutrality would not be used as a guise for the eventual control of the country by one faction. Finally, he suggested that a guaranteed neutrality such as that given to Austria might be the solution for Laos.[28]

Early in June the Thai government came to the conclusion that the Geneva Conference was moving toward a solution that would be unacceptable to Thailand. Also, the conference had not taken up the proposals put before it by Tanat Khoman. In addition, the Pathet Lao forces continued to improve their military position by making small advances in sporadic engagements. What finally caused the withdrawal of the Thai delegation was the growing suspicion that the conference was moving toward agreement on a coalition government that

[28]Collection of Principal Speeches of Foreign Minister Tanat Khoman, Bangkok, Ministry of Foreign Affairs, December 1961, pp. 44–54.

would include Communists in key positions without adequately safeguarding against their eventual control of the whole country. The Thai government was convinced that the Pathet Lao would ally itself with Souvanna Pouma against the rightist members in any coalition government and would soon turn Laos into a Communist satellite. On June 16 General Surachit Charuserani, Minister of Agriculture and also Director General of the Thai Public Relations Department, made an important statement that appeared to reflect the thinking of Prime Minister Sarit. Surachit said that the Pathet Lao now controlled most of Laos, and that if it was permitted to enter a coalition government, it would surely have the decisive voice in determining government policy. Asked whether SEATO forces would be used to check the Communist advance, he said that SEATO could not act without a request from the Laotian government; and that if it did send troops into Laos, there was great danger that the Chinese would intervene massively. The hopelessness of the situation, in General Surachit's view, was that "it is now too late for SEATO to do anything in connection with the Laotian crisis. Also, it is too late for the Laotian problem to be solved by political means. If any remedial measures to the situation were to be taken at all, it should have been taken while Captain Kong Lae was still in control." He was fearful that the International Control Commission, which had been sent to Laos to supervise the ceasefire, might have to withdraw its personnel because they had not been permitted to carry out their instructions. Speaking of the United States and its policy, Surachit said:

At the moment, Thailand feels that the western nations, especially the United States, are more interested in solving the Berlin problem than the Laotian problem. If one is forced to choose between Europe and Asia, one will choose Europe—an industrialized area which has greater military power than Asia. Asia has almost nothing.[29]

The Thai delegation returned to Geneva late in June and eventually agreed to accept in principle a coalition government in Laos with Pathet Lao representation. Thereafter the Thai government was principally concerned about what this solution would mean in terms of Thailand's security. Late in May a widespread Communist plot had been uncovered in the northeast area of Thailand along the Laotian border; its purpose was to detach that area from Thailand and join it with a Communist-dominated Laos. More than one hundred arrests were made, and two leaders of the conspiracy were executed. At the same time, it was reported that a Thai Exile Organization comprising several hundred men had been formed in the Communist part of Laos, and that they were being prepared for infiltrating Thailand after Laos was safely under Communist domination. These stories received wide publicity in Thailand and undoubtedly added to the apprehension that already existed about what would happen to Thailand if Laos were brought under the influence of North Vietnam and Communist China. Despite the strong assurances of the United States—including a personal letter from President Kennedy to King Poumipon—Thai leaders in June 1961 were not convinced that Thailand could survive the pressures that would build up along its borders if the Communists were successful in turning Laos into a leftist-leaning neutral country.

In a speech delivered to the American Association of Thailand on July 19, 1961, Foreign Minister Tanat Khoman deplored the Western powers' preoccupation with the developing Berlin crisis, which he believed was not so serious a

[29]*Seri Thai,* June 16, 1961. *Thai Press Summary* (translation), U.S.I.S., Bangkok.

threat to world peace as was the situation in Laos. Tanat was convinced that Laos would serve as an excellent jumping-off point for any power that planned to extend its control over Southeast Asia, and he believed that such efforts were already under way. The first step by the Communists was to undermine the Western position in that part of the world, and he thought that their efforts were being "greatly facilitated by the apparent lack of interest felt by the West and its unwillingness to assume direct responsibility." After Western influence had been undermined, he continued, the Communists would then impress on all the small nations of the area the inevitability of the "new order" in the area and of the desirability for them to cooperate fully with the future rulers. If any nation tried to resist the inevitable, military pressure and subversion would be used to bring the recalcitrants into line; large military forces would be held in readiness in case any nation called for help from outside or decided to fight rather than submit peacefully to the aggressor. Tanat felt that the situation was grim indeed, and that it was further aggravated "by those who want to be friendly but whose lack of interest and responsibility, indecisiveness, and even unwitting detractions contribute to bringing about the present deterioration and, God forbid, to the ultimate stage when all of us around here may be nibbled to death or simply gnawed to the bone." Tanat concluded his gloomy forecast by saying that Thailand had in the past relied too heavily for its security on nations far away from Asia, and that it should now place greater emphasis on its own resources and on building up closer ties with other Asian nations.[30] Few who heard this important statement of Thai foreign policy

[30]Collection of Principal Speeches of Foreign Minister Tanat Khoman, *op. cit.*, pp. 59–67.

doubted that a re-evaluation of that policy was then under way in the Thai government.

Effect on Thai-American Relations

By the summer of 1961 Thailand's confidence in the United States and in the SEATO alliance as a means of ensuring the security of Southeast Asia had reached a low point. The Thai attitude was commonly described as a "crisis of confidence," and many observers wondered what would result from the reappraisal that Marshal Sarit and his government were forced to undertake of Thailand's foreign policy since 1950. On May 11, 1961, a *New York Times* report from Bangkok indicated that there was a strong trend toward neutralism in official Thai circles; and although this story was officially denied by the Interior Minister, General Prapat, there was little doubt that SEATO and then United States inaction in the face of continued Pathet Lao advances in Laos caused many Thai leaders to question whether SEATO was not a "paper tiger," as the Communists had claimed.

The root of the crisis in Thai-American relations lay in the political overcommitment of the United States in Laos in 1960 and 1961; and when the critical situation precipitated by the Kong Lae coup in August 1960 forced the United States to take a hard look at its vital interest in Southeast Asia, neither the Eisenhower nor the Kennedy administration was willing to risk a major war to retain Laos as a strongly pro-Western stronghold. That the United States government vacillated for nearly four months in 1960 before giving its support to General Poumi in his effort to retake Vientiane was indicative of the deep division over United States policy in Laos that existed in Washington under the Eisenhower administration; and this division was equally sharp in the spring of 1961, when President Kennedy was faced with an even more difficult decision: whether or not to commit American troops to the defense of Laos. In both instances the debate revolved around the question whether the long-term cost and the short-term risks involved in preserving a pro-Western government in Laos were small enough to warrant committing American power to this area at a time when the Congo, Berlin, and Cuba were also major testing grounds of American and Soviet strength and will. The United States considered the possibility of accepting a neutral government headed by Prince Souvanna Pouma in the autumn of 1960 and then abandoned it; a few months later it was forced to give renewed thought to this alternative. One can only speculate whether the Eisenhower administration would have handled the 1961 crisis in a different way than did President Kennedy; the hard fact is that when Kennedy received conflicting counsel from his military advisers and was faced with nearly unanimous opposition to intervention from congressional representatives of both political parties, as well as strong disapproval from both of his European allies in SEATO, he found it difficult to decide in favor of sending American forces into Laos for an indefinite period and with no assurance that the Chinese would not also intervene as they had done in Korea. The irony of the Laotian crisis of 1960–1961 was that the United States was forced in the end to accept a much less satisfactory arrangement—a coalition government with Communists in it and half of the country under Communist military control—than it could have had in August–September 1960, when Souvanna Pouma was prepared to keep the Communists out of his coalition government, and when the Pathet Lao controlled only a small area.

For Thailand it would not be unfair to say that its government probably went too far in assuming that the United States would go to war to maintain a pro-Western government in Laos. Thailand's obsession with maintaining a friendly government in Vientiane caused it to believe that only Poumi Nosavan was capable of preserving Thailand's interests and that the neutralism of Souvanna Pouma was only a step along the road to Communist domination of Laos. From 1958 to 1960 Thailand was successful in persuading the United States of the correctness of this view; and so long as the United States agreed, the Thais were not concerned about what the British and French thought. When the United States began to waver, however—in August 1960 and again in April 1961—Thailand's bold position became untenable; thereafter its confidence in the United States began to decline as it realized that American policy might not always support its point of view on Laos. This was especially so when Poumi Nosavan's rightist forces, in which Thai leaders had placed such great faith, proved to be militarily and politically unequal to the task of defending the country against sustained Pathet Lao pressure. The major flaw in Thailand's policy was the assumption that the United States would support a pro-Western government in Laos under all circumstances, and that it considered the defense of Laos identical with the defense of Thailand. This assumption proved wrong when the Laotian crisis was dealt with in Washington in April and May 1961. It might be said that Thai policy was based to a large extent on wishful thinking—namely, that it could expect American support in every instance in Laos, regardless of the circumstances prevailing there at any given time. The reality of the situation, as the events of 1961 demonstrated, was that the United States, like any other great power, was not willing to let its policy, in a critical situation involving its armed forces, be determined by another country's national interest. In the case of Laos, the national interests of Thailand and the United States finally diverged because the latter was unwilling to accept the risk of a major war in defense of an area that it was not pledged to defend. In Korea in 1950, a somewhat similar situation existed, and the United States intervened. In Laos, where the aggression was much less flagrant and more difficult to cope with, the United States chose not to become involved militarily.

But even if one accepts the view that Thailand was under some illusion in thinking that the United States would put troops into Laos, there remained the key question that Thais felt they had a right to ask: Would the United States and the other SEATO allies be prepared to defend Thailand if the Communists used the same piecemeal tactics in launching subversion and guerrilla warfare against Thailand? If SEATO remained inactive in Laos because there was no outright aggression, what would it do if Thailand were not openly attacked but was threatened by Thai Communist guerrillas trained and supported by the Pathet Lao and Viet-Minh across the Mekong? It was this threat that brought Thailand into SEATO in 1954, and in the spring of 1961 it appeared that the Communists were increasing their infiltration in the vulnerable northeastern provinces of Thailand.

For Thailand, therefore, Laos was a barometer of Western intentions in Southeast Asia. If the West took a strong stand to preserve a non-Communist government in Vientiane, Thailand was confident that its own borders would be protected. When, however, the West faltered in Laos and began to compromise in 1960 and 1961, Thai leaders feared that Western will had begun to erode, and that eventually these nations would not be able or willing to hold back the Communist menace in Southeast Asia. It was this fear, this uncertainty of long-term American steadfastness in resisting Asian Communism, that the United States sought to overcome in the months and years following the retreat from the brink of war in Laos.

Chapter 7

Reappraisal and Readjustment in the Alliance

THE failure of the SEATO powers, particularly the United States, to take strong action to stop the Communist offensive in Laos during the first half of 1961 resulted in disillusionment and deep anxiety in Thailand. This led to a reappraisal of Thai foreign policy, the effects of which have been felt down to the present day. If Thai leaders had previously erred in their estimate that the United States would support Thai policy in Laos under all circumstances, there was danger during the latter half of 1961 and early 1962 that in their frustration they might swing too far in the opposite direction and assume that the United States could not be counted upon to halt the Communists under any circumstances. The statements and actions of the Thai government during this period indicated a certain schizophrenia, resulting from its uncertainty over how to deal with the multitude of problems that seemed to plague the nation in the wake of the Laotian crisis. The government began to dramatize the subversive threat that Laos represented, and gave full publicity to the uncovering of Communist cells and Communist activity in the north and northeast sections of Thailand. There were renewed

discussions with the Soviet ambassador in Bangkok concerning trade and cultural exchanges, and there was increasing
talk of an "independent" Thai foreign policy and even of
neutralism as an alternative to the SEATO alliance. The
government's frustration was exacerbated by the behavior of
Cambodia's chief of state, Prince Sihanouk, who seemed to
Thai leaders to be following the traditional Cambodian policy
of attacking Thailand when the latter was under pressure
from another quarter. The reaction in Thailand to Sihanouk's
emotional outburst showed its nervousness and tension during the autumn of 1961 and resulted in the breaking of diplomatic relations between the two countries.[1]

The mounting Berlin crisis in Europe and the prolonged
Geneva negotiations over the Laotian problem contributed
to Bangkok's anxiety about Thailand's exposed position in
the Cold War. This anxiety was magnified by the growing
Communist menace in South Vietnam, as Thai leaders were
not certain whether the United States would be as weak in
dealing with this threat as they believed it had been in meeting the Communist challenge in Laos. SEATO, the Thai
government had concluded, was nearly useless so long as the
unanimity rule prevailed in cases where individual members
wanted to deal with security threats to the former Indochina
states. Prime Minister Sarit stated the Thai case strongly in

[1]In his address to the nation on the third anniversary of the October
20, 1958, revolution, Prime Minister Sarit leveled a broadside against
the Cambodian leader, causing Cambodia to break diplomatic relations.
Sarit did not mention Sihanouk or Cambodia by name, but it was clear
whom he meant when he said, "Patience means forbearing the annoying
accusations and arrogance of a Head of a State who has constantly made
himself known as an enemy of Thailand." He said Thailand had to
"exercise restraint and to condone such arrogance by taking for con-
solation the old proverbial tale of a pig challenging a lion to a fight."
See Thailand, *Foreign Affairs Bulletin,* October–November 1961, p. 7.

a speech commemorating the seventh anniversary of the signing of the Manila Pact:

Some countries take only a lukewarm interest [in SEATO ideals
and objectives] as their real interest and worries are elsewhere.
So they are reluctant to take on additional responsibilities in this
part of the world. That is why they have been endeavoring to
dissuade SEATO from any attempt to do what by right it should
have done. As a result, instead of setting about our work in
complete unison we have before us a sad spectacle of filibustering,
contention and working at cross purposes.

Sarit said that he did not share the view of some who thought
that SEATO should be scrapped altogether, but he did think
the organization needed to be refashioned

in such a way as to inject into it a new sense of purposefulness
and dedication, to make it an organization composed of members
who completely share the same thoughts and interests, the same
hopes and aspirations, whose fundamental goal is to safeguard
and maintain peace and welfare in South East Asia and who are
ready to make common sacrifices to build up a bastion against
the impending danger.

If such changes could be brought about in the organization,
Sarit said, "it would definitely be the answer to our most
solemn prayer."[2]

On the diplomatic front this matter of reforming SEATO
to permit individual states to act without the prior agreement
of all other members became the vital question for Thailand
insofar as its relations with the United States were concerned.
When Foreign Minister Tanat Khoman was in the United
States in September to attend the United Nations General
Assembly session, he also conferred for several days in Washington with American leaders. The uppermost subject for
discussion was Thailand's demand that the United States give

[2]Thailand, *Foreign Affairs Bulletin*, August–September 1961, pp. 62–3.

an unequivocal guarantee to defend Thailand if Pathet Lao forces renewed their drive toward the Mekong, regardless of what other SEATO nations decided. The Thai government asked from the United States what it had sought and failed to obtain in 1954 at the time the Manila Pact was signed— namely, an American commitment to defend Thailand if it were in imminent danger of Communist attack. Without such a formal guarantee Thai leaders feared that what had happened in Laos could also happen in Thailand. Thailand really wanted a bilateral alliance with the United States, but it was willing to settle for any arrangement that ensured that the United States would act independently of SEATO, if necessary, to halt the further advance of Communist power in Southeast Asia. Thailand did not obtain this commitment from the United States in 1961; but it made its case abundantly clear to Washington, and there was a hint that unless Thailand obtained a guarantee of its own security, it would refuse to cooperate with the United States in its efforts to bring about a coalition government in Laos.

After drawing back from the possibility of war in Laos in April and May 1961, the United States also began to reassess its policy in Southeast Asia. One of its chief concerns was how to reassure Thailand of American determination to honor its pledge to defend that country without committing itself also to preserve a pro-Western government in Laos. Vice-President Johnson had emphasized American determination to defend Thailand during his visit in May, and this was followed by efforts to increase the military and economic strength of Thailand to meet threats to its security. President Kennedy, in his address to the United Nations General Assembly, cited Southeast Asia and Berlin as the two areas where real threats to world peace existed. Asserting that the Communists' guerrilla tactics in Laos and Vietnam had nothing to do with "wars of liberation" but represented outright aggression on sovereign states, the President said: "The very simple question confronting the world community is whether measures can be devised to protect the small and weak from such tactics. For if they are successful in Laos and South Viet-Nam, the gates will be opened wide." Warning that the end of the rainy season in Laos might see the renewal of fighting there, he concluded that "the world community must recognize—all those who are involved—that this potent threat to Laotian peace and freedom is indivisible from all other threats to their own."[3] Such words were reassuring to Thai leaders who had begun to fear that the United States was so preoccupied in Berlin and the Congo that the crisis in Southeast Asia must take second place; but they wondered whether these words would be translated into a firmer United States policy in Asia.

In October 1961 President Kennedy sent his special assistant on military matters, General Maxwell Taylor, to South Vietnam to appraise the deteriorating military situation there; afterward Taylor went to Bangkok for consultations with Prime Minister Sarit and other top Thai officials. Both the United States and the Thai governments attached the greatest importance to General Taylor's survey of the military situation in Southeast Asia. In Washington, Secretary of State Rusk told a press conference that the threats to the security of Laos and Vietnam were matters of great concern to other countries in that area, such as Thailand and Cambodia. "We are looking forward to General Taylor's report with the greatest possible interest," he said.[4] When it was announced some weeks later that the United States would give large-scale assistance to South Vietnam to help it to defeat the Viet Cong insurgency, Thai leaders were pleased and took this as a sign

[3]*Department of State Bulletin,* October 16, 1961, p. 623.
[4]*Department of State Bulletin,* November 6, 1961, p. 750.

of a toughening United States policy in Southeast Asia generally.

At the beginning of 1962 Thailand's attention was once again focused on Laos. After long discussions and negotiations the Geneva Conference had reached agreement on all important aspects of a settlement of the Laotian problem; but final agreement awaited the formation of a coalition government in Vientiane which could represent that nation at the conference table. Negotiations among the three factions—rightists, Neutralists, and Pathet Lao—had produced an agreement in principle that Prince Souvanna Pouma would be acceptable as Prime Minister of a coalition government; but the crucial question was which faction would get the posts of Minister of Defense, Interior, and Finance. The rightists insisted on controlling both the Defense and the Interior ministries, but the Pathet Lao refused to agree to such an arrangement. A Lao "summit" meeting among the princes representing the three factions (Boon Oum, Souvanna Pouma, and Soupanouvong) in December 1961 broke down after Prince Boon Oum, representative of the conservative faction, refused a compromise proposal to turn over these two ministries to Souvanna Pouma. This deadlock on the political front was followed within a few weeks by renewed Communist military pressure on government-held positions in northern Laos, and many observers believed that the Communists were fully prepared to break the ceasefire and use military force to achieve their objectives at the conference table. General Tanom Kittikachorn, Thailand's Minister of Defense, told the press that he did not understand why United States officials favored turning over both the Defense and Interior ministries to the Neutralist faction, saying that it was puzzling to him to see the United States giving large-scale assistance to South Vietnam to fight the Communists while in Laos it refused to support the Laotian government's position.[5]

The military situation in Laos became serious in February, when Pathet Lao forces with Viet-Minh support began a build-up in the northern Laotian province of Nam Ta, bordering on China. Thai forces were alerted, and on February 13 units of the Thai army were deployed to strategic areas near the Laotian border. The movement was carried out swiftly, and the government kept secret the locations and the numbers of troops involved. This was the first time since 1940 that army units had been moved to the Laotian border, and it indicated how seriously the government viewed the renewed Communist pressure in Laos, especially in an area so close to Thailand's northern border. The government justified its action by asserting that developments in Laos, especially the attack launched by the pro-Communist forces against the town of Nam Ta, threatened the security of Thailand and constituted a violation of the ceasefire agreement. The Thai government believed that if such an attack were to succeed, "the security of this country and the welfare of the Thai people may seriously be affected."[6]

This movement of troops, which reportedly was decided upon without consultation with the United States or SEATO, served notice that Thailand would not wait for foreign assistance before taking whatever action it deemed necessary to safeguard its security in the face of renewed Communist pressure in Laos. The action also set the stage for a later request for SEATO action if Communist forces pressed their attack to the Thai border.

Within a week of the Thai government's action, Attorney General Robert Kennedy visited Bangkok as a stage of his

[5]*Bangkok Post,* January 18, 1962, p. 1.
[6]Thailand, *Foreign Affairs Bulletin,* February–March 1962, p. 65.

journey to various Asian countries. Prime Minister Sarit used the occasion to impress on the President's brother the seriousness with which the Thai government viewed the renewed fighting in Laos, and sought to elicit from him some idea of what the United States government was prepared to do to support Thailand if its security was endangered. In a discussion with a group of university students, Mr. Kennedy insisted that the United States would stand by its commitments to defend Thailand; but he also made it clear that the Thais must have the will to defend themselves and to take whatever steps were required to build unity within their nation in the face of danger. In an obvious reference to Laos, Mr. Kennedy said: "All we can do is help. . . . If the people aren't interested, no matter what the United States or what some outside power does it is not going to make a difference." He added, "We are convinced that the people of Thailand want to preserve their independence and that is why there is this close relationship."[7]

United States Guarantee of Thailand's Security

At the end of February 1962, Foreign Minister Tanat Khoman was invited to Washington to discuss with President Kennedy and top American officials ways in which Thailand's security could be ensured within the SEATO framework. Before leaving Thailand, Tanat held a press conference and reiterated Thailand's anxiety over the political pressure being exerted by the United States and other powers on the Laotian government to join a coalition with the Pathet Lao. He said that although Thailand and the United States were agreed on basic objectives in Laos, they differed on methods in dealing with the situation there. "For us the stakes are indeed high," Tanat warned. "Others, further away, can afford to be more generous and liberal. It is no secret that we feel the

[7]Thailand, *Foreign Affairs Bulletin*, February–March 1962, p. 67.

situation in Laos is critical. If anything happens there, it affects Thailand directly." He criticized countries that claimed "to be Thailand's friends" but did not want to take the situation at Nam Ta seriously, because they failed to see that the aggression there was something new. "It is a new kind of imperialism which is serious and which can spread out violently, not only through all of Laos, but all over the region, because of the force and power behind it."[8] Thailand's frustration was dramatized when it was reported that Prime Minister Sarit had turned down a plan for holding a SEATO exercise in Thailand. According to press reports, Sarit believed that SEATO was spending too much time holding maneuvers and not taking effective measures to hold back the Communists in Laos.

Perhaps these and other statements by Thai officials were designed to enhance Thailand's bargaining position when Tanat held his important talks in Washington; but, in the opinion of this writer, the fears and frustrations expressed by the Thai government at this time were genuine. If the Communists succeeded in taking Nam Ta without provoking SEATO into military action, the Thais reasoned that they would then be emboldened to prepare for action against Thailand itself. In this situation, where Thai leaders believed that the safety of their own territory was at stake, they were prepared to act with or without SEATO's support, just as Prime Minister Sarit had predicted in September 1960, when the situation in Laos first began to deteriorate. Now, of course, the situation was much worse, and the critical question for Thailand, as it had been in April and May 1961, was how the United States would react, and what it was prepared to do to guarantee Thailand's security if the Communists continued to push.

[8]*Bangkok World,* February 24, 1962, p. 1.

The Foreign Minister spent five days in consultation with United States government officials, and on March 6 he held a forty-minute discussion with President Kennedy. The President assured Thailand of full United States support for its independence and territorial integrity, and he pledged American determination to meet any Communist attack on Thailand without requiring the prior agreement of other SEATO countries. This assurance was formalized in a joint statement issued the same day by Secretary of State Dean Rusk and Foreign Minister Tanat Khoman. The two key paragraphs of the statement said:

The Secretary of State reaffirmed that the United States regards the preservation of the independence and integrity of Thailand as vital to the national interest of the United States and to world peace. He expressed the firm intention of the United States to aid Thailand, its ally and historic friend, in resisting Communist aggression and subversion.

The second part read:

The Secretary of State assured the Foreign Minister that in the event of such aggression, the United States intends to give full effect to its obligations under the Treaty [SEATO] to act to meet the common danger in accordance with its constitutional processes. The Secretary of State reaffirmed that this obligation of the United States does not depend upon the prior agreement of all other parties to the Treaty, since this Treaty obligation is individual as well as collective.[9]

Other parts of the statement called attention to American efforts to help Thailand meet the threat of indirect aggression through economic and military assistance programs, cited agreement between the two governments on the necessity of achieving a "free, independent and truly neutral Laos," and

[9]*Department of State Bulletin,* March 26, 1962, p. 498. See also Thailand, *Foreign Affairs Bulletin,* February–March 1962, pp. 5–6.

recognized that "continued economic and social progress is essential to the stability of Thailand," and that Thailand would fully utilize its own resources in achieving economic and social progress. The United States agreed to give full support to Thailand's efforts to defend itself, but it also required a greater effort on the part of Thailand to increase the economic and social progress of the nation, in order to build national unity against the Communist internal threat.

The reaction in Thailand to this agreement was an emotional outpouring of praise and renewed confidence in the United States. The *Bangkok World* headlined its March 11 issue: "Premier Hails America as Thais' 'True Friend,' " in reference to the Prime Minister's report to the nation. Foreign Minister Tanat, whose prestige increased greatly as a result of his successful negotiations in Washington, said in a television interview that the United States pledge strengthened SEATO and increased Thai confidence in the organization. The Minister of Defense, General Tanom Kittikachorn, said: "It is good and suitable that the United States is willing to act on our behalf without consulting SEATO. There is much confusion in SEATO, and we cannot afford to wait in case of aggression. The assurance makes Thailand feel more secure."[10]

Prime Minister Sarit, in a nationwide radio and television address on March 10, spelled out why the Rusk–Tanat statement was so important to Thailand. Speaking of SEATO and its history, Sarit said:

During the seven years after its establishment, there had been some difficulties that prevented this Organization from being able to carry out effectively its tasks as it was expected. This fact has caused grave concern to Thailand because this country, being the outpost of the defense line of the Free World, must be the first to confront the danger.

[10]*Bangkok World,* March 9, 1962, p. 1.

On the matter of internal aggression through subversion, Sarit assured the nation that "the United States has also manifested its clear intention to support and contribute to our counter-measures in the same way as it is doing in South Viet-Nam at this moment." Praising the United States for its renewed pledge to Thailand, Sarit said: "All of you will agree with me that it is not so easy to find such a sincere friend who is concerned about our own well-being as the United States." He hoped that "This Joint Thai–U.S. Statement will stand as a symbol of the close and cordial relations which have long existed between the two countries and will further serve to promote the better understanding and cooperation between the peoples and Government of Thailand and the United States."[11] Several weeks later Sarit announced that the Australian Foreign Minister and the Philippine Foreign Minister had made statements in support of the United States position on obligations of members under SEATO, and these nations were also hailed as "true friends" of Thailand.

The Laotian political problem remained to be solved, however. The Pathet Lao, supported by an increasing number of Viet-Minh troops, were threatening to take Nam Ta and to push on to the Mekong River. Many observers believed that the United States had given its pledge to defend Thailand in return for assurance that the Thai government would use its influence with the Boon Oum–Poumi Nosavan faction in Laos to help bring about a coalition government among the three Laotian groups. It is not known whether the Thai government did in fact give the United States such an assurance; but the Rusk–Tanat declaration was a turning point in Thailand's attitude on the Laotian political problem and possibly was the key factor that caused the Thai government to accept, albeit reluctantly, the American plan to have Prince

[11]Thailand, *Foreign Affairs Bulletin*, February–March 1962, pp. 7–9.

Souvanna Pouma installed as head of a tripartite coalition government and to give him control of the disputed ministries—Defense and Interior.[12]

But it was one thing to obtain Thailand's agreement that Souvanna should lead a coalition government, and another to persuade the Laotian government headed by Prince Boon Oum to turn over the disputed ministries. To break the deadlock and to prevent the resumption of large-scale fighting— which the United States and Britain believed would ruin the chances of carrying out the Kennedy–Khrushchev Vienna agreement—the United States government sent the Assistant Secretary of State for Far Eastern Affairs, Averell Harriman, to Thailand and Laos. Harriman arrived in Bangkok on March 21 and then proceeded to Vientiane for talks with Laotian leaders. He had already seen Prince Souvanna in Rangoon. Prior to his arrival Thai officials were very wary of being used by the United States to persuade Boon Oum and Poumi Nosavan to join a coalition government, but after talking with him they showed some receptivity to the American point of view. In a press interview following a discussion with Harriman, Sarit indicated that they had reached agreement concerning a solution of the Laotian crisis, but that its implementation depended on certain actions being taken by both the Pathet Lao and the Laotian rightists, the most important being the complete cessation of fighting. Sarit admitted that Harriman had impressed on him the advisability of installing Souvanna Pouma as Premier and his conviction that Souvanna would not be dominated by the Communists. On the other hand, said Sarit, if events did not prove Harriman's assumption to be correct, the United States was pre-

[12]This view is held by Insor in his analysis of Thailand's policy at this time. (*Thailand: A Political, Social and Economic Analysis* [London, 1963], pp. 130–31.)

pared to take other actions to ensure the safety of the area, adding: "Mr. Harriman said he does not want Laos to fall into Communist hands. He said that America is taking actions concerning Laos because it has the interests of Thailand, its ally, at heart."[13]

The Assistant Secretary of State was less restrained than Sarit in his remarks to the press concerning the intransigence of General Poumi Nosavan. He indicated that all thirteen nations participating in the Geneva Conference were in agreement that Souvanna Pouma should be Premier in Laos, and that only Poumi was holding up final agreement by his refusal to turn over the two ministries of Defense and Interior to him. Harriman said, "We made it very plain that you could not have a viable government with either of these two wings [Pathet Lao or rightist] holding these two posts." The only solution, he insisted, was to deny control of both ministries to either side by putting them under Souvanna Pouma. Harriman said that the United States had suspended economic assistance to the Boon Oum government; and that if there were no agreement soon, military aid might also be cut off. "We do not have to support a government who does not follow the United States' policies," he asserted.[14]

Two days after Harriman's visit to Bangkok, the city editor of the *Bangkok Post,* who had exceptionally good contacts in the Foreign Ministry, wrote a front-page byline article in which he indicated that Thailand had lined up behind the United States position on Laos, with certain reservations: (1) the coalition government had to follow a genuinely neutral and independent policy; (2) that policy had to be effectively maintained in the future; (3) there would not be a *putsch* that would end in Communist domination of Laos. The Thai government, he wrote, did not believe that political or eco-

[13]*Bangkok Post,* March 26, 1962, p. 1.   [14]*Ibid.*

nomic pressure could force the rightist government to resign in favor of a coalition headed by Souvanna Pouma, but friendly persuasion might succeed if properly applied; Thailand would be prepared to do its part in helping to persuade the Laotians, but it did not want to press them on the composition of a coalition government, because the Laotians were a proud people and should be permitted to decide such matters themselves; Thailand would be prepared to support a government headed by Prince Souvanna Pouma on these conditions, but it continued to have reservations about Souvanna's ability to preserve his government's neutrality and prevent the Communists from dominating government policies; on this point, however, Thailand was willing to accept the judgment of the United States and Britain that Souvanna had a good chance of maintaining his independence, especially since the United States had given assurances that it would not allow the Communists to take over the whole country. According to the *Bangkok Post's* report, another factor in Thailand's decision to support the United States policy was the latter's belief that Soviet support for Souvanna Pouma as Prime Minister was based on its desire to prevent the Chinese from supporting a Communist government in Laos and pressing their offensive throughout Southeast Asia. Although Thailand was not so sure, this report said, that the Soviets and Chinese were working at cross purposes in Laos, the Thais were willing to give the American and British position a trial.

Whether the U.S. is right in its assessment of Prince Souvanna Phouma or of the likely turn of events in Laos remains to be seen. Thailand, mindful of the fall of small countries in Europe to the Communists, is watching the developments with anxiety. But, because Thailand alone cannot withstand a Communist onslaught and is aware of the U.S. obligation in this area, it is a risk that has to be taken.[15]

[15]*Bangkok Post*, March 28, 1962, p. 1.

By the end of March 1962, then, it seemed that Thailand and the United States were in agreement on measures for dealing with the Laotian problem, both politically and militarily, and that the Laotian rightists were isolated in their efforts to prevent Souvanna Pouma from assuming the premiership. Thai leaders were not enthusiastic about United States policy toward Laos, and they took every precaution to avoid giving the Laotian rightists the impression that Thailand had abandoned them. The American guarantee of Thailand's security and private American pledges that it would not permit the Communists to take over all of Laos were the main factors in bringing the Thai government into line with the United States position on Laos; but the American resolve still had to be tested before the Thais were convinced of the wisdom of their decision.

American Forces to Thailand and the Settlement in Laos

In April 1962 the Laotian military situation deteriorated considerably as the rightist faction continued its refusal to join a coalition government and the Pathet Lao with Viet-Minh support intensified its pressure on Nam Ta. Some observers believed that Poumi deliberately sought to provoke the Communists into a large-scale attack there so that he could then call on the United States for help to counter an open aggression by outside forces. In a showdown Poumi was said to be convinced that the United States would have to support him, just as it did in December 1960, when he forced Kong Lae's forces out of Vientiane.[16] The situation in 1962 differed

---

[16]Oliver Clubb writes that "the course followed by Boun Oum and Phoumi Nosavan indicated an attempt to scuttle the negotiated settlement, presumably in the expectation that if general hostilities were renewed, the United States would have no choice except to throw its full support behind their faction." (*The United States and the Sino-Soviet Bloc in Southeast Asia* [Washington, D.C., 1962], p. 67.)

from that of 1960, however, in that the Thai government was moving away from support for Poumi and into closer harmony with American efforts to bring about a coalition government, which most members of the Geneva Conference believed was the best hope of preventing Laos from setting off a larger war.

At the end of April a Laotian government delegation headed by Prince Boon Oum and including Poumi Nosavan went to Bangkok to obtain Thai support for its policy. The rightists were aware that the Sarit government was far from pleased at the prospect of having a neutralist coalition headed by Souvanna Pouma situated once again on its doorstep; and it therefore sought to exploit these misgivings by making an open and dramatic appeal for Thai support. Despite its private doubts over American policy on Laos, the Sarit government took a firm position on the question of further support for the rightist government. The day before Boon Oum arrived in Bangkok, the Director General of the Thai Public Relations Department, General Surachit, made a significant statement of the government's policy on Laos—the first public indication that Thailand now supported the United States position. Admitting that he could understand the anxiety of right-wing leaders about joining a coalition with the Pathet Lao, General Surachit said that the United States believed, after taking into account all factors—including the position of the Soviet Union—that a coalition government was the best alternative in Laos. "I therefore think that if an agreement is reached in line with the U.S. proposal, it would bring good results rather than bad," he continued. "If bad results follow this later, I believe that the U.S. will not deny its responsibility and might step in to solve the situation in time."[17] Following the Laotian visit, in which Prince Boon

[17] *Bangkok World,* April 25, 1962, p. 1.

Oum and his party were shown every courtesy, Generals Tanom and Prapat as well as Foreign Minister Tanat made statements indicating their belief that the visit would result in better relations between the United States and the Laotian rightist leaders. Thai leaders were careful to point out that they had brought no pressure to bear on the Laotians, but it was clear that the Thai government had counseled them to give the American plan a trial period. The government also showed its continuing friendship for Laos by making a gift of one thousand tons of rice and some building materials to the Lao government.

Before the effects of this Thai counsel could become known, however, the military situation in Laos took a turn for the worse in early May, when the Communists launched a heavy attack on Nam Ta and finally captured this outpost in northwest Laos near the Chinese border. Rightist forces retreated in disorderly fashion southward toward the Thai border; but, instead of regrouping and establishing a new defense line, possibly at Ban Houei Sai, the Laotian troops fled across the Mekong into Thai territory at Chiang Kham without making any attempt to engage the Communists. The government in Vientiane charged that Chinese troops had entered the battle for Nam Ta, and that government troops were badly outnumbered. It appears, however, that rightist forces were routed at Nam Ta by Pathet Lao and Viet-Minh forces and that they then fled eighty-five miles southward into Thailand. In so doing, the government forces abandoned much of northwestern Laos to the Communists and opened the way for the Pathet Lao to move down to the northern border of Thailand—an opportunity that the Communists did not choose to take. It was indeed a humiliating spectacle; and this episode convinced most observers, both Thai and American, that

General Poumi's forces would not stand up to the Communists in serious fighting.

Whatever the reasons for the collapse of the Royal Laotian Army, the event had a profound impact on the Thai government. Thailand charged that the Communists had deliberately broken the ceasefire at Nam Ta and were preparing to threaten the Thai border. As far as Thai leaders were concerned, the fall of Nam Ta could not be interpreted in any way other than that the Soviet Union was not willing, or able, to restrain the Communist forces in Laos, and that in this situation there was no possibility of reaching a political settlement. Thus, Thailand asked, in early May 1962, the same question it had put one year earlier: What was the United States prepared to do to stop the fighting in Laos and prevent the Communists from advancing to the Thai border?

The response of the United States was not long in coming. Secretary of Defense McNamara and Chairman of the Joint Chiefs of Staff Lemnitzer arrived in Bangkok on May 8 for urgent consultations with Thai leaders and then flew on to Saigon before returning to Washington. Within a week agreement was reached with the Thai government concerning the stationing of United States forces in Thailand. On May 17 a United States Marine Task Force of 1,800 men landed in Bangkok and was quickly transported to Udorn in northeast Thailand, only twenty-five miles from the Laotian border. The Marines were in addition to a thousand-man United States Army battle group that had participated in SEATO maneuvers in April but had remained at Korat because of the situation in Laos. This battle group was soon reinforced by additional troops flown in from Hawaii. Together with United States Air Force units and an army engineer battalion, the American military force in Thailand soon numbered more than 5,000 men, and it was clear that thousands more were prepared to move in if the situation in Laos warranted it. This was a dramatic show of power by the United States at a time when Thailand was convinced the Communists were about to swallow up Laos. Within a week of the arrival of American forces, the United Kingdom, Australia, and New Zealand sent small contingents of armed forces to Thailand to assist in its defense. It should be noted, however, that the Thai government was careful to avoid giving the impression, both before and after the arrival of the United States Marines, that either SEATO or Thai forces would be used in Laos. Thailand was as concerned as the United States about provoking the Chinese Communists into counter action in Laos. Thai leaders viewed the fact that Pathet Lao forces, following the fall of Nam Ta and the retreat of Poumi's troops from there into Thailand, had not pressed their advantage by moving into the area along the Mekong and on Thailand's border, as evidence that the Communist side was exercising considerable caution in this tense situation. Ban Houei Sai on the Mekong, for example, was not occupied by Communist forces even though it had been abandoned by government troops without a fight.[18]

The Thai and the American governments issued separate announcements concerning the agreement between them for the stationing of United States forces in Thailand. The communiqué issued by the Thai government on May 15 cited, as the reason for the action, that the Pathet Lao with the support of several Communist countries had "engaged itself in premeditated actions by the seizure of Muong Sing and Nam Tha in deliberate and flagrant violation of the ceasefire agreement"; and also that pro-Communist elements had

[18]The Thai government's caution at this time was outlined in a byline article by the city editor of the *Bangkok Post* entitled "Defense Without Provocation-Aim," which appeared to be based on reliable information from high government sources. (*Bangkok Post,* May 14, 1962, p. 1.)

pushed southward in the direction of the Thai border. Claiming that these circumstances constituted a threat to the security of Thailand and citing the Rusk-Tanat statement of March 6 and obligations under the SEATO treaty, the Thai communiqué declared that the governments had agreed that "some units of the United States forces be stationed in Thailand for the purpose of co-operating with the Thai Armed Forces in defending and preserving the peace and security of the Kingdom of Thailand."

The President's statement, issued the same day, said that following joint consideration by the two governments concerning the situation in Southeast Asia, "the Royal Thai Government has invited, and I have today ordered, additional elements of the United States military forces, both ground and air, to proceed to Thailand and to remain there until further orders. These forces are to help insure the territorial integrity of this peaceful country." The President emphasized that "this is a defensive act on the part of the United States and wholly consistent with the United Nations Charter." He reaffirmed that United States policy in Laos "continues to be the reestablishment of an effective cease-fire and prompt negotiations for a government of national union."[19] It is significant that the President's statement clearly indicated that there had been no change in American policy toward Laos; the implication was that United States forces had no purpose other than restoring peaceful conditions in which negotiations for a coalition government could proceed. In this way the President sought to reassure the Soviet Union and at the same time to warn the Chinese and North Vietnamese against further military action in Laos.

[19]The texts of both statements may be found in *Department of State Bulletin*, June 4, 1962, pp. 904–5, and in Thailand's *Foreign Affairs Bulletin*, April–May 1962, pp. 29–30.

Both the Thai and the United States statements emphasized that the action taken was in accordance with obligations assumed under the SEATO agreement of 1954; it was therefore interesting to note that the statement issued by the SEATO Council on May 16 simply took note of the United States and Thai action without giving any endorsement to it. Noting that the movement of American forces to Thailand "was entirely precautionary and defensive in character," the statement concluded with this innocuous sentence: "All SEATO member governments have on many occasions publicly stated their desire for a united independent Laos, with a truly neutral government, and for the establishment of an effective cease-fire."[20]

Despite General Poumi's last desperate efforts to win the support of various Asian countries for his stand against a coalition government, the defeat at Nam Ta and the diplomatic pressure from the United States finally brought him to the negotiating table early in June. On June 12, 1962, the three Laotian factions signed an agreement to form a coalition government with Prince Souvanna Pouma as Prime Minister and with his Neutralist faction holding the portfolios of Defense and Interior. After two more weeks of delay the new government finally came into being on June 23. In the cabinet of nineteen members, the Neutralists held eleven posts, and the rightists and the Pathet Lao held four each. General Poumi and Prince Soupanouvong were named Vice Premiers.

Thus, after a full year of fruitless efforts to carry out the intent of the Kennedy–Khrushchev agreement at Vienna, the three Laotian factions were persuaded to join in a "troika" political arrangement, which few people believed could work effectively but which nearly everyone agreed was the least dangerous solution to the Laotian problem. President Ken-

[20]*Department of State Bulletin,* June 4, 1962, p. 906.

nedy and Chairman Khrushchev expressed something of this sentiment in an exchange of letters on June 12. The Soviet leader was pleased that "good news has come from Laos" and hoped that the coalition government of Souvanna Pouma could be "the pivotal event both in the life of the Laotian people themselves and in the cause of strengthening peace in Southeast Asia." Asserting that the results achieved in Laos through cooperation among the powers was an example of how other international disputes might be settled, Khrushchev expressed satisfaction over the fact that "the mutual understanding we achieved while meeting in Vienna last June on the support of a neutral and independent Laos is beginning to be translated into life." In his reply President Kennedy agreed that the formation of a coalition government under Souvanna was "very encouraging," and that it marked a "milestone in the sustained efforts which have been put forward toward this end, especially since our meeting in Vienna." The President asked the Soviet leader to cooperate at the forthcoming Geneva Conference to bring about a final solution to the Laotian problem and to work together with the United States to implement the agreements. "I agree," said the President, "that continued progress in the settlement of the Laotian problem can be most helpful in leading toward the resolution of other international difficulties."[21] Both the United States and the Soviet Union were clearly pleased that their efforts had finally produced agreement on Laos and removed it, at least for the moment, as a major arena of international tension.

Thailand's Reaction to Laotian Settlement

If the Soviet and American leaders were pleased by the coalition government in Laos, the same could not be said

[21]*Department of State Bulletin,* July 2, 1962, p. 12.

for Thai leaders. Although earlier they had agreed with the
United States to support a coalition government and had
also indicated this view to the rightist government in Vientiane, they were nevertheless highly skeptical of the viability
of such a government and held serious doubts whether Souvanna would be able to resist the Pathet Lao, which clearly
had demonstrated its willingness to use military pressure
whenever political action did not achieve the desired results.
When the coalition was agreed upon,Thai leaders remained
noncommittal in public; but the press was less restrained.
The influential *Siam Rath* said in an editorial on June 14
that formation of the coalition government might stop the
fighting at least temporarily, but that the agreement was like
an armistice: the danger of civil war was still not over, and
the threat to neighboring countries therefore remained great.
Sarn Seri, Prime Minister Sarit's paper, asked editorially on
the same day whether Souvanna Pouma and Soupanouvong
would actually be willing to have the Chinese and North
Vietnamese cadres withdraw from Laos, since their participation in the recent fighting had been a major factor in forcing
the rightists to agree to a coalition government. If the Laotian
problem could not now be solved peacefully, the paper said,
the United States would "suffer the worst headache," because
it had been instrumental in bringing the coalition into being.
After the new government was actually installed later in June,
the Thai government was deeply disturbed by the charges of
the Lao Information Minister, a Pathet Lao man, that the
presence of American troops in Thailand constituted a threat
to the neutrality of Laos. That this official claimed to speak
for the whole Laotian government was taken as a sign that
Prince Souvanna Pouma would not be able to prevent the
Communists in his government from straining relations between Laos and Thailand. When the United States withdrew

approximately half of the United States Marine contingent early in July, just before the resumption of the Geneva meeting, some Thai papers complained that this showed the United States reacted more to propaganda from Laos than it did to threats to the security of Thailand.

The Thai government was sufficiently sensitive to the anti-Thai propaganda from the Pathet Lao faction that it delayed for some days its decision whether to participate in the final negotiations in Geneva to work out the Laotian accords. Subsequently the Laotian government's move to establish diplomatic relations with Communist China and with North Vietnam also disturbed many Thais, even though these moves did not surprise Thai leaders. Finally, Souvanna's decision to name Soupanouvong acting Premier during his absence in Europe was taken as an ominous sign. As a result of these actions by the new Laotian government, the question was raised in Bangkok whether it should be granted recognition by Thailand. *Sarn Seri* declared that Thailand should not simply follow the lead of the Western powers in extending recognition but should adopt an independent viewpoint. "It appears as if most of the western powers do not care whether the Communists swallow up Laos," said the paper editorially on June 30. "Their only thought seems to be to shove the garbage out of their way, and they do not care whether they shove it in front of anybody else's house." A few days later, when it was announced that the United States had appointed a new ambassador to Laos, *Sarn Seri* took it upon itself to offer him some advice: "When a coup was staged in Laos [Kong Lae's coup in August 1960], if Western diplomats had had a proper understanding of the situation, the results of that coup would never have led to all the current trouble and confusion." It was because Western diplomats did not believe that the coup was supported by the Communists that the crisis arose, the paper contended. If the representatives of some countries had not supported the Kong Lae coup from the start, the situation in Laos would not have deteriorated to the point where "the Communists have been able to dominate the country as they are doing to this day."[22]

Despite its misgivings, the Thai government finally decided to send a delegation to the Geneva Conference, after being persuaded, it said, by "some friendly countries" that its participation would contribute to the successful conclusion of the conference. Nevertheless, when the representatives of the fourteen nations had reached full agreement and had gathered on July 23, 1962, to sign the Declaration on the Neutrality of Laos and the Protocol to the Declaration, Thailand sent only its ambassador in Bonn to sign; all other signatories were foreign ministers, and in the case of Laos it was Prime Minister Souvanna Pouma. The document that the assembled representatives signed was an agreement to respect the neutrality and independence of Laos, as the latter had proclaimed in a declaration of policy on July 9. In essence this agreement pledged the signatories to withdraw all military forces, both regular and irregular, from Laos and not to interfere in its internal affairs either directly or indirectly; it provided that Laos would enter into no military agreements or alliances which were inconsistent with its neutrality, and that it would not allow any nation to have military facilities or bases in the country or use it as a base of operations against any other country. And Laos agreed not to call upon SEATO for protection, even though that treaty had made provision for such protection. The thirteen nations guaranteeing the neutrality and independence of Laos agreed to consult with the Laotian government and among themselves in case of a violation of the agreement "in order to consider measures which might

[22]*Thai Press Comment* (translation), July 1, 1962, U.S.I.S. Bangkok.

prove to be necessary to ensure the observance of these principles and the other provisions of the present Declaration."[23]

Within a week of the signing of the Geneva Agreements, it was announced in Washington and Bangkok that the remaining United States Marines stationed at Udorn would be "redeployed" to their Seventh Fleet stations; and President Kennedy told Prince Souvanna Pouma that the United States was prepared to give Laos economic assistance to help assure its independence and stability. In Bangkok, Marshal Sarit welcomed a statement attributed to Souvanna that Laos wanted to have friendly relations with Thailand because of the strong cultural ties between the two peoples. The Thai leader said there was no reason for Laos and Thailand to be angry with each other, and he indicated he believed that Prince Souvanna was sincere in his wish for good relations.

While the Western powers took comfort in the belief that war in Laos had been averted, the Thai government continued to view the situation with anxiety and frustration. In a long article entitled "Thailand at Crossroads," published on the day following the signing of the Geneva Agreement, the city editor of the *Bangkok Post* summarized what were probably the views of responsible Thai officials on the situation in Laos and in Southeast Asia. "Thailand feels," he wrote, "that the establishment of a coalition government of the current composition and the signing of the accords in Geneva, rather than improving it, have brought about a deterioration of the Southeast Asia situation *vis-à-vis* Thailand and other countries still free in this region." The Thai government doubted that the Communists had any intention

[23]For the texts of the Declaration and Protocol, see *Department of State Bulletin,* August 13, 1962, pp. 259–63. For a summary of the provisions, see Russell H. Fifield, *Southeast Asia in United States Policy* (New York, 1963), pp. 204–5.

of carrying out the provisions of the Geneva Agreement, but believed that they would use its provisions to build up their influence in key ministries of the government, while the Vietnamese Communist guerrillas camouflaged themselves as Pathet Lao troops and remained in the country. Thailand believed, the writer continued, that the Geneva Agreements were not strong enough to prevent the Communists from taking over Laos through continued subversion and outside assistance—that the SEATO umbrella had been withdrawn without replacing it with adequate guarantees against a Communist *putsch*. Thailand did not think the Western powers were naive about the situation; rather, what gave Thailand a "sinking feeling" was that it seemed the West was "trying gracefully to wash their hands of Laos." With the Communists in the government of Laos and with the neutralists leaning toward a pro-Communist policy, the writer believed Thai leaders feared that the Communists were in a better position to increase infiltration and subversion of northeast Thailand. "The threat to this nation will increase, of course, when the Communists finally take over complete control of Laos." The writer believed that Thailand had only two courses of action to protect its interests in this dangerous situation: a bilateral treaty with the United States or accommodation with the Communist powers. Thai leaders, he said, did not believe that SEATO was a reasonable alternative, because some members of SEATO would not be willing to fight to defend Thailand if the danger approached its borders. Only the United States had the power and the determination to stop the Communist advance in Asia, he said; and it had made bilateral treaties with the Philippines and the Republic of China and was carrying the full burden of the war against the Communists in South Vietnam.

If Thailand, with uncertainty and instability near its border, cannot get what it considers adequate and effective guarantees for the preservation of its independence, freedom and sovereignty, it may be forced into accommodating itself to the conditions surrounding it, in the hope that the Communists who are coming closer and closer will live and let live.

The continued presence of American forces in Thailand was considered to be a test of American determination to defend Thailand and to maintain a truly neutral government in Laos. If these troops were withdrawn without the conclusion of a mutual defense pact, the Thais might conclude that "the Western Powers, after getting off the hook in Laos, are also going to forsake Thailand and the rest of Southeast Asia."[24]

Troubles with Cambodia

Some observers found it difficult to understand why Thai policy seemed to harden on the question of a final agreement on Laos in the summer of 1962, after the Thai government had seemed so pleased by the Rusk–Tanat statement of March 6 and by the subsequent arrival of American troops in Thailand to warn the Communists against pressing their offensive toward the Mekong River. Although Thai leaders had never had any enthusiasm for a coalition government headed by Souvanna Pouma, they had nevertheless seemed willing in the spring of 1962 to go along with this plan after receiving assurances from the United States that it would take action if the Communists broke the truce or tried to take over the country by a *coup d'état*. The reason that Thai policy hardened was that in mid-June 1962 the International Court of Justice awarded to Cambodia a historic site in eastern Thailand known as Khao Pra Viharn. This event, unfortunate from the Thai point of view, had a profound effect on Thai

24*Bangkok Post,* July 24, 1962, p. 4.

national feelings and caused the government to become defensive and antagonistic.

The area in question, though small and uninhabited, contained the ruins of a famous temple which the Thai people had long cherished as their own. Thailand controlled the area following the treaties of 1904 and 1907 with France, under which the border with French Indochina was finally settled. After getting its independence from France in 1954, however, Cambodia contested Thailand's possession of the Pra Viharn area and finally persuaded the Thai government to have the case decided by the International Court of Justice. So sure were Thai leaders that their case would be upheld that they did not seriously consider the possibility that the court might rule against Thailand. Therefore, when the court on June 15, 1962, ruled in favor of Cambodia and the Thai government was faced with the obligation to surrender the disputed land to Cambodia, the news hit the public like a thunderbolt. Few issues have aroused such widespread public indignation, among even peasants and villagers, as did this decision of the court. In dealing with the popular outburst of emotion against the Cambodians, the Sarit government had to use all the power and persuasiveness at its command to keep the situation under control and to prevent dissident and subversive elements from using it to try to discredit and perhaps to upset the regime.

The situation was particularly distasteful and humiliating for Thailand because its relations with Cambodia had deteriorated steadily following the diplomatic break in October 1961. In addition, the Cambodian chief of state, Prince Sihanouk, had a way of infuriating the Thais with the numerous charges he made against Thailand during his visits to foreign countries as well as within Cambodia. The Thai government considered the Cambodian leader to be completely opportunistic in his foreign policy and hostile to Thailand, and strongly suspected that he found it useful to bait his Thai and South Vietnamese neighbors as a means of currying favor with the North Vietnamese and the Chinese Communists—especially when he believed that Chinese influence and Communism were making gains in Southeast Asia. The Cambodian brand of neutralism was anathema to Thailand, for it seemed to prove that Cambodia could get aid from all sides in the Cold War without having to make the adjustments that committed nations such as Thailand had to make in terms of less flexibility in foreign policy. Also, Thai leaders resented the fact that Sihanouk's voice seemed to carry so much influence in the world, despite the size and capabilities of his country, and that the United States gave him not only aid but also recognition as an important Asian leader. Why, asked many Thais, did the United States pay so much attention to a man who was constantly criticizing its policies in Asia and constantly attacking America's allies there? For months after the diplomatic break, the Thai government tried to maintain its composure in the face of Sihanouk's increasingly vitriolic anti-Thai outbursts; but by the eve of the International Court's decision on Pra Viharn, Thai tempers had become so frayed that the Foreign Ministry issued an official statement citing a number of speeches recently given by Sihanouk in a province near the Thai border.

On each occasion [the statement read] he [Sihanouk] launched into false and frenzied attacks against Thailand. He referred to the prime minister in terms which are not usual among civilized people. Such vile attacks and allegations denote such vulgarity and incoherence, they sound more like utterances coming from an inmate of a psychopathic ward.[25]

After two weeks of emotional speeches and public demon-

[25]*Bangkok Post,* June 9, 1962, p. 1.

strations by the Thai people against the court decision, Prime
Minister Sarit, who had so far remained relatively quiet, made
a nation-wide radio and television address to explain why the
government had decided to submit to the court's ruling, even
though it disagreed profoundly with it and also with the
factors that contributed to it. This was one of the most
crucial decisions of Sarit's rule as head of the Thai government, and it called for genuine statesmanship. Some Thai
leaders favored a military defense of Pra Viharn. In terms of
public awareness and emotional involvement, there was no
comparison between the Pra Viharn case and most foreign
policy issues the government had to face in its nearly four
years in power. Even the Laotian crisis of 1960–1961 did not
generate the kind of nationalistic fervor aroused by the International Court's decision. Sarit drew on a mantle of royal
sanction for his action by stating that the government was
indebted to the King, "whose concern for the welfare of the
country prompted Him graciously to give Royal advice and
words of wisdom to the Government." But in the final analysis it was Sarit who took responsibility for accepting the
court's ruling. He called on his countrymen to be "far-sighted"
and to exercise "our faculty to reason." He asked the nation
"not to be overcome by unruly and reckless emotions or to
think only in terms of forceful solutions." The court's order
was final, he said, and Thailand must honor its obligations
under the United Nations Charter. He cited Thailand's reputation in the world and concluded that the nation would
need many years to repair its loss of prestige if it failed to
abide by its obligations under international law.[26] Nevertheless Thailand reserved the right to initiate a review of its case
at some future time.

[26]For the text of Sarit's address and documents relating to the Pra
Viharn dispute, see Thailand's *Foreign Affairs Bulletin,* June–July 1962.

Had the Pra Viharn case affected only Thailand's relations with Cambodia, the matter probably would have receded in importance after Sarit's strong plea for reason. However, no sooner had the Thai government made the painful decision to abide by the court's judgment than it became known that Prince Sihanouk had requested additional military aid from the United States to suppress Viet Cong infiltrators. Prime Minister Sarit told the press on July 12 that according to his information Cambodia had asked for equipment to increase its army strength to ten divisions from four. Sarit said he doubted that Cambodia would use these extra forces to fight the Communists, and implied they would be used against Thailand. His announcement set off a rash of press and official comment to the effect that the United States would incur the displeasure of Thailand if it agreed to increase military aid to Thailand's enemy Cambodia. Foreign Minister Tanat Khoman said that Thailand's security would be affected if the Cambodian request was granted; and he doubted that such arms would be used against the Viet Cong because Cambodia actually was supporting the Viet Cong, he asserted, by allowing them transit its territory to South Vietnam. General Tanom Kittikachorn, Minister of Defense, hoped the United States would consult Thailand before giving any more arms to Cambodia; and General Prapat Charusatien, Interior Minister, said American help to Cambodia was "like giving meat to a tiger." By these and other statements Thai leaders made it plain that they would view any important increase in American aid to Cambodia as an unfriendly act toward Thailand. When Prince Sihanouk proposed that another international conference be called to guarantee Cambodia's security, Thai leaders were strongly opposed because of Sihanouk's assertions that the threat to his country came from Thailand and South Vietnam rather than from Communist nations. Thailand charged that Sihanouk planned to make an agreement with Peking by which the latter would obtain bases in Cambodia. Border incidents multiplied during the summer months of 1962, and there was increasing talk in Bangkok of the possibility of war.

By mid-September the crescendo of criticism reached a peak after it was learned that the United States had delivered to the Cambodian Air Force twelve T-28 aircraft under a previous agreement, and that additional equipment was scheduled for delivery later in the year. So loud and vehement was the outcry in Bangkok that the United States ambassador felt obliged to state publicly that American arms aid to Cambodia would never be used to kill Thais. What made the situation even worse was that the delivery of planes was announced within a few days after Prime Minister Sarit and the American ambassador had had a frank discussion about United States aid to Cambodia and after Foreign Minister Tanat Khoman's statement to the press that if the United States gave further military aid to Cambodia it would be tantamount to acceptance of Sihanouk's charges that Thailand had aggressive intentions against Cambodia. "This arms aid to Cambodia," Tanat said, "will affect good relations among the Free World countries and will bring about more tension and complexity in this region, which may lead to a greater danger to the whole of Southeast Asia."[27] Although the delivery of these planes to Cambodia was one of those cases where military deliveries are not coordinated with United States foreign policy objectives, and even though this fact was carefully explained to the Thai government, the timing could hardly have been worse. Thai leaders chose to believe that the United States had deliberately sought to embarrass them after they had made an issue of telling the United States that they

[27]*Bangkok World,* September 11, 1962, p. 1.

would consider further military aid to Sihanouk an un-friendly act. Commenting to the press, Tanat Khoman said it was unfortunate that the United States had bowed to Prince Sihanouk's "blackmail" and that the "bad timing" of the planes' delivery, whatever the motive, could only worsen the situation in Southeast Asia. He pointed out that Cambodia had never indicated a willingness to fight against the Communists but rather that it considered Thailand and South Vietnam the real enemies. As for assurances made by the American ambassador that such arms would never be used against the Thais, Tanat said the only way this could be assured was if the Americans themselves handled the arms. Tanat concluded by stating sadly: "There is no real partner-ship between America and Thailand."[28]

Within a few days the Thai government announced that it would negotiate a formal trade agreement with the Soviet Union, and Prime Minister Sarit told newsmen that the time was "appropriate" for the two countries to formalize the trading that had been going on for some time on a private basis. A few days later he told the press that conclusion of a trade agreement with the Soviet Union was not a retaliatory move against American arms shipments to Cambodia; but he admitted that the delivery of planes was "untimely" and said that "a good friend does not do such things." Commenting on talks he had had with the American ambassador, Sarit said the United States was fully aware of Thailand's dissatis-faction "and now knows that this is a serious thing." He told the press that the United States should suspend any agree-ment, old or new, that provided arms aid to Cambodia, and that he had made his views clearly known to the American ambassador.[29] General Prapat, Minister of Interior, also de-

[28]*Bangkok Post,* September 18, 1962, p. 1.
[29]*Bangkok World,* September 28, 1962, p. 1.

nied that the decision to conclude a trade agreement with the Soviet Union was in retaliation against United States arms aid to Cambodia; he said that the action was more in line with the policy of "Thaism" which the government was emphasizing in its foreign policy. But Prapat was nevertheless critical of the United States for its policy toward Cambodia:

This boy Cambodia has been trying to provoke us, an adult. He spits at us, tells lies about us, tries to provoke us into some action so that he could cry that a man has hit him. But we do not succumb to the provocations. This boy throws bricks on our roof. Now a friend supplies the boy with bricks.[30]

Thus did a secondary issue arise in the latter half of 1962 to spoil the good work that had been done during the first half of the year to mend the rift in Thai-American relations resulting from a divergence of views over how to handle the Laotian crisis. It is not the purpose here to ascertain whether Thailand's attitude toward United States policy in Cambodia was justified and whether the facts as stated by Thai leaders were accurate. The important aspect of this situation is that Thai leaders were embarrassed and humiliated first by the International Court's decision to award Pra Viharn to Cambodia and then by what they believed was Prince Sihanouk's effort to embarrass Thailand further by asking for additional military aid from Thailand's ally, the United States. As Sarit said, American willingness even to discuss the Cambodian request was not the way a good friend and ally should act. This view underscored once again the basic frustration of the Thai government in dealing with the United States: for despite its firm adherence to the SEATO alliance and its strong support for the United States in such crises as Berlin and Cuba, Thailand felt the United States government did not always give its views the same respect and support when Thai-

[30]*Bangkok Post,* September 21, 1962, p. 1.

land was faced with what it viewed as equally important challenges to its security. What made the Cambodian case even more irritating to the Thais was that the United States apparently did not realize at first how its discussions with neutralist Prince Sihanouk would affect the feelings of its staunch ally Thailand. As a Thai official said in a conversation with this writer, "If an elephant steps on your toe, it will hurt. But if he doesn't even know that he stepped on your toe, it hurts even more."

This is the real problem in Thai-American relations: how to adjust the worldwide commitments and concerns of a great world power to those of a small ally which is much more immediately threatened by events on its border than is its powerful ally. This was the problem that the United States and Thailand had to resolve if the alliance was to be meaningful to both countries in protecting their vital interests in Southeast Asia.

Chapter 8

Outlook

THE period 1963–1964 saw a gradual improvement in the immediate security problem facing Thailand and a decline in Thai frustration and apprehension over United States policy in Southeast Asia. Among the factors accounting for this improvement in relations between Thailand and the United States were the apparent success of the 1962 Laotian political settlement in preventing the Pathet Lao from gaining control of the government in Vientiane, the increasing American involvement in the defense of South Vietnam against Communist insurgency, and the firmness with which the United States confronted the Soviet Union in the Cuban missile crisis as well as in the face of renewed Soviet pressure on Berlin. Another contributing factor was the apparent willingness of Washington to refuse additional military assistance to Cambodia. These added up, the Thai government believed, to a renewed determination on the part of the United States to stand by its friends in Southeast Asia. As a result, Thailand's confidence in the United States as an ally began to increase and the Thai government cooperated more closely with the United States to improve the internal security of its northeast provinces along the Laotian border and to build up the capability of the Thai armed forces. Although the death of Field Marshal Sarit in December 1963 caused some uneasiness, in both Thai and American circles, over the possibility of a new power struggle within the ruling military group, the transition to the new government of General Tanom Kittikachorn was remarkably smooth; and at the time of this writing there was no indication of any serious threat to its controlling position, either within the armed forces or from the outside.[1]

Despite the gradual improvement in U.S.–Thai relations after the disillusionment felt in Bangkok during 1961 and 1962, the longer-term outlook for Thailand's relations with the United States and Thailand's policies toward neighboring countries in Southeast Asia was clouded by the increasing political instability in South Vietnam, after the overthrow of the Diem government late in 1963, and the growing confrontation between Thailand's two southern neighbors, Malaysia and Indonesia. In South Vietnam, the Thai government viewed with apprehension the struggle for power among the various factions and the increasing effectiveness of the Viet Cong in infiltrating important areas and in undermining the authority of the Saigon government. Thailand was also fearful that war between Malaysia and Indonesia might cause a serious security problem on its southern border and that the country might be caught in a "nutcracker" between unfriendly forces in both the north and south. The Thai government made a great effort to mediate the dispute between Malaysia and Indonesia, but to no avail. It also took great pains to increase cooperation with Burma along the lengthy Thai-Burmese border and to im-

---

[1]Although the Tanom government has stated as its goal the granting of a constitution and the holding of general elections, there appears to be no more enthusiasm on the part of this government than of the Sarit government to institute constitutional reforms while the security threat to Thailand remains great.

prove relations with the government of Prince Souvanna Pouma in Laos. Thus, while the internal security of Thailand had improved during 1963 and 1964 and American policy in Southeast Asia had proved to be more palatable to the Thais than it had been during the preceding two years, there remained an uneasy feeling in Bangkok that the long-term security of the country would hinge largely on the outcome of events elsewhere—in Vietnam and perhaps in North Borneo.

The hard reality for the Thais, as for every country in East Asia at the end of 1964, was the growing power of China under a disciplined and ruthless regime whose goal was the imposition of Chinese hegemony over all of East Asia. The detonation of China's first nuclear device at the end of 1964 only served to underline the fact that a new great power was rising in Asia and that the countries of Southeast Asia would be unable to stop this threat from overwhelming them without protection from the outside. This threat was not new; it had existed ever since the Red Army had driven the Nationalists off the mainland in 1949, had fought the American forces to a standstill in Korea, and had supported the Viet-Minh in their struggle to oust the French from Indochina. What was new in 1964 was the clear indication that the Chinese and their North Vietnamese allies were extending their power southward by tactics which did not bring into action the SEATO alliance or massive intervention by the United States. The advance of the Pathet Lao and their Viet-Minh allies had been checked in Laos in 1962 by the deployment of American forces to Thailand; but it soon became apparent that the immediate objective of Chinese and North Vietnamese strategy was the conquest of South Vietnam, or at least a settlement that would place the Viet Cong in a position from which they could extend control over the country by political means. If this strategy succeeded, Laos and Cambodia would be outflanked and Thailand would then bear the full force of the Chinese thrust southward. To underscore this point, the Chinese broadcast a clear warning to Thailand early in January 1965 that they supported a newly formed Thai "patriotic front" whose objective was to overthrow the Thai government and replace it with a neutralist regime that would rid the country of American influence. The Thais had no doubts that if the Communists won their struggle in Vietnam, Thailand would quickly come under the same kind of pressure and guerrilla warfare from the north. What happened in Vietnam was, therefore, crucial to the future of Thailand.

At the beginning of 1965, another climax was fast approaching in the struggle for power in Asia between Communist China and its allies on the one hand, and the nations of the Free World, led by the United States, on the other. The first test of strength between the Communist powers and the Free World had occurred in Korea fifteen years earlier; and there the United States had demonstrated that it would resist Communist aggression in Asia, just as it was prepared to resist it in Europe. However, the seeming unwillingness of the United States to bomb Communist China in the Korean War led to an inconclusive settlement there and caused many Asians, including the Thais, to question the effectiveness of the nuclear deterrent in preventing the expansion of Communist influence in Asia. A second test of the American will to resist the spread of Communist power in Asia came in 1954, when the French were on the brink of military disaster in Vietnam and called for American intervention. Despite its previous vast support of the French war effort with arms and equipment, the United States was unwilling in 1954 to use its own military forces to prevent the Communists from ousting France from its position in Vietnam. Although the United States joined the Manila Pact and committed itself for the first time to defend the mainland of Southeast Asia against Communist attack, it avoided committing permanent forces in order to retain flexibility in dealing with any situation that might arise. Therefore, although the United States warned of its intention to use force to prevent further Communist aggression in Southeast Asia, it also left in doubt whether it was prepared to use its overwhelming power, if necessary, to defend Southeast Asia.

A third test of American determination to prevent the spread of Communist power in Asia came in April 1961, when Washington had to decide whether to intervene in Laos to prevent that country from being overwhelmed by Pathet Lao and Viet-Minh forces. Here again the United States appeared to be indecisive in the face of a clear Communist threat and chose to negotiate in Geneva rather than to escalate the war in Laos by introducing American forces there. Although the United States sent its troops into Thailand a year later when the Communists again threatened to take over Laos, doubt remained in the minds of many Asian leaders as to what action the United States would take if confronted with a Communist threat which did not appear to warrant the use of massive American power.

The current test in South Vietnam is, therefore, a continuation of a policy of Chinese Communist expansion which began as soon as the Red Army swept to victory in China in 1949.[2]

[2]Some observers may argue that the Communist conquest of China was itself a test of American will to resist the spread of Communist power in Asia—that the failure of the United States to use its vast power to prevent the Communists from taking over China was the first indication that the United States could be forced to withdraw its

There are, however, two important differences between the present test in Vietnam and the previous confrontations in Korea and in Vietnam. First, in Korea and to a lesser extent in the 1954 Vietnam crisis, Soviet and Chinese policies were in reasonable harmony, with the result that the United States would have had to face the combined power of China and the Soviet Union if it had decided to escalate either of these conflicts. In the current struggle for Vietnam, there is reason to believe that the Soviet Union is not prepared to risk nuclear war and that it may not be willing to support the Chinese if the latter pushes the United States into a larger war over South Vietnam. In this sense, the current struggle in Vietnam is much more of a test between the United States and China than was the case in previous East-West confrontations in Asia. Second, the current crisis in Vietnam, unlike the one in 1954, finds the Vietnamese themselves fighting the Communists. In 1954, the Viet-Minh had the support of nearly all the Vietnamese people in a national struggle to oust the colonial power of France. Now, however, the South Vietnamese are struggling to prevent their country from being overrun by the North Vietnamese. If the United States must fight in Vietnam, it is far better politically as well as militarily to fight in support of an indigenous people which has demonstrated its willingness to carry the brunt of the war, rather than in support of a colonial power which is fighting to reimpose its rule on the local people, as was the case in 1954.[3]

---

influence from Asia if it was faced with sufficient impediments in the use of its nuclear power.

[3]Despite this obvious difference in the two situations, however, President de Gaulle apparently chooses to equate the French position in 1954 with the United States position in Vietnam today and to ignore the huge casualties suffered by the South Vietnamese forces during the past several years in the defense of their country.

One of the most disturbing aspects of the war in Vietnam, insofar as Thailand and all other countries in Southeast Asia are concerned, is the inability the United States has so far shown to devise an effective means of coping with the new kind of warfare developed by Mao Tse Tung and used with alarming success against the French and in the current struggle for control of South Vietnam. Despite its vast superiority in modern weapons and delivery systems, the United States at the beginning of 1965 seemed unable to find the means of effectively countering the guerrilla tactics of the Viet Cong. For three years the United States sought ways to bolster the South Vietnamese forces with modern equipment and technical assistance, only to find that the military situation in South Vietnam had deteriorated markedly during 1964, to a point where a Communist victory seemed imminent. President Johnson was then faced with the harsh choice of either accepting a humiliating defeat of American policy in Vietnam or of changing the ground rules to permit the United States and its allies to fight the Communist powers on terms that were more favorable to the United States, namely by using naval and air power to convince the aggressors that the price they had to pay for a continuation of the war was too high. Such a change in rules could well include the deployment of a sizable force of troops from the United States and its allies; but it seemed reasonably clear early in 1965 that fighting the war only in South Vietnam was a losing proposition and that the guerrilla tactics perfected by the Vietnamese Communists had been strikingly successful in winning for them large sections of South Vietnam. The new policy introduced by the United States was, of course, warmly endorsed by the Thai government and by other Asian governments that feared the repercussions of a Communist victory in Vietnam. In fact, Thai leaders found it difficult to understand why the United

States had waited so long before it adopted the tactics of making the North Vietnamese pay a price for their continued guerrilla warfare against South Vietnam.

But even if the war in South Vietnam were to be concluded on terms which prevented the Communists from gaining control of the country, this would not be the end of the Chinese menace in Asia. As the military strength of China grows and as the Communists entrench themselves ever more firmly in control of this power base, new tests will confront the United States and its allies in their efforts to contain Chinese power. Always the test will come at a time when the Chinese believe that the United States and its allies are unlikely to resist their pressure firmly. The main hope, for countries such as Thailand, the Philippines, and Malaysia, of remaining outside the Chinese sphere of influence will be for the United States to stand as firm in resisting Chinese and North Vietnamese encroachments in Southeast Asia as it has stood in Europe against Soviet pressures. Certain Asian countries have recently drawn closer to Peking in the belief that the United States will not remain steadfast against an extension of Chinese power, and have concluded that it is only a matter of time until Chinese hegemony is extended over the whole area. These nations hope to receive better treatment than the Thais and Malaysians if this situation occurs and American power is withdrawn from the area.

In the foreseeable future, therefore, the security of Thailand and of other nations in Southeast Asia will be decided not in Hanoi or Peking or Moscow, but in Washington. The United States in the mid-1960's is by far the most powerful nation in the world, and its scientific capability and economic strength give every promise that it will be able to maintain this pre-eminent position for some time to come, perhaps indefinitely. The real problem in Southeast Asia is not whether the United States has the power to force Communist China and North Vietnam to halt their pressure on their neighbors, but rather how it should use this power to counter the unconventional and highly effective type of warfare that is being waged in the jungles of South Vietnam and which will surely be employed against Thailand and other neighboring countries if it succeeds in Vietnam. The new tactics adopted by the United States early in 1965 may, hopefully, bring about meaningful negotiations on the future of Vietnam and Laos; but the risk of a larger war must also be calculated. The escalation of the war will be meaningless unless the United States is prepared to match every Communist move in this critical struggle. In the past, the Chinese apparently were not convinced that the United States would pay a high price to defend the countries on the mainland of Southeast Asia, especially if the aggression was camouflaged as a "war of national liberation" fought by the people against foreign domination. The current crisis in Vietnam is, therefore, a test of how far the United States will go to defend a country which is thousands of miles away and in which the United States has been very cautious about committing its power.

In the final analysis, the question whether the United States remains in Southeast Asia and continues to defend the free countries of that area against the growing menace of Chinese Communism will be decided by the American people and by Congress. President Johnson has now taken a bold stand and proclaimed to the Communist powers as well as to America's friends that the United States will not be pushed or negotiated out of Vietnam nor forced to renege on its commitments elsewhere in Southeast Asia. The President has thus shown leadership in rallying the nation to the challenge of Chinese and North Vietnamese aggression in

Asia. But what price are the American people prepared to pay to defend this area? Is the country ready to have American ground forces tied down indefinitely, as in Korea, to give South Vietnam time to develop its own resources and sense of nationhood sufficiently to cope with the internal political problem? And how much American power can be brought to bear in the Far East to contain the power of China without endangering the defense of Europe, or the Near East, or Latin America, to the point where these areas could become subject to pressures from other forces, both Communist and non-Communist, which seek to upset the balance of power in these areas?

It seems to this writer that a greater American commitment to the defense of Southeast Asia is a logical outgrowth of American policy in Asia since 1941, when the United States decided it would not permit the Japanese to dominate this whole area. The Korean War was a further step along the road to American involvement on the mainland of Asia, and the Southeast Asia Treaty (Manila Pact) brought this country into the defense of mainland Southeast Asia for the first time. The withdrawal of the British, French, and Dutch after World War II left a power vacuum in this region. The United States had either to fill this vacuum or to recognize the area as falling within Communist China's sphere of influence. Since 1950, the key question asked by leaders of all the countries in Southeast Asia, and in other areas as well, has been: Will the United States exercise sufficient power and determination to convince the Chinese that they should turn their energies inward? Some leaders in Southeast Asia are not convinced that the United States is willing to pay the price of remaining over the long term and have therefore adopted neutralist or pro-Peking policies in order to adjust to what they believe is a new power situation in Asia. Other nations, such as Thailand, continue to have faith in the ability and determination of the United States to check Chinese imperialism, just as it was able and willing to hold back Soviet imperialism in Europe and the Near East. In mid-1965, there was a growing confidence in Thailand and elsewhere that the United States would not abandon its responsibilities in Southeast Asia and that the Chinese would eventually have to shift their aggressive policy or risk disaster. However, an American presence in South Vietnam and in Thailand will probably be required for a long time if these areas are to be permitted to develop as non-Communist states living in the shadow of the Chinese mountain.

It is imperative, therefore, that Americans as well as Asians come to understand the long-term nature of the present struggle for Southeast Asia and make the adjustments that will be required to carry out their commitments. Without a clear understanding by the American people of our long-term goals in this area and of the resources that will be required to reach those goals, the President will find it difficult to chart a steady course over the period required in order to maintain the security of Southeast Asia. It is to be hoped, therefore, that a better understanding of the hopes and aspirations of the peoples of Southeast Asia, such as the Thais, will result in a better appreciation among the American people of the need to be steadfast in Southeast Asia.

One generation is a remarkably short time for a nation to readjust completely its thinking about foreign policy, to move from isolationism to an acceptance of world-wide responsibility for the maintenance of peace in a revolutionary world. Historians may well record that this transformation of the United States into a world power whose strength was used for preserving freedom rather than enslaving lesser powers was among the most significant events of the twentieth century. If the United States is indeed equal to the task, small countries in Asia such as Thailand will continue to live and grow according to their own traditions and culture; if not, these countries are destined to live under a Chinese Communist system.

Selected Bibliography

Bartlett, Norman. *Land of the Lotus Eater.* London, 1959.

Blanchard, Wendell, ed. *Thailand: Its People, Its Society, Its Culture.* New Haven, 1957.

Brimmell, J. H. *Communism in South East Asia.* London, 1959.

Busch, Noel F. *Thailand: An Introduction to Modern Siam.* Princeton, 1959.

Buss, Claude A. *Southeast Asia and the World Today.* Princeton, 1958.

Butwell, Richard. *Southeast Asia Today and Tomorrow: A Political Analysis.* New York, 1961.

Chakrabongse, Chula. *Lords of Life.* New York, 1960.

———. *The Twain Have Met.* London, 1957.

Champassak, Sisouk Na. *Storm over Laos.* New York, 1961.

Clubb, Oliver E., Jr. *The United States and the Sino-Soviet Bloc in Southeast Asia.* Washington, D.C., 1962.

Coast, John. *Some Aspects of Siamese Politics.* New York, 1953.

Collective Defense in South-East Asia. New York and London: Royal Institute of International Affairs, 1956.

Crosby, Sir Josiah. *Siam: The Crossroads.* London, 1945.

DeYoung, John E. *Village Life in Modern Thailand.* Berkeley, 1958.

Dommen, Arthur J. *Conflict in Laos: The Politics of Neutralization.* New York, 1964.

Emerson, Rupert. *Representative Government in Southeast Asia.* Cambridge, Mass., 1955.

Fifield, Russell H. *The Diplomacy of Southeast Asia, 1945–1958.* New York, 1958.

———. *Southeast Asia in United States Diplomacy.* New York, 1963.

Foreign Affairs Bulletin. Bangkok: Thailand Ministry of Foreign Affairs, 1960.

Graham, W. A. *Siam: A Handbook.* 2 vols. London, 1924.

Griswold, A. B. *King Mongkut of Siam.* New York, 1961.

Hall, D. G. E. *A History of South-East Asia.* London, 1955.

Harrison, Brian. *Southeast Asia: A Short History.* London, 1954.

Ingram, James C. *Economic Change in Thailand since 1850.* Stanford, 1955.

Insor, D. *Thailand: A Political, Social, and Economic Analysis.* London, 1963.

Johnson, John J., ed. *The Role of the Military in Underdeveloped Countries.* Princeton, 1962.

Jordan, Amos A. *Foreign Aid and the Defense of Southeast Asia.* New York, 1962.

Kahin, George McT., ed. *Governments and Politics of Southeast Asia.* Ithaca, N.Y., 1959. 2d ed. 1964.

Kaufman, Howard K. *Bangkhuad: A Community Study in Thailand.* Locust Valley, N.Y., 1960.

King, John K. *Southeast Asia in Perspective.* New York, 1956.

Landon, Kenneth P. *Siam in Transition.* Chicago, 1939.

MacDonald, Alexander. *Bangkok Editor.* New York, 1949.

Mende, Tibor. *South-East Asia between Two Worlds.* London, 1955.

Modelski, George, ed. *SEATO: Six Studies.* Melbourne, Australia, 1962.

Moffat, Abbot L. *Mongkut, the King of Siam.* Ithaca, N.Y., 1961.

Pauker, Guy J. "U.S. Foreign Policy in Southeast Asia," *U.S. Foreign Policy—Asia.* (U.S. Senate, Committee on Foreign Relations, Report No. 5, section 3.) Washington, D.C., 1959.

Pendleton, Robert L. *Thailand, Aspects of Landscape and Life.* New York, 1962.

Phimphisan, Chamni. *The Siam Directory 1962.* Bangkok, 1962.

Pye, Lucian W. "The Politics of Southeast Asia" in Gabriel A. Almond and James S. Coleman, *The Politics of the Developing Areas.* Princeton, 1960.

Sarasas, Phra. *My Country Thailand.* Bangkok, 1956.

Sayre, Francis B. *The Passing of Extraterritoriality in Siam.* New York, 1928.

The Siam Society Fiftieth Anniversary Commemorative Publication. Bangkok: Siam Society, 1954.

Skinner, G. William. *Chinese Society in Thailand.* Ithaca, N.Y., 1957.

———. *Leadership and Power in the Chinese Community of Thailand.* Ithaca, N.Y., 1958.

Smith, Nicol, and Blake Clark. *Into Siam: Underground Kingdom.* New York, 1946.

Stanton, Edwin F. *Brief Authority.* London, 1957.

Suthiwart-Narueput, Owart. *The Evolution of Thailand's Foreign Relations since 1855.* Unpublished Ph.D. dissertation, Fletcher School of Law and Diplomacy, 1956.

Sutton, Joseph L., ed. *Problems of Politics and Administration in Thailand.* Bloomington, Ind., 1962.

Textor, Robert B. *From Peasant to Pedicab Driver.* New Haven, 1961.

Thailand Past and Present. Bangkok: Ninth Pacific Science Conference, 1957.

Thompson, Virginia. *Thailand the New Siam.* New York, 1941.

Thompson, Virginia, and Richard Adloff. *The Left Wing in Southeast Asia.* New York, 1950.

Trager, Frank (ed.). *Marxism in Southeast Asia.* Stanford, 1959.

Vadakarn, Luang Vichitr. *Thailand's Case.* Bangkok, 1941.

Vella, Walter F. *Siam under Rama III.* Locust Valley, N.Y., 1957.

————. *The Impact of the West on Government in Thailand.* Berkeley and Los Angeles, 1955.

Vistas of Thailand. Bangkok: Thailand Public Relations Department, 1963.

Wilson, David A. *Politics in Thailand.* Ithaca, N.Y., 1962.

Wolf, Charles, Jr. *Foreign Aid: Theory and Practice in Southeast Asia.* Princeton, 1960.

Wood, W. A. R. *A History of Siam.* Bangkok, 1933.

Index